THE SOCIOLOGY OF SOCIAL WORK

Although there have been previous titles designed to introduce social work students to sociology as a relevant discipline, *The Sociology of Social Work* is unique in its focus on the sociology *of* social work. The writers, all qualified sociologists with an active involvement in social work, look at different aspects of the subject from a variety of perspectives. There are chapters on child abuse, informal caring, family therapy, residential care and probation interviewing, while Lena Dominelli tackles the twin issues of race and gender. Nor is sociological theory ignored. The reader will find up-to-date reviews of the relationship between recent theoretical perspectives in sociology, welfare and social work.

The book considers some of the key issues in social work; it explores how sociology can be used to understand the role of social work in society; and it contributes to the clarification of some major sociological issues – methodological, substantive and theoretical.

Thorough, relevant and sophisticated, *The Sociology of Social Work* will be of interest to social workers and sociologists.

THE SOCIOLOGY OF
SOCIAL WORK

Edited by
MARTIN DAVIES

LONDON AND NEW YORK

First published 1991
by Routledge
11 New Fetter Lane, London EC4P 4EE

Simultaneously published in the USA and Canada
by Routledge
29 West 35th Street, New York, NY 10001

First published in paperback 1994

© 1991 Martin Davies

Typeset in Baskerville by
Mews Photosetting, Beckenham, Kent
Printed and bound in Great Britain by
Biddles Ltd, Guildford and King's Lynn

British Library Cataloguing in Publication Data
A catalogue record for this book is available from the British Library

Library of Congress Cataloging in Publication Data
A catalog record for this book is available from the Library of Congress

ISBN 0-415-11521-3

CONTENTS

CONTENTS

CONTRIBUTORS

Graham Allan is Reader in Sociology at the University of Southampton. He is the author of *Friendship: Developing a Sociological Perspective*, Harvester Wheatsheaf, 1989, and (with Graham Crow) *Community Life: an Introduction to Local Social Relations*, Harvester Wheatsheaf, 1984.

Brian Corby is Senior Lecturer in Applied Social Studies at the University of Liverpool. He is a qualified social worker, with a special interest in child abuse, and has written *Working with Child Abuse*, Open University Press, 1987.

Martin Davies is a qualified probation officer and Professor of Social Work at the University of East Anglia, Norwich. He is the author of *The Essential Social Worker* (third edition), Arena, 1994, and (with Gwyneth Boswell and Andrew Wright) *Contemporary Probation Practice*, Avebury, 1993.

Lena Dominelli is Professor of Social Work at the University of East Anglia, Norwich. She is a qualified social worker, and author of *Anti-Racist Social Work*, Macmillan, 1988, and (with Eileen McLeod) *Feminist Social Work*, Macmillan, 1989.

David Howe is Senior Lecturer in Social Work at the University of East Anglia, Norwich. He is a qualified social worker, and has written *An Introduction to Social Work Theory*, Wildwood House, 1987, and *On Being a Client: Understanding the Process of Counselling and Psychotherapy*, Sage, 1993.

Peter Huxley is Professor of Psychiatric Social Work at the University of Manchester. A qualified social worker, he is author of *Social Work Practice in Mental Health*, Gower, 1985 and (with David Goldberg) *Common Mental Disorder: a Biosocial Model*, Routledge, 1992.

John Offer is Senior Lecturer in Social Administration and Policy at the University of Ulster, Coleraine. He has written *Informal Welfare: a Sociological Study of Care in Northern Ireland* (With R. Cecil and F. St Leger), Gower, 1987.

Roger Sibeon is Director of MA courses in the Department of Sociology at the University of Liverpool. He is the author of *Towards a New Sociology of Social Work*, Gower, 1991.

Stephen Stanley is Intelligence Officer in the Inner London Probation Service. He has written *A Survey of Social Enquiry Reports* (with M.B. Murphy), ILPS, 1984, and *Alternatives to Prison* (with M. Baginsky), Peter Owen, 1984.

ACKNOWLEDGEMENTS

Plans for this book emerged from discussions made possible by the award of small grants from the Central Council for the Education and Training of Social Workers and from the University of East Anglia, Norwich. The University also contributed significantly to the costs incurred in the preparation of the finished volume.

An earlier version of Chapter 5 and a short section incorporated into Chapter 1 were first published in the *British Journal of Social Work*.

Chapter One

SOCIOLOGY AND SOCIAL WORK

A misunderstood relationship

MARTIN DAVIES

I

This book can be approached in two ways. Most obviously, and as
its title implies, the reader will find an exploration of social work seen
through the analytical eyes of sociology. The range is not comprehensive but illustrative: each author takes one or more aspects of social
work practice and subjects it to a sociological critique.

But there is another way of viewing the material here presented,
and it is one that is difficult to resist: the various chapters that make
up the collection not only illustrate the multi-faceted nature of social
work, but also demonstrate beyond any doubt that sociology itself has
many aspects and many styles. Thus, the reader can use this book
to reflect upon the different ways in which sociologists approach a
common topic. By taking social work as an exemplar, we can check
out what contribution sociology has to make to our understanding of
a complex social phenomenon and how it goes about the task.

Sociology in the late twentieth century is not an easy subject: not
only does it have to cope with the multi-dimensional nature of human
society that has always confronted those who would seek to understand it; but increasingly it has also had to accommodate itself to a
range of complex philosophical perspectives that are partly to do with
the influence of political theory as it impinges on all levels of human
society, that partly stem from an increased sensitivity to the significance
of language in social relationships, and that in particular reflect
sociologists' own concern with problems of methodology.

Sociology's felt need to take account of methodological hazards and
to develop analytical systems that go some way towards an understanding of verbal and non-verbal human interaction has at times

1

tended to make the subject unduly introspective. Some sociological debates seem to go not only beyond empiricism, but beyond theory and into realms more reminiscent of theology and metaphysics. The struggle of sociologists to accommodate not only social complexity, but the near-mystical dimension of time and the invisible cross-currents of power and knowledge, can make heavy demands on the student; but, by inviting sociologists to apply their intellectual perspectives to a relatively restricted and tightly focused subject-area like social work, this book aims to provide an accessible illustration of the discipline's relevance and applicability in an important area of public interest.

Of course, social work itself is not as straightforward a sphere of activity as some of its apologists or critics have tended to assume. 'I want to help people', says the well-intentioned would-be social worker when applying for training; if only it were so simple!

Those in the job usually have a clearly observable daily routine: it involves office work – record keeping, report writing, attending meetings; home visiting; interviews with clients; telephone calls to public- and private-sector agents (like the unemployment benefit office or next-door neighbours); attendance at court, in tribunal, or at case conference; running groups; arranging or, more rarely, giving practical aid; and so on. But what is it all for?

Outside observers – councillors, MPs, journalists, even sociologists new to the field – may have ideas about the nature of the social worker's occupational brief that differ significantly from those held by practitioners who may, in any case, not agree among themselves. Clients will see it differently again; while, to further complicate matters, senior managers have tended to exaggerate social work goals (for example, with regard to delinquency reduction) in order to command more resources in their annual battle for the budget. It has proved remarkably difficult to achieve a reliable and empirically sustainable idea of what public-sector social work is corporately paid to deliver. The problem of who defines social work – and whether the definitions are compatible with empirical reality – is both sociologically and politically of interest.

There are other puzzles in social work that suggest fertile ground for sociological analysis. For example, why is it that a field of activity that has tended to be regarded unfavourably by politicians on both left and right and that is generally viewed without enthusiasm by the electorate has nevertheless experienced unprecedented growth – in both relative and absolute terms – as a public-sector profession? Or again, how is it that, as a number of studies have shown (for example, Boswell 1985), many social workers enjoy a remarkably high degree of personal job autonomy – not only affecting *how* they do their work (which is not uncommon in other occupations) but also *what* they do and how they prioritise it (which is much rarer)?

It might be thought that the political significance and the conundrum-like nature of its purpose would have drawn sociologists to study social work on a massive scale. In fact, the sociology of social work cannot be said to exist as a field of study in the United Kingdom at the present time; it was conspicuous by its absence from a list of subject-areas drawn up by the discipline's leaders when they reported in 1989 to the University Grants Committee.

II

Attempts to trace the processes of intellectual development are notoriously hazardous, and there is no simple way of characterising the pattern of affinities between sociology and social work. But there have been only two occasions in recent times when sociologists have had a significant impact upon mainstream social work theory.

The first was in 1959 when Wootton published her book, *Social Science and Social Pathology* which aimed a body-blow at social casework by attacking its more pretentious absurdities:

> Happily it can be presumed that the lamentable arrogance of the language in which . . . social workers describe their activities, is not generally matched by the work that they . . . do: otherwise it is hardly credible that they would not constantly get their faces slapped. . . . Without doubt the majority of those who engage in social work are sensible, practical people, who conduct their business on a reasonable matter-of-fact basis. The pity is that they have to write such nonsense about it.
>
> (Wootton 1959: 279)

Wootton's writing had the effect, in the 1960s, of making social workers more aware of the impact of social and economic factors in the lives of their clients, though they never responded warmly to her pleas that they should keep it simple and develop practical skills directly relevant to service delivery and social advocacy.

The second time sociologists impacted on social work to a significant extent – indeed, to the greatest extent yet – came during the 1970s when there emerged a clear identification of sociology with a left-wing (or radical) critique of state capitalism. For a time, we saw a vibrant interaction between knowledge, theory, and literature on the one hand and practice on the other, with social workers particularly concerned to minimise the damaging consequences of their own intervention strategies, as highlighted by deviance theory and the associated notion of a labelling process.

Corrigan and Leonard (1978), moving smoothly from theory towards praxis, argued that the best interests of the clients of social work were at odds with those of the ruling class in any capitalist society and that they could be served only by social workers willing to enter into conflict with the existing system. Not surprisingly, Heraud (1970) had warned of the need to document 'the ideological impact of sociology on social work'.

Simpkin took the radical critique to its logical conclusion. 'Social work', he said, 'is at best a flawed and limited way of helping people, and at worst descends to sheer deception.' He referred to himself as a revolutionary seeking to extend his way of life into his work and grateful that social work was 'one of the few occupations which carries a licensed mandate to seek change', and could 'therefore be used as a base for experiments towards a new social philosophy' (Simpkin 1979: 152–60).

Whatever the strength of the arguments used by those who saw in social work an unacceptable vehicle for the oppression of the poor, the radical idea of using social workers as agents of political reform seemed to reveal – then, as now – an astonishing naïvety about the sociology of organisations, the relative powerlessness of individuals within them, and the importance of self-interest as a motivating force in any occupational group. There was bound to be a bitter harvest of disillusionment.

It was left to Cohen (1975) to identify ruefully the internal contradictions inherent in the radical approach to social work in an essay that proved unexpectedly influential in promoting the new realism that was to become the hallmark of social work writing in the eighties. He recognised that sociology had offered 'remarkably few prescriptions that [can] actually be followed by social workers in any practical sense', and saw a clear conflict between the Marxist's desire not to blunt the contradictions in the system and the client's need for urgent help. 'The mothers of autistic children, suicidal housewives in tower blocks, derelict old vagrants' should not, he said, be written off by radical practitioners impatient with the system (Cohen 1975: 94–5). His solution was for the social worker to act under cover, to 'stay unfinished', to live with ambiguity, to draw a clear distinction between short- and long-term objectives.

There is therefore always a potential conflict between the role of the welfare state agents and the imperfections of the allegedly iniquitous system that employs them, and this has been a recurring hazard for radical sociologists offering advice to practitioners – especially for those like Cohen who admits to having escaped from 'a career in psychiatric social work into the safe world of sociology' (1975: 87). Even Simpkin, having taken pot-shots at almost everyone in sight, confesses that, as a social worker himself, he has to employ in the course of his duties 'quite harsh measures, including use of statutory powers'. He reconciles himself to this, he says, by not identifying with the role (1979: 157).

Radical sociology's colonising forays towards social work foundered eventually on just such examples of blatant self-deception. The problem was that the logic of the argument ought to have led to calls for the abandonment of state-sector social work. But, partly for reasons of self-interest and partly because most were not wholly persuaded that the abandonment of social work would bring about political improvement, those who were actively engaged in or employed by social work always pulled back from the brink of drawing such a conclusion. When it came to the crunch, they settled for an eclectic or a clandestine solution, and were inevitably compromised as a result.

The retreat from radicalism, however, has brought no comfort for social work. During the 1980s, sociologists, heavily influenced by Foucault's work (1975) on power and punishment, sought to interpret and understand the changing shape of modern society, with particular reference to the part played in it by public-sector operatives – like social workers. The central role of welfare officials is clearly spelt out:

> The concept of 'the social' . . . refers to a quite specific historical event, the emergence of a network or relay through which power is exercised over populations, a power of administration. It denotes an increase in the importance of mechanisms of insurance and security.
>
> (Smart 1989: 80)

But, although social workers loom large in post-Foucaultian writing, the messages remain fundamentally pessimistic. On the one hand, they are presented as puppets of a macro-system employed, not for well-intentioned 'helping' purposes, but as critical agents of state power:

> Those welfare workers who perceive themselves as operating somehow 'outside' the system of juvenile justice misunderstand both the system itself and their own role in it. . . . They are firmly within the system, their activities and influence crucial for its development. . . . Hence for the experts to seek *more* power and influence as a means of providing more care is to base an action on an analytic error.
>
> (Harris and Webb 1987: 176)

On the other hand, social work systems themselves are seen as self-perpetuating, self-serving organisations whose primary concern is with the welfare of their own employees:

> Wherever one looks, one discovers that under the pressures of administrative convenience, progressive innovations . . . [have] served merely to advance the self-interest of the care-taker professionals, or, as with social work, virtually to create the profession that perpetuated them.
>
> (Scull 1989: 150)

The post-Foucaultians go a long way towards reinforcing the cynical views of social work's critics; if Conservative politicians read more sociology, they could claim scholarly support for the idea that social work is a bureaucratically superfluous, self-seeking accoutrement to modern life. And yet, as I have argued in *The Essential Social Worker* (Davies 1985), when you talk to clients who have benefited personally from social work help, such a conclusion seems to be wildly at odds with empirical reality.

A fundamental problem lies in the macro-perspective towards which many sociologists (especially those concerned with theory) are inexorably drawn. Macro-perspectives, by their very nature, exclude the interests of individuals; indeed, the very idea of 'individualism' is often presented as methodologically unsound. But the world of social work – like the intimate world of ordinary men and women – is almost wholly taken up with the lives and fortunes of individuals. Sibeon, in Chapter 2, makes a strong case for sociology needing to develop more theories of the middle range; but to do this means accepting social, psychological, and economic imperfection as a fact of life (or, in research terms, as 'givens'); understandably, many sociologists would find such a constraint intolerable if it were to 'limit radically the questions which can be asked' (Garland and Young 1989: 17).

The fact that social workers *have* to live with imperfection, restrict their vision, and limit their questions does, I guess, simply highlight a major difference between the two activities. Sociologists ask questions; social workers must act as though they have answers. The problem has been that, in the past, social workers have assumed that there might be a dynamic relationship between the two, and that they could therefore aspire to be applied sociologists – a conceit that can now be seen to have been misguided.

There is, of course, a political dimension to this. The sociological critique identifies oppression, economic exploitation, and inequality, and advocates a process of social planning designed to change things. The social worker may be seen either as a potential front-line troop in the battle for a new society or as an obstacle – propping up and prolonging the existence of an iniquitous system. In empirical reality, however, the social worker is a revolutionary irrelevance – a mere employee in the welfare industry, with a range of quite specific skills to learn, tasks to perform, services to deliver, a professional identity to maintain, and a career to pursue. Changes in social work practice will tend to *follow* statutory developments, rather than the other way about.

Even though many social workers are politically left-of-centre, only a small number would think of their occupation as representing socialism in practice. To the extent that sociological theory hints at that as an appropriate organisational goal for social work, it is likely to misrepresent a significant part of what social workers do.

III

The work of sociologists, then, has had less of a direct impact on social work than historically might have seemed likely, given the fact that the two subjects are often bracketed together and even, at times, mistaken for each other.

Sociology and social work are totally different entities; in some ways, their historical links and their consequent juxtaposition in higher education have been both misleading and unfortunate. It is essential that sociology should be protected to undertake its critical work – almost inevitably and always exposing weaknesses in the way society currently operates. Sociology can hardly avoid being reflective and controversial, having as it traditionally does the role and status of an intellectual opposition party, exposing flaws and shortcomings in any establishment. It is hard to imagine a sociologist either content with the *status quo* or prepared to settle for an imperfect world. As Scull puts it, 'I think a realistic pessimism is to be preferred to . . . modest illusions about the possibilities of humanising a fundamentally inhuman system' (1989: 164)

But, of course, this style poses problems for the doers of the world – those who are employed to fulfil agency expectations and to undertake duties to the best of their ability. There is always a risk that sociology, by highlighting weaknesses, will undermine the self-confidence and the legitimacy of social work managers and practitioners alike.

Let me explore this matter further. Sociologists identify elements in the social world which prompt their critical attention: the plight of poor people, of women, of blacks, of Catholics; they expose the ineffectiveness of therapeutic intervention, the reality of state power, corporate privilege, or male domination. Fine, we can understand and appreciate that.

But, if such an analysis is presented – as generally it is – with the idea of 'somebody doing something about it', there follows the immediate problem of deciding *what* should be done, and by whom.

The sociologist knows that critics have derided the discipline's own tendency to stop short of prescribing improvements. Scull concludes one of his critical essays like this:

> I am well aware of the pressures to be more than 'negatively critical'. It is not enough, according to the conventional wisdom, to speak harsh words about contemporary institutions. One 'should have the decency to provide a detailed blueprint for change and improvement, and should offer his suggestions in the spirit of one who is thankful for our collective blessings and, at all costs, hopeful' (Boyers 1979, p. 28). This I cannot do, for I lack the necessary faith in the managerial approach to the problem. . . . Perhaps the best I can do is to persuade others to share my sense of discomfort.
>
> (Scull 1989: 164–5)

But if the sociologist lacks faith in a managerial approach, how is any improvement to be achieved?

The very scale of much sociological analysis – dealing, for example, with class inequality – makes an individual response difficult to contemplate. Moreover, in a sociological sense, it is highly unlikely that those in positions of superiority will freely concede their status or forgo its perks. Thus the achievement of change through individual behaviour cannot be regarded as a sound sociological strategy. Only a political campaign can have face validity, and, even then, experience teaches us that the nature of the reforms gained will not be in precisely the form demanded by the original sociological critique – chiefly because other conflicting social forces will have come into play.

Now, if we apply this model specifically to the world of social work, we discover a double-barrelled dilemma: for, not only does the social worker find himself overwhelmed by the enormity and the often irremediable nature of the problems identified by sociologists; he discovers that, all too often, he himself is said to be a, or even *the*, party responsible for the problem. For example, it is the social worker who is the front-man for state oppression, or who acts out policies of institutionalised racism, or who ameliorates unacceptable living conditions only to the point where political rebellion is discouraged, or whose very offer of help carries with it the poisoned chalice of social stigma. Under this scenario, the more the social worker tries to accommodate the sociological analysis, the more oppressed he becomes by self-doubt.

In this situation, as Simpkin (1979) recognised, social workers cannot avoid the compromises that characterise their occupational role. They know that those aspects of social life that are subjected to critical analysis by sociologists are not the personal possession of any one individual, but are the product of an organisation, a social class, a religious or political group, an industrial firm, a cultural tradition, or an economic system. They have no option but to play out their role upon a complex social stage, not, as the radicals would have it, as a temporary expedient, but because that is the nature of their job.

The agency, too, has to develop a *modus operandi*. What seems to happen is that management issues policy directives that are held to be sociologically sensitive. Two recent examples have been seen in the probation service's instructions to its officers to avoid custodial recommendations in their social inquiry reports and in some local authorities' restrictions on the placing of black children in white families. Such steps might be said to confirm that sociologically inspired action *can* be taken at the level of corporate management, but detailed

9

consideration of both examples would suggest that other factors are involved as well – in these cases, concern over the rising cost of imprisonment in the first instance and sensitivity to the growing influence of ethnic minority pressure groups in the second. Moreover, and significantly, both examples are to do with social work's *own* internal behaviour, and not with its impact on external agencies.

Not only, then, are sociology and social work different entities; social work practice and policy are developed under the influence of a wide range of complex factors, of which sociology is only one, and, in the direct sense, probably a very minor one at that.

It looks as though social workers – though sometimes attracted by macro-analyses – have learnt to operate independently of them. Indeed, it could hardly be otherwise, given the nature of their role and their traditional working methods. Even the switch from worker autonomy to a more bureaucratised model (as reported by Howe in Chapter 10) is unlikely to affect it one way or the other. Social workers have a job to do, and the way they do it reflects statutory requirements, agency guide-lines, the professional office culture, and their own personal style and inclinations. There is precious little scope for theoretical sociology to exert much direct influence on that.

To argue that sociology and social work have little in common with each other is not to detract from either; nor is it to suggest that sociological enquiry has nothing to contribute to social work. On the contrary. Within social work, there is a need for more research that starts from the *given* nature of the enterprise. Maybe sociology is only one part of the academic tradition that will feed into this; social psychology, market and operational research, and economics all have a part to play. But social work research certainly needs the discipline and the style of social science; the quality of empirical work undertaken in the field – especially a lot of that done 'in house' – is abysmal, and often appears to have been undertaken by people unaware of even the most basic debates that have taken place in fifty years' development of sociological research methods.

A programme of research undertaken by sociologists with a sympathetic interest in social work – preferably with a social work background themselves – can throw light on many key issues relevant to policy development and practice. The massive growth in social services budgets has meant rapid expansion in public-sector staffing; the emergence of private-sector homes has introduced ambiguities of meaning in the world of welfare; media interest in social work has brought new tensions and led to changed practices – often more to do with deflecting criticism than with improving service delivery; bureaucratic hierarchies have got longer and the work of social services managers has begun to look more and more indistinguishable from that of managers in business or industry; 'community care' as a concept has assumed the status of a political dictum without much realisation of what it means in practice or what it might cost; social workers spend more and more time writing records and reports to the point where the written word may be assuming more social significance than the events described; gender distributions inside social services have followed predictable lines, with mostly men appointed to the top jobs carrying the biggest salaries.

Sociologists have not appreciated the many potential fields for study and analysis that have developed in the wholly non-radical arenas of local authority social services departments, health districts, and probation offices during the 1980s and beyond. But in order to capitalise on that opportunity, researchers will have to acknowledge that they cannot always be in the business of wholly redefining other people's worlds. Social activities take many forms and not all are easily explicable, but all have internal and external systems, and all have functional attributes which are open to study and development.

In 1981, I wrote:

That there is scope for research investigation into and theoretical debate about welfare systems, goes without saying but a phrase such as '*the* sociology of social work' conjures up an impression of something far more specific, more reified than anything that can yet be envisaged.

(Davies 1981: 279)

Nothing has changed. Of course, as will become clear to any reader of this volume, the idea of *the* sociology of social work is certainly erroneous. But even *sociology of social work*, as Sibeon punctiliously puts it in Chapter 2, is strangely underdeveloped.

IV

There seem to me to be three major issues facing social work that lend themselves to sociological exploration.

The first is one that I have tried to grapple with elsewhere (Davies 1985), and that still seems to me to be fundamentally a sociological question: What is the function (in Merton's sense) of social work in society? What part does it play in the order of things? If it didn't exist, would it have to be invented? Is it a mark of consensualism – or of conflict? In an increasingly mobile, even fluid community is social work likely to assume more and more of the traditional roles of the family? What is the nature of the relationship between social work and ethnic (or other) minority groups?

The second is different, but, if answered successfully, should provide vital clues to enable us to answer the first (which is, I think, the more difficult question). What constitutes good social work practice? Who is to be the judge of that? How much freedom should social workers themselves have to define it (or to re-define it)? What rights or powers do clients have in answering the question? Could a form of consumerism be introduced to good effect? Is it essentially in the hands of those in power – political or managerial? Sociological theory would suggest that the latter option is the one most likely to be close to social reality, but it is not impossible for it to be so answered as to incorporate a high level of client satisfaction as a fundamental criterion.

The third question flows, not only from post-Foucaultian writing, but also from the work of Goffman (1961) and Miller and Gwynne (1972). It is this: once social work organisations are created, what can be done to restrict the apparent tendency for some employed within them to utilise the relative vagueness of agency objectives to maximise the congeniality of their own work position irrespective of its impact on the interests of agency or client? How can a situation be prevented in which workers are free to re-define goals for their own limited benefit?

Of course, the ultimate irony is that the radicals have explicitly said that social workers *should* set out to re-define the goals – though with an eye on revolution rather than on self-interest. Such a circumstance only brings us back to the second, or even to the first question. Can social workers in the public sector be allowed, under any circumstances, to override political policy making in profiling their own functions – and, if so, are they likely to model their work on activities likely to be of greater benefit to clients or of maximum value to themselves? This is a question that lies at the heart of much public disillusionment with social welfare.

Even the act of asking questions like this is sometimes said to be indicative of a reactionary approach to welfare; on the contrary, concern with worker efficiency, a critical approach to the vested interests of unions and professional associations, and a commitment to strive for the development of *relevant* practice skills are all crucial for the maintenance of a reputable social work service – whether it is operating within a fully fledged socialist state or under a mixed economy.

The chapters of this book do no more than hint at some of the answers to these questions. But if, as seems likely, the business of social work continues to grow rapidly – and especially if new relationships between the public sector and private development emerge – then the need for research investigation and programme monitoring will become even more pressing. Whether sociology offers a primary vehicle by which improved patterns of service can be achieved in social work seems, on its track record to date, rather doubtful. It is a question that is of as much interest to sociologists as it is to social workers.

© 1991 Martin Davies

NOTE

A short part of Section II of this chapter incorporates an extensively revised extract from an article originally published in the *British Journal of Social Work* (Davies 1981).

Part One

SOCIAL WORK AND SOCIOLOGICAL THEORY

Chapter Two

THE CONSTRUCTION OF A CONTEMPORARY SOCIOLOGY OF SOCIAL WORK

ROGER SIBEON

This chapter explores issues at a general level in the construction of a sociology of social work. The reason for selecting theory as the main focus for the chapter is that a seeming lack of awareness of developments in modern sociological theory has been one of the major deficiencies in accounts of social work, including a number of professedly 'sociological' accounts. Theory, as will become apparent in the following pages, has connections not only to methodology; theory influences decisions in the selection of particular social work topics for empirical inquiry and also influences subsequent analysis and interpretation of the data produced by empirical research.

AN OPERATIONAL DEFINITION

Sociology of social work explicitly employs *sociological* theoretical, empirical, and methodological perspectives as a resource for analysing the nature of social work; its ultimate objective is to increase sociological understanding of social work *as a whole* rather than of only a single dimension or 'component' of social work (e.g. its organisational structure) viewed in isolation from other major components which together form the world of social work. This composite definition will suffice for the moment in identifying a sociological sub-field that can accurately be described as *sociology of social work*.

Earlier work by Leonard (1966) and by Heraud (1970) in formulating a holistic, comprehensive sociological overview of social work has been overtaken by events both in sociology and in social work. At the present time, sociology of social work is acutely underdeveloped (Howe 1988: 65). Almost all existing sociological analyses of social work exhibit at least one of two distinctive features. First, even ostensibly 'sociological' accounts of social work have a tendency to be detached from recent major theoretical and empirical developments in 'mainstream' sociology. For example, Sullivan's (1987) *Sociology and Social Welfare* is mistitled; the specifically sociological content of the book is sparse. Distance from sociology is even more evident in Day's (1987) *Sociology in Social Work Practice*. Webb in a critical review suggests that Day's depiction of sociology is superficial and inadequate (Webb 1987: 157), outdated (158), and one which 'owes virtually nothing to sociology, but almost everything to a string of commonplace observations and homilies that could be derived from any quarter' (158).

The reasons for a low level of development in sociology of social work are complex. They include: schismatic responses to hotly contested disputes centred on the politics of welfare, reflected in a long history of tension and 'distance' in the relationship between sociology and social work (Webb and Evans 1976) which was heightened in the 1970s and early 1980s by Marxist sociology's rejection of 'bourgeois' social work professionalism (Pinker 1983a: 153); wider perennial and also contemporary problems (Lee 1982) in the general relationship of social science knowledge to social work discourse, including 'abstract' academic theory on the one hand, and, on the other, evidence of social workers' occupational preference for common-sense reasoning (Karpf 1931), experientially acquired 'practice wisdoms' (Carew 1979), and a tendency in their everyday practice and in their way of thinking about the nature of social work to draw very little upon sociology or upon formal social science knowledge generally (Kadushin 1959; Bartlett 1970; Stevenson 1970, 1981: 22–3).

Another reason for the torpid rate of progress in this field of study is the general lack of interest in, or knowledge about, social work on the part of most sociologists and perhaps also a general reluctance among sociologists to spell out the empirical applications (not only with regard to social work) of theoretical ideas (Bryant 1976: 347).

A second distinctive feature in sociological accounts of social work is the tendency to focus not upon the profession *in toto* but upon specific, delineated themes, topics, or individual 'components' of social work. These include the structure and forms of knowledge employed by social workers; the relation of 'theory' to practice; professionalisation processes; social work education and training; professional socialisation; moral-political dimensions of social work; organisational and service-delivery issues; and the relation of social work to the welfare state and to the wider society. At the present time, there is no developed sociology of social work in the sense of a holistic contemporary sociological overview of social work, encompassing all of the various components just referred to. This signifies not only a failure to assess sociologically whether one or more of these components has greater 'centrality' or causal significance than others in determining the general shape of social work in Britain today, but also a contemporary failure to examine sociologically the ways in which some of these individual components may *interact* and perhaps have strong mutually 'shaping' influences one upon the other.

In defining sociology of social work, to specify that the analysis has to be explicitly and identifiably *sociological* is, in one sense, a fairly straightforward proposition. Some social science accounts of social work, whatever their merits as contributions from other disciplinary perspectives, are patently not sociological. For example, Timms and Watson's (1978) text on social work is written from the standpoint of philosophy, Sutton's (1979) from the standpoint of psychology. Neither of these texts is, nor were they intended to be, a study in *sociology* of social work. In another sense, however, the term 'sociological', when used to describe the *modus operandi* appropriate to sociology of social work, is problematic. Sociology is multi-paradigmatic: ethnomethodology, symbolic interactionism, Marxist sociology, and structuralism are (in terms of their epistemological and ontological assumptions and methodological precepts) antithetical sociological perspectives (Urry 1981: 32). This leaves open the question of *which* sociological perspectives (or combination of perspectives) should be selected, and there is no reason to suppose all sociologists of social work will adopt the same sociological approach to their subject matter. This is not necessarily a bad thing; in Reed's terminology, acceptance of paradigmatic pluralism within any field of social science discourse is a way of recognising complex ambiguities that exist in the social world and in the relation of observers and social investigators to that world (Reed 1985: 206). However, positions do, of course, have to be taken at the level of individual contributions to the corpus of knowledge that constitutes sociology of social work. As will become apparent later, particular 'types' of sociology will be advocated in this chapter and some other types criticised. This reflects the importance of making explicit the grounds for selecting particular sociological perspectives and methodologies and the need to *demonstrate how the particular approach adopted contributes theoretically, empirically, and methodologically to the future development of sociology of social work.* A crucial implication of this is that sociologists of social work should engage in critical analysis of sociological perspectives; without such analysis the grounds for selecting particular perspectives will remain unclear. One of the main arguments of this chapter is that a *reflexive* sociology of social work, in consciously choosing and fashioning its own sociological tools against a background of theoretical and methodological pluralism in sociology, has to also be, in Friedrichs's (1970) terms, a *sociology of sociology*.

The second strand in the definition provided at the beginning of the chapter also requires attention. Sociology of social work aims, as its ultimate and primary objective, to increase sociological understanding of the social work profession *as a whole*, including the various components listed earlier and patterns of interrelation between them, and also patterns of interrelation between them and the wider society. This does not mean that detailed sociological studies of specific, individual components or of particular social work topics, undertaken without reference to other constitutive components of social work, are not an integral part of a sociology of social work. As in most other fields, in sociology of social work it is necessary to build upon an academic division of labour and upon specialist academic and research interests, in particular, narrowly defined areas of inquiry; and it is necessary also to distinguish between short-term and longer-term objectives in constructing a contemporary sociology of social work. Tightly focused sociological analyses of specific topics or particular components of social work are no less important to the future development of sociology of social work than other work undertaken at the level of broader, globalistic sociological 'overviews' of social work examined in its entirety in a way that encompasses all of its major constitutive components. Indeed, topic specificity in theoretical or empirical research is a necessary way of providing depth of topic 'penetration' and close, detailed sociological knowledge of particular social work processes, problems, and practices. Examples of sociological topic specificity are Smith's (1979) work on social work organisations, Heraud's (1981) account of social work education and training, and Hardiker's research on the structure and forms of social work knowledge (Hardiker 1977, 1981; Curnock and Hardiker 1979). On the one hand, it is necessary to construct detailed sociological knowledge of each of the major constitutive elements that comprise social work; on the other, it is also necessary to develop sociological frames of reference for viewing the assemblage of elements from a wider vantage point.

Therefore future development in this field requires that sociological analyses should be undertaken at two distinct levels. Future progress in sociology of social work *is dependent upon the continuation of detailed sociological investigations of particular social work topics, as well as work at the level of a more global sociological overview which aims both to formulate its own procedures and hypotheses and to bring together material produced by other, topic-centred studies.* In constructing a contemporary sociology of social work it is essential that efforts should be made to ensure that the patterns of influence between global sociological perspectives and detailed sociological topic-centred studies are dialectical; in the future it seems at least possible (and certainly desirable) that an accumulation of theoretical and empirical sociological studies of specific social work topics will increasingly be shaped by and in turn modify the more holistic, 'global' perspectives developed as part of the construction of a modern sociology of social work.

SOCIOLOGICAL THEORY AND METHOD: OPPOSITION BETWEEN MICRO-SOCIAL AND MACRO-SOCIAL PERSPECTIVES

All of the major sociological perspectives in one way or another address the 'micro–macro problem', described by Outhwaite as 'the most important opposition in contemporary social theory' (Outhwaite 1983: 17). This is variously expressed as tension between epistemological idealism and materialism, or between non-determinist and determinist theories of behaviour and consciousness as in the debate of 'human agency versus structure'. These oppositions have created 'a widening gap between micro- and macro-social theories and methodologies' (Knorr-Cetina 1981: 41). There have been innumerable attempts to bridge this gap. Bendix (1984) advocates an integration of 'subjectivist' and 'positivist' methodologies. Thomason (1982) suggests that both idealist (constructionist) theories and realist (materialist) theories contain theoretical deficiencies. Wuthnow et al., in adopting the term 'Bergerian sociology' (Wuthnow et al. 1984: 21), indicate a renewal of interest in earlier sociological attempts to construct a dialectical theoretical integration (Berger and Luckmann 1967) of micro- and macro-social variables, an interest also revealed in Giddens's (1984) elaboration of the concepts 'duality of structure' and 'structuration' developed in his earlier work (Giddens 1976, 1977, 1982). Hindess rejects the idea of building theoretical integrationist bridges around the concept 'duality' (Hindess 1982: 499), but it is nevertheless sharply critical of the reductionisms inherent in methodological individualism and in structural theory based on methodological collectivism (Hindess 1986a: 113–14).

It is possible to transcend conventional formulations of the micro-macro theoretical opposition through use of the concepts 'sites', 'space-time', and 'materials'. Sites are particular places such as a social services office or a professional training course at a university or polytechnic. If it is heuristically assumed that sites and what goes on within them are not wholly insulated from events, ideas, resources, or policies that exist outside any particular site(s), it can be inferred that individual sites are locations in space-time. An argument developed later is that social work *materials* flow between sites: 'materials' is a convenient shorthand expression used throughout the chapter as a generic term encompassing social work values, forms of thought, policies, practices, organisational and service-delivery conventions, or any 'problems' or controversies associated with social work. Some social work materials are temporally disseminated in the sense that they travel across social work sites through time. Though the notion that materials 'travel' might at first sight seem curious, there are significant analytic empirical advantages in thinking about social life in this way. An example of a particularly problematic social work material that has travelled far through time is 'theory–practice' (controversies surrounding the relevance or otherwise of academic social science to social work practice). Current constructions of the 'theory-practice' problematic have perennial dimensions going back to the first attempts to 'professionalise' social work at the turn of the century (Jones 1979; Lee 1982).

Social work materials are not only disseminated temporally. At any particular period of time, such as the present, social work materials (ideas, policies, forms of practice, etc.) are disseminated spatially across contemporaneously existing social work sites. This is not to say that social work forms of thought, practices, policies, and organisational conventions are likely to be wholly identical in every social services office (or probation office) throughout the country: but it is to say that social workers in a particular local place or at a particular local time employ at least some *shared* forms of thought and procedures likely to be recognised as something called 'social work' by spatially (and temporally) dispersed social workers. Actors, for example, speak of 'professional social work' (BASW 1977: 20) as something (a 'material') that exists over and above any particular social work site; to say this is to say that the material must have been disseminated, by whatever means, across sites through space and time.

There are a hundred and one ways in which at least *some* of the things that happen in a local (social work) site may be relatively unique and idiosyncratic at the level of the particular site itself or at the level of personal biographies and personalitier (Lave 1986). Site-specific idiosyncrasy implies a degree of spatial and temporal insulation from structure and history. Some forms of psychological reductionism (Bottomore 1975: 50) and, in sociology, micro-situational theories such as symbolic interactionism rest on a precept that personal consciousness, meanings, intentions, and actions in particular sites, far from being predestined local unfoldings of a grand historical script or predetermined 'expressions' of a macro-structural order, are largely *emergent* site-specific 'productions'. Microsociology and, in particular, symbolic interactionism rests on a theoretical framework based on *methodological situationalism* (Meltzer, Petras, and Reynolds 1975: 54). This statement, however, returns us to the 'micro–macro problem'. Methodological situationalism, based on a theoretical assumption that a large element of 'emergent', situationally produced material is the 'stuff' of social life and based methodologically on '*in situ*' research techniques such as participant or non-participant observation, is well suited to the task of producing data on situationally specific material. Methodological situationalism is not suited, though, to the task of empirically producing and analysing data referring to much larger configurations of materials of the type *that circulate spatially and temporally across sites and which may 'enter into' a local site and to a greater or lesser extent shape local actors' ways of thinking and acting.*

Some meanings may be widely disseminated and become an established part of the 'language habits' (Sapir 1966: 68–9) of an occupational 'speech community' (Whorf 1956) or of particular segments of an occupational community. Examples of trans-situational collectivised constructs in professional social work are the 'presenting problem' thesis (Haines 1975; 39–40) and the client 'emotional ventilation' thesis (Moffett 1972: 85). Microsociology is neither conceptually nor methodologically equipped to account in non-reductionist terms for these or any other temporally and spatially dispersed social work materials (Knorr-Cetina 1981: 28). Structural theory attempts unsuccessfully to 'solve' this problem: it offers a macro-reductionist axiom (methodological collectivism) which claims that micro-events, cognitions, and practices in local sites are predetermined expressions ('necessary effects') of history and of social structure. An example is Philp's structuralist theory of social work discourse under capitalism: according to his theory, what social workers 'say' and do is an 'effect' of a historically institutionalised discourse which *determines* local social work 'speech' and practices (Philp 1979: 89). Once again, we are returned to the 'micro–macro problem' and the debate of 'human agency versus structure'. Ultimately, the theoretical opposi-tions between micro-social and macro-social theories pivot on the problem of reductionism (Craib 1984: 220–1). To attempt to account for 'structure' *in terms of* agency is (micro) reductionist, as in methodological individualism and, in a different sense, in methodo-logical situationalism: equally, to attempt – as in Philp's theory above – to 'explain' human agency *in terms of* structure is (macro) reductionist, as in methodological collectivism. Social life is not reducible to a single reductionist principle of 'micro' or 'macro' explanation. Neither is it possible to arrive at an 'accommodation' or 'compromise' based on a *synthesis* of both these forms of reductionism: this is because it is not logically possible to construct a theoretical synthesis out of opposed, mutually contradictory theories (Leonard 1984: 75).

MICRO-SOCIAL THEORY AND THE PROBLEM OF REDUCTIONISM

Although micro-situationalist sociology breaks with the Garfinkelian ethnomethodological rubric (Garfinkel and Sacks 1970) of a chain of (re)accounting occasions (Wilson 1971: 69) which refer to no ontologically prior order of phenomena (Bruce and Wallis 1983; Gilbert and Mulkay 1984), some versions of microsociology never-theless remain phenomenologically close to actors' 'own' data. An example is 'grounded-theory' methodology formulated by Glaser and Strauss who argue that explanatory theory should emerge from the actors' own data rather than be 'generated by logical deduction from a-priori assumptions' (Glaser and Strauss 1967: 3). Though it is not suggested that 'structural' aspects of social contexts have no con-sequences for the constructs and forms of awareness developed by actors (Glaser and Strauss 1964), grounded-theory methodology is none the less more narrowly situationalist ('site-specific') than many other microsociological perspectives: some grounded-theory case studies resemble Eckstein's (1970) category of configurative-idiographic studies which Mitchell notes 'do not easily lead to . . . general theoretical interpretations' (Mitchell 1983: 195). In contrast, Becker's interactionist methodological prescriptions suggest that the function of a micro-empirical case study is that it 'attempts to arrive at a comprehensive understanding of the group under study. At the same time the case study also attempts to develop more general statements about the regularities in social structure' (Becker 1968: 233). The frequent criticism that microsociology is 'divorced from structure' is, therefore, not wholly accurate (Williams 1986). A related and important point is that microsociology is not individualist; it is not a form of methodological individualism (Cooley 1902: 36). Microsociology is 'situational', and focuses on the study of face-to-face *interactions* (Simmel 1971: 23) through which meanings and practices are negotiated *intersubjectively* among individuals in local sites. Microsociology in the form of methodological situationalism is intersubjectivist (Mead 1967: 78) and interactionist: it is not concerned with individuals as single actors but with interactions and negotiations in social situations and regards social action as arising from the interlocking of intentionalities rather than from their singular existence (Knorr-Cetina 1981: 8–9 and 16–17).

The point was made earlier that micro-situationalist sociology is reductionist if it tries to account for certain types of phenomena: specifically, it is neither conceptually nor methodologically equipped for engaging in non-reductionist explanatory analysis of *linkages* between spatially and temporally dispersed sites or for investigating the temporal and spatial passage of material across sites and its possible 'entry' into some of these sites. As will become clearer later, this is an argument not for replacing but for supplementing micro-ethnographic data by other forms of analysis based on other methodologies including the use of social survey and statistical data, contemporary and historical documentary sources, and 'co-ordinated ethnographies' (Duster 1981: 132–3). An important reason for retaining micro-situationalist studies in sociology of social work is that they provide data on the handling of social work materials in local sites without requiring macro-reductionist interpretations of those data as 'necessary effects' of social structure (Smith 1965; Strauss *et al.* 1973: 308; Hill 1982).

Structural theory portrays welfare professionals as relatively passive, predetermined agents (Burrell and Morgan 1979: 368) implementing a pre-given 'macro' discourse of welfare (Philp 1979; Sharp 1980). Structural theory is rejected in micro-situationalist empirical research, as in Sudnow's (1965) study of the 'situated' nature of plea-bargaining in the American criminal justice system. In this judicial system plea-bargaining takes place between the prosecuting counsel (the District Attorney), the defence counsel (the Public Defender), and the accused person. Sudnow shows that whether plea-bargaining can produce agreement leading to a plea of guilty to a less serious charge partly hinges on *negotiation* of the concept 'normal crime': 'normal' burglaries, for example, involve no use of weapons, little damage to property, theft of only low-priced items, and an 'amateur' as opposed to 'professional' *modus operandi* in carrying out the offence (Sudnow 1965: 260). Wootton (1975), in a commentary on Sudnow's data, makes the point that definition of what in any *particular* instance constitutes an actual example of a 'normal crime' cannot be determined with reference to general conventions, but, rather, has to be situationally negotiated on each occasion that the question arises. For this reason Wootton refers to 'expressions whose meaning relies on the context in which they are used in such a way that attempts to delineate the meaning of words in some more general way are both misleading and incomplete' (Wootton 1975: 19).

Wootton's contention that language, meanings, and practices are contextual gains a measure of support in Carlen's (1977) detailed investigation of magistrates' courts where she examined interactions between police officers, probation officers, magistrates, solicitors, and social workers. The situated, particularistic ebb and flow of meanings and negotiations between judicial and welfare professionals in Carlen's study has a contextuality and situated significance that it would be difficult to infer from a knowledge of formal law, abstract rules, official conventions, or from an uncontextual general knowledge of the formal professional and occupational functions and tasks of the participants observed '*in situ*' by Carlen. Other ethnographic empirical studies have revealed important interactive processes in the construction of social policies (Carrier and Kendall 1973; Young 1977; Ham 1980) and in social work practice (Kuhn 1962; Barbour 1985; Pratt and Grimshaw 1985). A useful micro-situational account of social work cognitions and practices is provided in Smith's (1977) investigation of the construction of meanings in social work decision making on child care issues, and in Rees's (1978) empirical study of interactions between social workers and their clients. Empirical 'micro' social work studies of this type are not always explicit in stating their underlying theoretical assumptions, but it is clear that such studies draw in one way or another upon the situationalist perspectives of microsociology. In short, a micro-situational approach to the study of social work language and

26

cognition rests on the methodological rubric, 'Don't ask for the meaning: ask for the use' (Ryle and Findlay 1972: 7), which in turn is derived from a theoretical postulate that practice and speech in micro-settings are not 'signifiers' of macro-structures (Heller 1986: 155–7).

In the light of the preceding remarks there are grounds for suggesting that the importance of situational microsociological studies in sociology of social work lies in their capacity to provide data which, when *placed alongside other types of data*, contribute to a fuller understanding of which social work materials are idiosyncratic, site-specific, and interactively 'emergent', and which materials are local variations or local applications of much 'larger' general patterns of material that are temporally and spatially dispersed across a very large number of social work sites. Put another way, methodological situationalism is a necessary but not sufficient perspective in sociology of social work: for investigating the larger space-time dimensions of social work, other theoretical perspectives and methodologies and other forms of data are required. To attempt to 'explain' the existence and space-time dissemination of these larger ('macro') configurations of material in micro-situational (or 'emergent') terms is reductionist; as already briefly noted, however, theories that try to account for these larger patterns (and their consequences for micro-happenings) in terms of macro-structural theory are no solution to 'the micro–macro problem' for they merely substitute one form of reductionism for another.

MACRO-SOCIAL THEORY: IMPORTING ANOTHER REDUCTIONISM

It is intended in this section of the chapter to assess critically some of the distinctive properties of macro-social theory in a general way rather than attempt to provide a highly detailed account of sociological variations in uses of the term 'social structure' (Rex 1973: 113–20). Some of the ideas examined below refer to 'structural analysis' which rests on a definition of social structure as the recurring, patterned features of social life, described by Cohen as the 'characteristics of lateral and temporal standardisation and recurrence' (Cohen 1972: 95). Another version of macro-social theory is structural*ist* analysis; it will be useful to begin with a critical review of structuralism because this type of macro-social theory provides a sharply focused contrast with the micro-situationalist perspectives discussed earlier.

Structuralist theorists' interpretations of micro and macro

phenomena involve an analytic movement from subject to structure: human actors are 'decentred' from their own meanings and for structuralists it is structure, not human actors as products of structure, that is the main focus of inquiry (Smart 1985: 16). Theoretical movement from subject to structure rests on a claim that structure is self-regulating and synchronic. The idea of a self-sustaining social totality is explicit in Scholes's comment 'At the heart of the idea of structuralism is the idea of system: a complete, self-regulating entity that adapts to new conditions by transforming its features whilst retaining its systematic structure' (Scholes 1974: 10). This postulate is a feature of structuralist linguistics, which may be regarded as the antithesis of the micro-situationalists' view that language, meaning, and practice are largely context-dependent. Lévi-Strauss (1963, 1974) argues that language and meaning are an autonomous, objective cognitive system. A cognitive system as defined in structuralist theory has a 'deep' inner logic that exists independently of its referential aspects or its situated, contextual usages by actors in local sites. In this sense, language is determinist: cognitive and practical activities are predetermined instances (parts) of wholes. The classic formulation of structuralist linguistics is elaborated in Saussure (1974). Saussure accords primacy to *langue* (language) over *parole* (speech). The core of Saussure's theory is that language is an objective facticity with a 'deep logic' of its own, a corpus of knowledge that is historically and structurally 'given' and that is hidden from actors' consciousness. Because the relationship of parts to wholes, of speech to language, is absent from consciousness, the actor's conscious reflection will not 'reveal' the deep logic of language which can never be grasped in its totality. In Saussure's theoretical scheme, the meaning of a word (or concept or theory) is not its relation to an object (Rojeck, Peacock, and Collins 1988: 119) but its relation to other words (i.e. the totality of language), and, because language (*langue*) is an unconscious universal structure which is unknown to human actors, the 'deep' (or 'real') meaning of words, cognitions, and practices is a surface-level expression which cannot be penetrated or decoded in speech (*parole*). In this objectivist, autonomising conception of language, 'it is not we who think and then use words but our language that thinks for us' (Sharp 1980: 99). Therefore (social work) practice and speech (*parole*) in a local site are, on this view, predetermined and humanly unrecognisable expressions of *langue*. *Langue* has, as it were, a life of 'its' own. This notion that (e.g. social work) *langue* is an autonomous entity existing independently of its situational practice by individuals or groups is part of a general structuralist theory that human actors are unbeknowingly 'inserted' into language (Barthes 1967).

Structuralist linguistics breaks sharply away not only from situationalist approaches but also from social constructionist conceptions of social work language and practice (Sibeon 1981: 59). In Bergerian constructionist sociology, language (e.g. social work language) is regarded as having a key role in processes of objectivation and socialisation (as in, let us say, the professional socialisation of social workers): this is because 'language is capable of becoming the objective repository of vast accumulations of meaning and experience, which it can then preserve in time and transmit to the following generations' (Berger and Luckmann 1967: 52). However, structuralist theorists believe that the objective facticity ('autonomy') of language and of structure is 'real'. For Berger any apparent objective facticity of language, structure, or culture is actor-imputed, i.e. is an *actor-reification* produced through processes of socialisation and the internalisation of humanly objectified, institutionalised meanings absorbed into consciousness and taken for granted (routinised) during 'everyday' interactions in the course of ordinary life. In Berger's terms, structure can be reproduced only through its *legitimation* in the habitualised thoughts, preferences, and practices of socialised *actors* who, however, may in some circumstances de-legitimate and change structure.

Theoretical possibilities for what constructionist sociologists call *de-reification* (Berger and Luckmann 1967: 226) and *de-objectivation* (Berger and Luckmann 1967: 144) are removed in structuralist analysis. Pro-Saussurian theories of language, as in Culler's concept of the 'closed circle of culture' (Culler 1975: 254), imply that there are no possibilities for discursively re-defining and changing the social (work) world. For sociology of social work, the central methodological implication of structuralist linguistics is that, because language has an underlying structure of its own, and because speech (*parole*) is derived from language (*langue*) and given meaning by it in ways beyond the conscious grasp of human actors, the study of (social work) knowledge should never begin with the micro-situational study of local, derivative 'speech instances' (*parole*) but instead should begin with the study of social work *langue* as a whole, i.e. as a 'deep', autonomous, and objectively 'real' facticity that exists independently of its situational expressions. This methodological rubric stems from the theoretical assumptions of structuralist linguistics; these assumptions centre on the idea that social work language (*langue*) does not depend on local social work speech practices (*parole*) for its reproduction nor can speech (*parole*) act upon or modify social work language. Determinist concepts of language and practice are also found in some other theoretical traditions, such as Foucault's earlier writing on 'clinical discourse'. In his 'archaeology' of knowledge, Foucault refers to 'a body of anonymous, historical rules, always determined in the time and space that have defined a given period' (Foucault 1972: 117). This reduces actors to the role of passive exponents of a pre-given mode of discourse (Searle 1969; Sadock 1974) and moves towards an endorsement of Saussure's rejection of a 'competence' model of language: by implication there is here a determinism of the kind rejected in social work terms by Webb (1985) and rejected in sociology by Habermas who argues that at least some limited space exists for actors to develop emancipatory linguistic and communicative 'competence' (Habermas 1972: 197).

For reasons that will be clarified later, the concept 'interests of capitalism', a key concept in Marxist versions of macro-social theory, may be regarded as a rhetorical construct; it is a reification that has no empirical explanatory significance. A case in point is the failure of Althusserian structuralist Marxism to transcend the economic determinism of conventional structural Marxism; this is revealed in, for instance, the Althusserian claim that 'no class can hold state power over a long period without at the same time exercising its hegemony over and in the Ideological State Apparatus' (Althusser 1971: 139). A useful critical overview of problems associated with the concepts 'relative autonomy' and 'determination in the last instance' is provided by Hindess (1981, 1983a: 39–42, 1983b). The problems noted by Hindess are exhibited in 'revised' Marxist accounts of social work. For example, Bolger *et al.* criticise 'crude' Marxist functionalism (Bolger *et al.* 1981: 3 and 17–19) then a few pages later announce 'the dominance of capitalist social relationships . . . exert their *dominant* interest in the development of social policy' (Bolger *et al.* 1981: 41, italics added). The familiar revisionist denunciation of Marxist welfare functionalism followed by its reintroduction in disguised form (Sibeon 1982) is evident in Leonard's Marxist account of social work. Having warned his readers that there is no simple 'direct correspondence' (Leonard 1984: 25) between social action and the 'needs' of capitalism, it soon becomes clear that Leonard has a very close 'indirect' correspondence in mind. He criticises Mitchell's (1975) Althusserian

Marxism (Leonard 1984: 49–52) on the grounds that 'the separation of ideology from economic imperatives leads . . . to . . . problems' (Leonard 1984: 49). These 'problems' only arise, however, when it is claimed that the empirical complexities of social life are reducible to the view that 'economic production is determinant "in the last instance" ' (Leonard 1984: 104). Caveats such as 'relative autonomy' or 'in the last instance' cannot remove the reification inherent in theories predicated on the idea of structural imperatives.

Problems of theoretical reification prompted Dahrendorf to observe that 'Society is patently not a person, and any personification of it obscures its nature and weakens what is said about it' (Dahrendorf 1968: 44). These problems are manifest in Marxist notions that 'structural contradictions' exist, and that these have an 'objective' structural existence independently of actors' forms of thought and actions. In Marxist theories of social work, contradictions are presumed to exist *within* structure; thus 'for . . . marxists, the concept of contradiction *within* social structures is essential . . . *the structure* is in constant tension' (Bolger *et al.* 1981: 3, italics added). This contrasts sharply with Berger and Luckmann's observation that ' "functional integration", if one wants to use this term at all, means the integration of the institutional order by way of various legitimating processes. In other words, *the integration lies not in the institutions but in their legitimation*' (Berger and Luckmann 1967: 224, original italics). The converse of 'legitimation' in the sense just referred to is that any 'crisis' of structural arrangements is *not a matter of 'contradictions' among or within the structures themselves, but a crisis of legitimation of those structures by actors*. A 'legitimation crisis', as in the legitimation crisis of the modern welfare state (Offe 1984), is in the true sense of the word a crisis of *legitimation*, not a situation of 'structural contradiction' or systemic ('objective') structural tension. Hypothesised 'structural' contradictions are no more than cognitively produced theoretical contradictions (i.e. explanatory failures) contained within theories of 'structural contradiction' themselves rather than existing 'in' the empirical reality to which such theories refer (Holmwood and Stewart 1983: 235).

Pierson refers critically to simplistic Marxist reductions of struggles surrounding 'race', gender, generation, and social movements to, ultimately, an expression of class struggles (Pierson 1984). In the next section of this chapter it will be shown that classes are not social actors; only actors can struggle and classes as such do not struggle (Hindess 1988: 27). A commonplace Marxist assumption has been that any division or 'fracturing' (Jones 1983: 54–9) of the working class along, say, 'race' or religious lines, is not 'real' conflict but instead is conflict promoted by the ruling class in defence of its interests. Empirical confirmation of this class-based 'divide and rule' hypothesis is conspicuously lacking. Wallis and Bruce note that for its confirmation it would be necessary to provide evidence of deliberate ruling-class attempts to ferment intra-class conflict: to show that these attempts were successful in producing or exacerbating conflict independently of (say) 'race' or gender or religious or regional factors: to show why the working class is 'blind' to the ruling-class strategy and why the working class is unable to understand its own values, intentions, and actions: to provide evidence that the ruling class *believes* it is in 'its' interest to promote intra-class antagonisms among the working class, and to provide evidence that this is done to further *class* interests rather than, for instance, the racial or gender or religious interests of the ruling class (Wallis and Bruce 1983: 101).

Despite these and other problems associated with reified conceptions of structure, the 'interests of capitalism', and 'objective' structurally given 'interests', theories based on these assumptions have accumulated in organisational studies (Marglin 1980; Burrell and Morgan 1979), sociology of medicine (see Bury 1986), sociology of education (Sharp 1980), sociology of welfare (Cockburn 1977) and also in the sociology of professions (Poulantzas 1975; Braverman 1974; Ehrenreich and Ehrenreich 1979). These theories empirically ignore or else reductively displace the role of actors.

An instance is the claim that capitalism and 'authoritarian' social work organisational hierarchies are synonymous (Bolger *et al.* 1981: 65). To claim that the construction of hierarchical 'bureau-professionalism' (Parry and Parry 1979: 43) in the Seebohm social services department is a representation or effect of 'the interests of capitalism' is either to ignore the self-formulated interests, purposes, and actions of the actors involved or reductively to suppose that these purposes are 'objective' 'necessary effects' of a social totality ('capitalist society'). In fact, there is fairly good empirical evidence (reviewed in Whittington and Bellaby 1979) that the construction, dissemination, and practical application of the organisational concept 'bureau-professionalism' in the 1970s gained major impetus through the research, consultancy, and far-reaching 'public relations' activities of individuals and groups influenced by the 'Brunel studies' (SSORU 1974: 14–15; Billis *et al.* 1980). Bureau-professionalism was socially constructed; it did not appear 'out of nowhere' as a predetermined expression of 'the interests of capitalism'.

Similarly, intense struggles throughout the 1980s among competitive social (work) actors over the construction of education and training policies were not a predetermined 'effect' of capitalism or the unfolding of a grand historical 'macro' script. These struggles centred on proposals to 'reform' social work education and training. The British Association of Social Workers had in 1977 warmly applauded (BASW 1977: 18) the Central Council for Education and Training in Social Work (CCETSW) for having introduced in 1975 a new two-tier, binary system of qualification that seemed likely to reinforce the Seebohm vertical task-stratification model in the social services departments (Lee 1982). In 1975 the existing full professional qualification for professional social workers (the Certificate of Qualification in Social Work) was supplemented by a new, more practical qualification (the Certificate in Social Service) designed for 'sub-professional' social services workers. The new two-tier system of training and qualification was attractive to professional actors because it seemed that the introduction of this binary system of training would buttress and maintain the hierarchical demarcation line (BASW 1977: 18) that had emerged in the social services departments between professional social workers ('CQSW work') and social services workers ('CSS work').

Some years later, for a complex mixture of reasons that cannot be explored here, the CCETSW proposed abolishing this two-tier system in favour of a *single* qualification that, as professional actors were quick to spot, would also mean fusing together the categories 'professional social workers' (CQSW workers) and 'social services workers' (CSS workers) and abolish the hierarchical dividing line between the two groups in the social services departments. These proposals were welcomed by the CSS lobby who wanted the same training, pay, and status as professional social workers, and also welcomed by employers who desired more practical, less 'professional' forms of training (Harbert 1985a, 1985b). However, the developments were fiercely resisted by social work academics and professional actors (Bamford 1984; Pinker 1984a, 1984b, 1986; Measures 1986). The intensity of the conflict between these competitive social (work) actors led Sainsbury to suggest that the future of social work itself was gravely threatened by intractable internal divisions (Sainsbury 1985: 9).

These conflicts were not 'a necessary effect' of the social totality, or of 'objective' structural 'needs', or of structurally 'given' interests;

the conflicts arose because different social work actors held different and opposed *self-formulated* interests and perspectives.

Another empirical illustration of a non-reductionist interpretation of policy construction processes is Clapham's (1986) rejection of Cockburn's (1977) claim that the failure of local authority 'corporate planning' techniques in the 1970s was an 'effect' of ruling-class 'objective' interests enshrined in the 'interests of capitalism'. Clapham shows that the demise of this management technique was largely a function of mobilised organisational resistance against it by 'threatened' professional actors within local authorities; in an illuminating aside Clapham suggests that any predictions concerning the fate of social work decentralisation ('community social work') should also be based on non-reductionist empirical analysis which does not reductively displace the proactive role of actors nor 'underestimate the power of the organisational interests involved' (Clapham 1986: 41).

TOWARDS AN ANTI-REDUCTIONIST SOCIOLOGY OF SOCIAL WORK

The term *actor* is central in non-reductionist sociology. Harre (1981), in a reference to biology, observes that animals have *emergent* structural properties, in particular *causal powers*, that are 'more than' the sum of the individual component parts (molecular cells). In social life, individual human actors have causal powers, but there are also other entities which have emergent structural properties: these entities have emergent capacities and types of causal efficacy that accrue by virtue of their structure and which are *in addition* to (or 'more than') the sum of the capacities possessed by individual persons. Harre calls these entities *supra-individuals*: examples of supra-individuals are committees (e.g. the cabinet or a local authority social services committee) and organisations such a local probation or social services departments, central government departments, professional associations, organised pressure groups, etc.

Supra-individuals do not exist above the middle-range ('organisational') level of social life. For an entity to be definable as a supra-individual it has to satisfy three criteria. First, it must be continuous in time. Second, it must occupy a distinctive and continuous region of space or a distinctive and continuous path through space. Third, it must have causal powers (Harre 1981: 141). Only 'structured collectivities' are supra-individuals with causal powers: a structured or 'relational' collectivity exhibits empirically 'real' relationships among its members (Harre 1981: 140). Non-relational taxonomic collectivities (e.g. 'the state', 'classes', 'men', 'white people', 'black people', 'women') have none of the emergent properties of structured collectivities (supra-individuals). To impute the existence of entities with causal powers above the level of supra-individuals ('organisations') is a rhetorical personification of something which cannot be empirically proven to 'exist' (Harre 1981: 141).

Rejection of personificationist conceptions of structure is also evident in Hindess's definition of an *actor* as 'a locus of decision and action where the action is in some sense a consequence of the actor's decisions' (Hindess 1986a: 115). Actors may be individual human actors, but there are also '*social actors*, other than human individuals' (Hindess 1986a: 115, italics added). For convenience, the term 'individual actor' is employed here and later to refer to individual human actors, the term *social actors* being used to refer to what Harre calls supra-individuals ('organisations' of various kinds). In Leonard's Marxist theory, social work under capitalism has an underlying function, said to be 'the justification of the present structure of class, gender, and ethnic relations' (Leonard 1983: xiii). Leonard's sociology and Hindess's anti-reductionist sociology are incompatible. Hindess observes that the possibilities for engaging in the social and political analysis of social reform are thoroughly obscured when the concept 'actor' is 'extended to aggregates that have no identifiable means of formulating decisions, let alone acting on them . . . [such as] . . . classes, racial, or gender categories' (Hindess 1986a: 124). Taxonomic collectivities are aggregates that do not have causal powers and therefore cannot 'cause' (be causally responsible for) any existing state of affairs (including those adjudged 'bad'), and for the same reason are not entities that can take remedial action to alter any existing state of affairs.

Major problems arise if it is assumed that 'objective', structurally 'given' interests are vested in taxonomic collectivities ('capitalist society' or the 'social totality', 'classes', 'men', etc.). Social work professionals, for example, are not unwitting 'agents of capitalism' (Edwards 1981: 307–8). Unless there was some intentional planning involved by someone, somewhere it is a teleological fallacy (explanation of a 'cause' in terms of its effects) to begin with a social work outcome, policy, or mode of practice and then 'work backwards' to impute the outcome or practice as the 'realisation' of someone's interests – such as the interests of other individual or social actors, or of taxonomic collectivities (Betts 1986: 50–1). If it is claimed that actors (e.g. professionals or their clients) have 'real' or 'objective' structurally given interests by virtue of their structural location in the social totality or their membership of a social category, it is unclear how the empirical researcher should distinguish these 'objective' interests from other interests, such as those specified by the actor concerned and by various other actors, or by the same actor in different circumstances (Hindess 1986b: 116). Hindess's sociology directs the researcher's attention to empirical investigation of the ways in which interests are *the product* of actors' assessments, decisions, and their framing of objectives in particular situations; this empirical orientation becomes necessary when it is recognised that interests 'do not appear arbitrarily, out of nowhere, they are not structurally determined and they cannot be regarded as the fixed or given properties of actors' (Hindess 1986b: 120).

Reductionist conceptions of actors' interests, preferences, and actions are not confined to conventional macro-structural theories. Recent advocates of the 'rational choice' approach formally denounce macro-structural theories and methodological collectivism. Rational-choice theory explicitly endorses methodological individualism (Hechter 1988: 264) and rests on the notions, first, that individuals normally act 'rationally' in maximising their personal gains and preferences in the face of structural constraints, and, second, that some preferences are not individually idiosyncratic but are group-patterned (Mason 1988: 17). Hindess's critique of recent Marxist versions of the rational-choice approach shows that these approaches, though formulated on an avowed commitment to methodological individualism, nestle on a tacit theoretical assumption that actors' forms of thought are structurally determined in so far as it is presumed that what counts as 'rational' action is a function of the actor's membership of a social collectivity (Hindess 1988: 22–4).

Hindess's conceptual framework predicts that actors' forms of thought and modes of assessing and acting upon their situation are not structurally determined, i.e. they are not a function of the actor's location in a social totality nor a function of the actor's membership of a social category. This formulation has a close empirical approximation in the policy struggles between competitive social work actors referred to earlier. In the earlier account it was noted that professional and 'academic-professional' actors perceived that a major de-professionalising threat was posed by the CCETSW's proposals to abolish the distinction between professional social work ('CQSW work') and social services work ('CSS work'). One way of responding to a perceived threat is to formulate a position of opposition, stick to it, and 'resist to the end'. This was Pinker's response to the perceived threat of de-professionalisation. He disseminated his 'professional' counter-definition through papers in academic social work journals (for example Pinker 1984a), and attempted to mobilise support via the popular journals that circulate widely among social workers. In 1984 he proclaimed that 'the balloon has reached bursting point' (Pinker 1984b: 18), and by 1986 he was advocating active sabotage of the proposals: he called for collective efforts to 'stop this initiative in its tracks . . . it is surprising that CCETSW has been allowed to get as far as it has done' (Pinker 1986: 21).

A different response from Pinker's is to 'see the writing on the wall', to view the CCETSW as a currently powerful actor operating in circumstances favourable to its policies, and to decide that if a new, threatening policy seems inevitable it may be better to 'go along with it' and perhaps even be seen to endorse it in principle while tactically attempting to avoid 'losing' too many interests to the new policy: one way of doing this is to try to ensure that 'second-order' negotiations at lower levels of policy detail can later be entered into in a way which brings as little damage as possible to (and as many advantages as it is possible to 'recoup' for) the threatened actor's constituency. This was the strategy adopted by the Association of Teachers in Social Work Education (ATSWE). The ATSWE, like Pinker, was strongly committed to an academic-professional model of social work education. In 1984 the ATSWE objected that a new single form of 'practical' training and qualification could not shoulder the 'incompatible burdens' that would be placed upon it (ATSWE 1984: 2). By 1985 the ATSWE, though still expressing strong reservations, had shifted its position and stated that it was 'broadly in favour' of the new practical training proposals (ATSWE 1985: 4). Twelve months later, in June 1986, the ATSWE recognised the seeming inevitability of a new training system and went as far as 'recommending' that the proposals be accepted (Report to Joint Working Party 1986: 4. para. 3). However the ATSWE also engineered some important caveats designed to safeguard its academic-professional interests and perspectives. These caveats insisted that only qualified staff be described as 'social workers' (Report to Joint Working Party 1986: 4, para. 2), that the existing 'academic' professional knowledge base for social work should not be significantly eroded (Report to Joint Working Party 1986: 5, para. 12), and that the regional committees set up to implement the details of the new scheme should not be dominated by employers and should have independent chairing (Report to Joint Working Party 1986: 6, para. 28).

In the course of the events just described, social actors employed strategies to achieve self-formulated interests and perspectives but neither the interests involved nor the modes of assessment and strategies employed for securing these interests were 'given' by the actors' structural location or membership of a social category. Pinker's professionalist response was similar to that of the British Association of Social Workers who strongly attacked the CCETSW proposals and criticised them as a 'back-of-the-envelope sketch' (Bamford 1984: 21). The ATSWE, though a member of the same academic-professional constituency as Pinker and the BASW, took an altogether different line and in doing so showed that there is no 'necessary' connection between actors' structural locations and their forms of thought or modes of 'assessing' and acting.

At a theoretical level, there are at least three reasons why the empirical description provided above cannot legitimately be criticised as resting on a 'new' epistemological idealism of the middle range. First, it is not assumed that actors 'know everything' when they make assessments and engage in action. Nor is it assumed that actors' decisions are always based on fully crystallised 'discursive' knowledge. Earlier, reference was made to Berger and Luckmann's descriptions of processes whereby knowledge may become habitualised, routinised, and 'taken for granted': a similar point is made in Giddens's distinction between 'discursive consciousness' and *tacit* or 'practical consciousness' (Giddens 1982: 9). The boundary between these categories of knowledge is neither structurally determined nor static. Tacit knowledge may sometimes become 'discursive' (Berger and Luckman 1967: 144) and discursive knowledge may sometimes become internalised and 'tacit' through regular usage (Hardiker 1981: 104).

Second, actors' capacity to shape events is limited by differentials in actors' access to strategies and resources, although actors' power – as we shall see shortly – is highly variable and may 'shift' from one actor to another,

Third, and crucially, actors' capacity to 'impose' their definitions, preferences, and perspectives is limited by the operation of unintended consequences. For instance, when the BASW and other professionalising actors in the 1970s enthusiastically supported the introduction of the new binary training system referred to earlier, the BASW had no idea that this new training system would later present unanticipated 'de-professionalising' opportunities to employers who decided the whole pattern of future training should become more 'practical' and based on the new less academic, less 'professional' CSS model. The BASW and employer associations are part of an 'actor network', and the outcomes of struggles among competitive actors within this network during the 1980s were partly a product of the unintended consequences of actions and responses to outcomes.

The concept 'unintended consequences' has important theoretical implications (Burns 1986: 10) and an important explanatory role in non-reductionist empirical sociology (Baert 1989). Hindess's criticisms (Hindess 1986c) of some applications of the concept relate to his rejection of Elster's (1985) methodological individualism, and to his more general rejection of reductionism (Hindess 1988: 25). Hindess's criticisms are supplanted elsewhere (Sibeon 1989) as part of an argument that the concept *is an essential analytic tool in non-reductionist analyses of the reproduction and change of social (work) situations.* There is no necessary or inevitable connection between use of the concept and methodological individualism, whether the latter is of the 'individuals make society' variety or in the form of a supposition (Rex 1988: 81) that constraints upon individuals are the effects of the actions of countless *other individuals.* In methodological situationalist research the concept's analytic potential is neatly illustrated in Collett's empirical study of probation officers (Collett 1989: 60–1), and at the trans-situational middle-range level of analysis use of the concept is in some instances crucial to an understanding of interactions between social (work) actors (Sibeon 1989: 4–5). Some unintended consequences are trivial, some are far-reaching, this being a matter for empirical assessment in each instance. Unintended consequences may extend far beyond localised 'actor networks' (Pakulski 1986), but this need not involve any endorsement of methodological collectivism: non-reductionist use of the concept does not involve a teleological assumption that unintended outcomes perform hidden ('latent') functions for system 'needs' (Giddens 1982: 10) or function to sustain 'objective', structurally given 'interests'. Empirical investigation of struggles over social work professionalism and training policies reveals (Sibeon 1989: 8–11) that there are sometimes highly significant situations of fortuitous coincidence between an observed intended *or* unintended outcome of an actor's actions and the self-formulated interests of another actor(s), *in which case the other actor(s) may wish to – and sometimes be able to – 'retain' the outcome and further disseminate it across a wide range of sites*: this empirical occurrence requires no teleological explanation because the interests in question did not 'produce' or 'cause' the outcome (Betts 1986: 50–1; Sibeon 1989: 5). One of the core arguments in this section of the chapter is that interactions between competitive social (work) actors, and the outcomes of those interactions, are not 'necessary effects' of social structure. Social events are highly contingent and relatively unpredictable: they could, usually, have 'happened otherwise'. This is partly because actors do not have a structurally 'fixed' or 'given' set of 'objective' interests and partly for the reason that actors' power is not a fixed-capacity attribute determined by their structural location within an overarching social totality. In social work, as elsewhere, 'struggles over divergent objectives really are struggles, not the playing out of some pre-ordained script' (Hindess 1982: 506). An understanding that social actors' power is an *emergent* outcome of interactions among actors rests on the view that social analysis should 'treat power as an *effect* of sets of variegated and differentially successful strategies to enrol others rather than as *cause* of that success' (Law 1986a: 5, original italics).

This is illustrated in a 'middle-range' empirical case study by Callon and Latour (1981) who investigated interactions within an actor network comprising two central competitive social actors. The actors were Renault, which had invested heavily in petrol-driven vehicles and stood to lose financially if the other major actor, Electricity of France (EDF), succeeded in its attempt to formulate and disseminate technical, economic, and environmental arguments in favour of its prototype electrically driven vehicle. In their investigation of the strategies employed by these social actors, Callon and Latour are critical of the idea that actors have a fixed or structurally predetermined 'size' (Callon and Latour 1981: 280). Social actors grow or reduce in size and influence contingently by means of specific transactions and 'translations' and according to the extent that they can successfully enlist ('enrol') the greatest number of durable materials in the form of ideas and discourses, practices, written contracts, laws, and conventions (Callon and Latour 1981: 284). Growing actors attempt to *consign* an ever-increasing number of issues ('materials') to the category of having been settled, established, or dealt with, so that *re-inspection* or re-negotiation of issues that have been 'consigned' is no longer regarded as necessary: once issues have been consigned and made *durable*, the social actor may address a wider range of issues and audiences and thereby produce relatively long-lived asymmetries in size between the growing actor and other social actors (Callon and Latour 1981: 187). In Callon and Latour's study asymmetries in size were later reversed and the once 'growing' actor (EDF) diminished in 'size'.

During the early 1970s the EDF successfully deployed a powerful range of 'enrolment' strategies. These strategies 'appealed' to a large variety of social, economic, and environmental considerations (noise, pollution, etc.) that made the EDF's arguments seem unassailable. The EDF employed techniques and media for disseminating materials that influenced public opinion and a wide variety of social and political institutions. Definitions shifted so markedly in favour of EDF that even Renault, faced with what seemed to be an inevitable decline in its field of operations, decided that it should march with the times and 'gear up' in advance for the lucrative possibility of supplying components (chassis for electrically driven vehicles) to EDF as part of the movement towards the future all-electric technology. In these processes a new 'line of reasoning was being unfolded . . . a chain of sequence . . . [which defined] . . . the margin for manoeuvre . . . by the other actors, their positions, desires, knowledge and abilities, what they will want and be able to do is channelled' (Callon and Latour 1981: 289). The electric vehicle 'is thus "real" . . . [and] Renault goes along with what EDF wants, just like the rest of France, moving towards an all-electric future' (Callon and Latour 1981: 289).

If, as suggested here, Callon and Latour's empirical conceptualisation of these events bears some resemblance to Berger and Luckmann's theoretical description of the processes of externalisation, objectivation, and transmission of ideas and practices, what happened next in the course of events described by Callon and Latour was the beginnings of a process of 'de-consignment' (roughly analogous to Berger and Luckmann's concepts 'de-reification' and 'de-objectivation', referred to earlier in the chapter). Renault became sensitised to perceived dangers in becoming an economic appendage of EDF, and began to 'fight back'. Renault suggested that consumer preferences had been exaggerated by EDF and pointed out that, despite rises in oil and petrol prices, demand for petrol-driven vehicles was in fact increasing. A chink had appeared in the idea-influencing armour of EDF: as Callon and Latour put it, *'the word was out'* (Callon and Latour 1981: 290) and a sceptical mood developed, encouraged by Renault, that perhaps *other* aspects of EDF's successful 'consigning' of issues could be critically re-opened for fresh interpretation. Renault went 'back to the drawing board', re-examined many previous studies, and began to reveal a series of technical shortcomings in the EDF electrochemical assumptions about battery power. Renault succeeded in arguing that electric-driven propulsion would be suitable only for certain types of vehicles (lorries of a particular kind) and that even this development lay far in the distant future. After the confrontation, the future of Renault seemed assured and EDF had to 'retire from the field . . . withdraw its troops' (Callon and Latour 1981: 291), tarnished with the reputation of having backed the wrong technical revolution.

In Callon and Latour's empirical study, EDF as a social actor 'failed' because it did not define and 'structure' the social world *irreversibly*. An analogous process is revealed in social work's recent history of policy struggles in the actor network referred to earlier: an outcome of these struggles was the 'failure' of professional(ising) actors in the academic-professional constituency in the 1980s to 'lock' professional education and the organisational division of labour in social services departments irreversibly into the professionally expansionist policies that 'expanding' professional(ising) actors had successfully formulated and implemented in the late 1960s and early 1970s (Sibeon 1989: 11). Power viewed as capacity to shape social events is an effect, not a cause, of strategic success in *irreversibly* enrolling and 'consigning' (making durable) a large number of related conventions, ideas, policies, and practices (Callon and Latour 1981: 293). Struggles and flux in the relationships that develop between social actors are not overarched by any historical or functional 'necessities' inherent in social structure; neither the actors' formulations of 'interests' and selection of strategies nor the outcome of struggles are predetermined by the location of the actors within any larger social system. In many, perhaps most, social situations, events and outcomes 'could' have taken quite a different turn. Interactions within actor networks are not insulated from larger patterns of general cultural and political meanings and practices, but actors 'read' and respond to, handle and sometimes re-shape these more pervasive materials in ways that are not structurally predetermined.

Social actors not only do not have structurally 'given' ('objective') interests, they also do not have a structurally 'given' size or given capacity to shape social events: their 'size' waxes and wanes and the processes and strategies through which this occurs are relatively indeterminate, shifting and precarious; sometimes, as in the recent history of British social work and in the EDF/Renault illustration, the outcomes of these processes are reversible. If relatively enduring asymmetries of size and power occur, this is itself contingently produced, not a 'necessary effect' of the social totality in the way claimed in macro-reductionist theories of welfare such as those examined in the previous section of the chapter. Callon and Latour's empirical conceptualisations, developed in their EDF/Renault study and also in Callon's 'St. Brieuc' study (Callon 1986), point to a more general postulate that decision making and action in the construction of public policy – for example in transport, health, welfare, housing, and education – are the outcomes of contingent, variable, and sometimes shifting patterns of interaction in the relationships that develop between a variety of social actors (Rose 1989; Rein 1976: 17 and 25). This means that the shape of social policy and social work is potentially highly variable and shifting: the shape of major social work materials at any moment in time is not a 'necessary effect' of any hypothetical 'needs' of social structure, but an *emergent* product of interaction among social actors who strategically disseminate material across sites and who interact and negotiate with each other (sometimes co-operatively, sometimes competitively) in pursuance of their perspectives and self-formulated interests and objectives.

To the extent that a 'new' sociology of social work shifts towards an anti-reductionist sociology of the middle range, this will also require a corresponding shift of attention towards the study of *media* and of the types of *transformative concepts* employed in different types of media by individual and social actors in their handling and *dissemination* of materials (ideas, policies, practices, etc.). Vance, in an account of American psychotherapy, suggests that routine dissemination of experientially acquired 'practice wisdoms' is achieved almost entirely through oral transmission; in his role as a practising psychotherapist, he writes, 'published materials . . . are of no help in increasing one's therapeutic skills . . . . Those of us really concerned about training practitioners are living in a world where our skills are transmitted by an oral tradition' (Vance 1968: 115). According to Vance, 'the only really effective channel . . . available for distributing clinically useful information is word-of-mouth' (Vance 1968: 117).

In British social work, an unwritten, oral tradition containing 'practice wisdoms' is a feature of large areas of social work practice based on the professional casework model (Paley 1984; Carew 1979: 36; Kakabadse 1982: 132–3; Curnock and Hardiker 1979: 10, 11, 159, 161). An oral tradition is also part of the psychotherapeutically oriented 'process' learning model in social work education (Simon 1967: 10; Jones 1982: 151; Haines 1985: 127; Harris *et al.* 1985; Greenwell and Howard 1986). Modern social work contains both oral and written traditions, though the former is given special emphasis. The idea of engaging in locally produced ('site-specific') idiographic constructions of emotional and cognitive insights in social work education (Harris *et al.* 1985; Coull 1986) and in everyday practice situations with clients (Gammack 1982) is a highly developed normative commitment in professional social work (Shaw 1975). This raises questions about whether and how the *contents* of locally produced ('emergent'), experientially constructed cognitive and emotional insights (Timms and Timms 1977: 119) can be written down in professional literature (Jamous and Peloille 1970) and *disseminated* spatially and temporally to other social work sites in a form that is meaningful to others 'who did not take part in the action' (Parsloe 1985: 159). Arising from this is the related question of what is meant by *professional* social work knowledge and whether a common, identifiable, and transmissible knowledge 'core' exists in the sense claimed by, for example, the British Association of Social Workers (BASW 1977: 25, para. 3.31).

In future research on the processes involved in the spatial and temporal dissemination of different types of social work materials, there are grounds for suggesting that a potentially significant empirical hypothesis is the possibility that actors for particular purposes employ mainly *written* media during special 'non-routine' periods such as the construction of major 'new' social work materials (e.g. 'child abuse') and during periods of professional turbulence. Routine 'oral' circulation of practice materials during tranquil professional periods is not the same thing as the production and dissemination of major 'new' materials nor similar to 'crisis-management' situations such as those which occur during major struggles over social work policy issues. Carew, Paley, Kakabadse, and the other writers referred to above were describing the strength of an oral tradition during social work's equivalent of a Kuhnian period of 'normal science' (Kuhn 1970: 5). In contrast, *written* media appear to have a very significant role in the professional construction of 'new' social problems facing the profession and in the construction and dissemination of arguments that extra professional resources and new professional 'responses' are required to combat new or previously 'hidden' social problems: this is evident in the influential role of written media (texts, reports, articles, written policy statements, etc.) both in the social construction of 'child abuse'

(Sharron 1983) as a major social and therefore 'professional' problem (Parton 1979: 442) and in the social construction of 'violence towards social workers' as a large but previously undetected problem (Small 1987: 43).

The strategic use of written media for 'consigning' materials and disseminating consigned materials across sites in an effort to enrol, enlist, convince, persuade, criticise, or attack opponent-actors also appears to be given special emphasis by actors during periods of internal conflicts and struggle when professional or other social work actors experience a sense of having their interests, objectives, and aspirations 'threatened' in some way. A historical example is the early efforts by the Charity Organisation Society to establish a 'new' social work paradigm ('professional casework') in the face of strong opposition from the social reformers of the day, particularly the Fabians. In struggling to establish an embryonic casework professionalism, the society's monthly journal was a key factor in the construction of an information network through which the society attempted to disseminate and legitimise its defence of 'good' casework principles (Jones 1983: 83). More recently, the struggle over 'traditional' versus 'radical' social work in the 1970s was accompanied by a veritable flurry of social work books, papers, and articles attacking – or defending – the virtues of 'radicalism' and 'professionalism' respectively. Actors' strategic use of written media was also a prominent feature of the previously described struggles over the relationship between education and training policies and the division of labour in social services departments in the 1980s, and in the 1990s may become an increasingly visible feature of conflicts over professional casework 'versus' decentralised community social work (Weinstein 1986).

In periods of professional conflict, unwritten informal communications are not unimportant (Knorr-Cetina 1982) but written rather than oral dissemination is a more effective 'consigning' medium for securing 'long-distance' and 'large-range' cognitive or practical control in professional communities (Law 1986a: 33). Writing is a more powerfully convincing, persuasive way of presenting and communicating arguments than is possible in conversations; that is, writing has greater *schematisation capacity* (Law 1986a: 14). Talk is neither as spatially and temporally *mobile* nor as *durable* a material as writing and, through the strategic use of written media, power is not a cause but 'an effect of the creation of a network of mobile, durable [materials]' (Law 1986a: 34).

Law's sociological analysis of the scientific community has implications for sociology of social work. Competitive actors' strategies for securing 'long-distance' control of social work ideas and practices may be regarded as resting on actors' attempts to convert materials that are *less* mobile and durable into materials that are *more* mobile and durable: 'it is only by so doing that it is possible to make a link between the large and the small-scale, to collapse the distance, so to speak, between the macro and the micro, and *exert influence upon the world from a particular place*' (Law 1986a; 32, italics added). Relatively little research has been undertaken into the processes involved in the strategic construction and dissemination across sites of social work ideas, policies, and practices.

The 'politics' of (social work) research is itself an important research topic. This is not to say competitive social work actors invariably commission, produce, or cite only those 'data' that conveniently support their own value position, but certainly enough is known in sociology about issues of reciprocity between 'data' and 'values' to justify empirical investigation of the production, interpretation, and dissemination of social work research data as socially constructed activities (Friedrichs 1970: 77–91). The construction and interpretation of data are tacitly or overtly influenced by theoretical assumptions and values of various kinds. For example, in a comment on research into 'community social work', Tuson makes the point that different researchers within the same institution, the National Institute of Social Work, have sometimes employed different underlying assumptions and therefore arrived at quite different data conclusions (Tuson 1989). In sociology of social work virtually no empirical data exist on readership networks or 'readership clusters' (Hagstrom 1965; Cole 1970) that may be associated with particular social actors and possibly also with influential social work academic or professional leaders, or with particular social work research, practice, or educational institutions; nor do very many data exist on the relationships that may develop between these idea-influencing networks and the competing interests and perspectives that exist in the various 'constituencies' that reflect social work's heterogeneous, segmental form (Heraud 1981: 17–20). Once reductionist notions that social work materials are a 'necessary effect' of the social totality are abandoned, empirical investigation of the proactive roles of actors and of processes in the construction and dissemination of materials across sites becomes a crucial research orientation in sociology of social work.

A point made earlier was that in moving away from the 'rigid' predeterminations of structural systems theory, many recent versions of sociology focus on empirical variation and indeterminacy in social life. A view of social life as almost totally 'processual', highly indeterminate, and in a constant state of flux and change is a feature of Elias's (1978) figurational sociology that has attracted critical attention (Bogner 1986; Layder 1986; Rojek 1986). Elias constructs a theoretical dichotomy between 'total statis' and 'total flux', and opts for the latter (Layder 1986: 378). There is no empirical justification for this 'either-or' dichotomy: the extent to which 'continuities' and 'discontinuities' exist in social life should be treated as an empirical question for investigation on each occasion that the question arises. Hindess rejects notions of 'essential structures' or a 'self-sustaining totality' but he does not claim that there are no 'relatively pervasive or enduring conditions' (Hindess 1986a: 123) or generalised meanings that may extend to a wide range of sites (Hindess 1986a: 121). A broadly similar point is Callon and Latour's observation that there are no valid a priori reasons to assume that the social world is either wholly 'static', systemically 'rigid', and structurally predictable or in a wholly chaotic state of endless flux and variation (Callon and Latour 1981: 282). Nevertheless, a high degree of flux and variation may sometimes occur *during* the 'passage' of material through time and space.

Reflecting on the structure and forms of scientific knowledge, Fleck, a practising microbiologist, observes that 'knowledge changes *unpredictably* and ideas alter *in* the process of . . . [their] . . . communication' (Fleck 1979, quoted in Jacobs 1987: 269, italics added). If this happens in science, which has a relatively epistemologically 'firm' knowledge mandate (Barnes 1985: 63), its occurrence is perhaps even more to be expected in social work which is a 'normative' (rather than 'scientific') profession (Halliday 1985), characterised by a relatively high degree of cognitive indeterminacy (Sargent 1985). Fleck's observation highlights the need for empirical investigation of the *transformative concepts* employed by individual and social actors who 'handle' materials that have come from elsewhere and who may 're-shape' the material before 'enacting' it or before passing it on to others. This does not mean that materials are not sometimes transmitted temporally and spatially in relatively unchanged form. Callon and Latour observe that successfully *institutionalised* ('consigned') materials travel far across a wide range of sites and become 'what everybody is saying' (Callon and Latour 1981: 298).

The 'unpredictable' possibility noted by Fleck is only one among many: some institutionalised materials may be spatially and temporally pervasive without much alteration of their form. To speak of the *transmission* of material implies relatively stable, ordered material circulating around a social system or, in the non-reductionist terms employed here, across a range of (social work) sites through space and time. Theoretical underpinnings for a *sociology of transmission* are implicit in Berger and Luckmann (1967) who describe the social world as relatively stable, made up of objectified, habitualised ideas and practices transmitted in relatively unchanged ('institutionalised') form: this implies that in the normal course of events social work materials, once created and institutionalised by actors, travel in relatively stable form to local sites where the materials are routinely actor-reproduced and further transmitted to other sites. This may be contrasted with Callon and Latour's criticisms of a sociology of transmission and their preference for a *sociology of translation* (Callon 1986: 196). Latour's sociology of translation is highly critical of diffusion models of culture; his performative rather than ostensive definition (Latour 1986: 269) raises large questions for sociological researchers involved in the study of the 'passage' of materials in social work (and in other professions also). Latour criticises notions that materials in the form of ideas, policies, and practices continue to 'travel' spatially and temporally by virtue of having a massive *initial impetus* from a powerful original source.

In criticising this notion of power, Latour introduces his 'sociology of translation' by drawing an analogy between materials dissemination and a rugby match. In rugby the first throw of the ball has no more significance than the fortieth or four-hundredth throw as the game proceeds and the 'material' (the ball) is passed from actor to actor. The material has no energy of its own that persists after the first kick or throw: the energy is given to it not by the first kick but by everyone in the chain who does something with it afterwards. In social life, material passes along chains of actors; but because these actors may have different values, priorities, interests, objectives, etc., each of them might 'act upon' the material *in a different way* so that the form of the material is continually changing *during* the course of its passage along actor chains (Latour 1986: 267). Material typically *'changes as it moves from hand to hand* and . . . transmission . . . becomes a single and unusual case among many, more likely, others' (Latour 1986: 268, italics added). This is because 'the spread in space and time of anything . . . is in the hands of people; . . . faithful *transmission* . . . is a rarity . . . and if it occurs it requires explanation' (Latour 1986: 267, italics added).

In Latour's terms, to refer to 'the' social work material (or 'it') is a misnomer, because that which is continually transformed is never for long the same object: the material that is 'reproduced' by individual or social actors in particular sites or situations is a shifting, continually transformed entity inscribed into further situations where it is further routinely transformed. Latour, like Berger, rejects structuralist conceptions of material as *autonomous*. However, in contrast to Latour, a Bergerian sociology of knowledge suggests that, although in modern pluralist societies there are multiple meaning-systems, large accumulations of material are relatively stable and routinised and transmitted in more or less the same form spatially and temporally for long periods until something unusual happens and the material is suddenly checked, stopped, and 'de-legitimated'. This is not to say that transmission-model theorists suggest that the empirical world is a completely stable ordered reality, nor do translation theorists construct a *completely* processual, indeterminate social world of continuously transformed ideas, policies, and practices ('materials'). None the less, each approach gives much greater emphasis to one or another of these ontological polarities. Critical attention to questions raised by these models and their opposed ontological assumptions is a crucial form of theoretical sensitisation in the construction of a contemporary sociology of social work, but *in an empirical not theoretical arbitrationist sense*. In sociology of social work, materials should be empirically investigated in ways that may reveal that both continuities ('transmissions') *and* discontinuities ('translations') exist in the contents and forms of those social work materials that appear to persist across social space and time. This empirical orientation requires an explicit methodological framework; the integrated framework described below is intended to have a role in hypothesis building and in identifying conceptual and methodological issues relevant to non-reductionist empirical analysis of social work materials.

AN INTEGRATED THEORETICAL AND METHODOLOGICAL FRAMEWORK

A synthesis of opposed theories is not logically possible where the theories remain in their original antithetical form; this is because 'it is in principle not possible to effect a theoretical integration of viewpoints which logically exclude each other . . . each theory is exclusive . . . [and this] . . . positively prevents integration' (Hamilton 1974: 150). However, it is possible to re-define concepts ('actors', 'sites', etc.) as they are moved from one paradigm or theory to another. The meaning of a concept may be re-defined (Kasius 1950: 7) when it is incorporated into or combined with concepts from other theoretical sources, a point noted in social work terms by Timms (1983: 79) and in Marxist terms by Leonard (1984: 104–5). Berger and Luckmann combine ideas from Marx, Durkheim, Weber, and Mead. A consequence of re-defining concepts drawn from (in this example) antithetical theories is that Berger and Luckmann 'are not and cannot be faithful to the original intentions of these several streams of social theory themselves' (Berger and Luckmann 1967: 29). Re-contextualising the ideas of other theorists involves 'integrating their thought into a theoretical formulation that some of them might have found quite alien' (Berger and Luckmann 1967: 29). The point being made here is that an integrated conceptual or methodological framework is theoretically legitimate provided the integration, if it combines otherwise unaligned or mutually exclusive concepts, does not contradict itself through failure to re-define (Ricoeur 1971: 532) the cluster of imported conceptualisations so as to make them mutually compatible. There are also some instances when a *multi-dimensional* comparison of different theories may reveal that in their original form they are 'already' similar in *some* dimensions (e.g. methodology, field of study, or unit of analysis) but dissimilar in other dimensions, such as epistemology, or substantive world-view (Glucksmann 1974: 231–2). Though these issues cannot be pursued here, it is worth observing that clarification of whether multi-dimensional comparative classifications of social work theories should be based on 'objectivist' or 'subjectivist' conceptions of human knowledge (or some non-reductionist fusion of these) is unexplored territory in the sociology of social work knowledge. Further work in this area would illuminate unresolved political, theoretical, and practical social work issues raised by, for example, Richards and Righton (1979), Webb (1981, 1985), Davies (1982), and Whittington and Holland (1985).

The idea of theoretical and methodological 'integration' is significant in other ways. It should by now be clear from the earlier parts of the chapter that the term 'macro' in its non-reductionist usages is a convenient way of showing that integration of micro and macro variables is a routine actors' accomplishment (Cicourel 1980). When social workers in their everyday practice assess clients' situations, formulate plans of action, write reports, etc., neither social workers' forms of thought and practices nor the organisational and service-delivery conventions surrounding practice are insulated from larger 'collective representations' that circulate temporally and spatially within social work and in the wider society. Furthermore, in many special non-routine circumstances such as major conflicts among social work actors over policy issues, 'integration' of micro and macro variables becomes an actors' strategy in consigning and disseminating materials across sites: collapsing the distance between micro and macro is a way of 'exerting influence upon the world from a particular place' (Law 1986a: 32). Cognitive and practical integration of micro and macro variables is not only an attribute of 'lay' actors; *it is also an attribute of sociological actors*. It is a routine 'sociological accomplishment', whether this is done explicitly as in the integrated framework outlined later, or whether it is done tacitly. A mundane example of the latter is an observer's or researcher's description of a person walking into a bank and cashing a cheque. The researcher's description of this commonplace activity tacitly invokes 'macro' assumptions; the researcher in his or her account is describing an activity (exchanging money in return for a slip of paper) that would seem bizarre unless the researcher tacitly assumes that s(he) and the reader both share a general background ('cultural') knowledge of the workings of the banking system. Everyday 'micro' activities in social work include assessing clients' situations and writing court reports on offenders or reports to case conferences. In these activities social workers do not wholly 're-invent the wheel each time': extra-situational cognitive materials and assumptions are already 'in' these micro-events. They are also 'in' sociological descriptions of these events. The point of these observations is that the *unavoidable* invoking of assumptions about (the existence of) 'macro' variables in sociological descriptions and interpretations of 'micro' data on social workers' cognitions and practices should, instead of remaining latent, be made fully explicit and open to analytic empirical scrutiny, as also should the invoking of 'micro-assumptions' in the interpretation and analysis of 'macro' data. Saying this is one thing; achieving it conceptually and methodologically is another matter.

Hindess, in rejecting the reductionisms of methodological individualism (Hindess 1986a: 117) and methodological collectivism (Hindess 1988: 37), acknowledges that 'these were not the only forms of social analysis on offer' (Hindess 1986a: 113), but he does not

proceed to an assessment of the possible role of *methodological situationalism* in contemporary non-reductionist social analysis. Earlier, the point was made that microsociology from Cooley onwards is interactionist and 'situationalist', not a form of methodological individualism. It was observed, too, that micro-situational methodologies are necessary both for investigating instances of the construction ('emergence') of materials (some of which may turn out to be relatively idiosyncratic and 'site-specific') in local sites and for investigating situational 'handling' of larger patterns of material that may 'travel' spatially and temporally across sites and 'enter into' sites in a variety of ways.

Callon and Latour's middle-range methodology in their EDF/Renault study was not micro-situationalist; though they interviewed some of the relevant participants, the researchers relied to a large extent upon analysis of documentary sources such as 'articles, reports, and accounts of meetings' (Callon 1986: 227). Their empirical conceptualisations and methodological procedures were well adapted to the analysis of *inter-situational interactions between social actors* and analysis of the spatial dissemination of material *across* sites: this could not have been achieved through use of ('intra') situationalist perspectives focused on interactions and negotiations of meanings among individual persons *within* a particular site(s) or through the use of intra-situationalist methodologies such as participant observation. In the 'middle-range' trans-situational sense just stated, methodological situationalism has a serious inherent limitation. The converse of this is that Callon and Latour's and other similar studies also have an inherent limitation in so far as they tell us very little about the intersubjective, interactive processes involved in the negotiation of meanings, intentionalities, and practices *within* the sites under investigation (EDF, Renault, etc.). If it is accepted that researchers cannot legitimately 'read off' micro-processes as a reflection or effect of reified 'macro' structures (as in structuralism and Marxism), it is also the case that we cannot 'read off' micro-processes within sites from a (middle-range) 'public' knowledge of the strategic interactions that become visible in the relationships that develop between social actors and in their disseminations of materials across sites. On the one hand, methodological situationalism is a necessary perspective, but, on the other, it is not a perspective that can portray non-reductively 'the *interrelation* between situated social events . . . [and] . . . the *linkage* between the happenings of diverse micro-situations' (Knorr-Cetina 1981: 28, original italics). Because of this, a multi-methodological approach is required for investigating the ways in which particular materials are empirically manifest at different 'levels' of social process.

An example of a methodologically multi-layered approach is Duster's study of American medical screening programmes for inherited disorders. Duster's research objective was to study empirically the ways in which the phenomenon under investigation is manifest ('can be found') at different levels:

> Three levels of entry are (1) direct observation of behaviour in the local setting in which it routinely occurs, the grounding for the 'micro' base of the study, (2) observation and analysis of the administrative, bureaucratic, or organisational unit(s) that are interposed between the local scene and (3) the 'macro' trends, rates, or perhaps law, or federal social policy development.
>
> (Duster 1981: 133)

Duster's precepts, reformulated in the terms introduced earlier, may be regarded as an indication that micro-situational methodology is necessary for investigating the construction and emergence of 'new' materials and for investigating local applications of pre-existing materials. Organisations are both social actors and local 'sites'. But organisations are not internally undifferentiated entities: knowledge of internal organisational processes is a relevant step in building up different types of data on the social construction and dissemination of policies. Knowledge of patterns of intentionality and meanings formulated in committees, work groups, and working parties may in some situations be highly relevant to an understanding of the relationships that develop in public between organisations as social actors. An instance is Harris's illuminating insider account of internal tensions and committee politics in the Central Council for Education and Training in Social Work at the time it was formulating the controversial new training policies referred to earlier (Harris 1984). The construction of data on these internal processes requires situationalist methodologies, such as participant or non-participant observation, capable of producing (from the inside) relevant ethnographic or other data that illuminate processes at one level (the micro) among the various other levels in which the particular material under investigation is extant in different forms.

This and the previous observations may now be summarised: in sociology of social work *a combination of methodological situationalism and middle-range methodology is required for non-reductionist empirical investigation and analysis of actors' 'handling' of social work materials within-and-across contemporaneously existing social work sites.* Another important dimension has to be added to (intra) micro-situational and (inter-situational) middle-range perspectives: this is the temporal dimension. The point at issue here is illustrated in Callon and Latour's study which described interactions between social actors in an actor network across a relatively short period of time. Though contemporary theorists of the middle range do not suggest that historically institutionalised continuities of ideas, policies, and practices are empirically insignificant, far greater emphasis is placed on investigation of flux, variability, innovation, and the relatively indeterminate, processual nature of current transactions among social actors viewed ahistorically within a relatively compressed period of time. The importance of history is recognised by Rein, who observes that in sociological studies of social policy 'one useful approach to understanding policy is to examine *recurring* issues' (Rein 1976: 23, italics added). A point briefly made earlier was that some major recent problematics articulated by social work actors have a perennial dimension: how these materials are constructed and responded to varies in time and place, but the existence of any such contextual variations does not mean that no long-term historical continuities exist in the ways in which these materials have been defined and handled in different times and places.

History, though, should not be interpreted reductively. Some phenomena in local social work sites, including forms of thought, policies, and practices, may be *shaped by and in turn shape* social work materials in other places and other times, but none of the sites in question have a historically or structurally 'given' dominance over other sites:

> All social action can be conceived as local in the sense that it must occur in settings bounded by local time and local space and the local constitutive expectancies of social exchange. It may ramify and serve as a future point of reference for many other local scenes, both temporally and spatially . . . But the question of whether . . . [a particular] . . . local scene has some future historic import is a problematic matter for empirical assessment.
>
> (Duster 1981: 114)

The empirical assessment called for by Duster is always necessary, because there is no structurally 'given' hierarchy of sites or hierarchy of actors with some always having total dominance over others (Hindess

1986a: 122). This emerged very clearly in Callon's (1986) and Callon and Latour's (1981) empirical demonstration that social actors contingently grow or reduce in size: social actors have no structurally determined capacity to enrol other social actors 'irreversibly' or to *consign* material and successfully propel it spatially and temporally across sites to a widening 'enrolled' audience.

Even relatively long-lived asymmetries in size and power are contingently produced and contingently sustained. Power is an effect, not a cause, of success in strategically consigning materials and making these consigned materials *spatially and temporally mobile and durable*. Sometimes, as Callon and Latour show, materials can be 'de-consigned'. This point was made earlier with reference to professional(ising) actors' failure in the 1980s to irreversibly 'lock' social work into the professionally expansionist policies that had been successfully cultivated by professionalising actors in the 1970s.

Methodological historical reconstruction requires, therefore, an explicitly non-reductionist theoretical and methodological integration based on the idea of combining contemporary micro-ethnographic data and middle-range 'documentary' data (Callon 1986: 227) with reconstructions of historical documentary data (Reed 1985: 146) relating to the particular topic under investigation. Integrating and analysing data produced by these different methodologies so as to bring different spatial and temporal levels of social process into focus simultaneously (Geertz 1979: 239) is difficult, but not impossible given some analytic imaginativeness and conceptual flexibility on the part of the researcher (Ball 1989). It is not suggested that every sociological empirical study of social work need have the breadth of theoretical and methodological scope just referred to, though it is desirable that some studies of this scope be undertaken.

More generally, the case argued in this chapter is for the construction of a 'new' non-reductionist sociology of social work that is geared to the ambitious task of bringing together theoretical conceptualisations and empirical data produced in a variety of separate studies many of which are likely to be concerned with micro or middle-range levels of analysis or with methodological historical reconstruction, rather than with these three levels simultaneously. The least conceptually developed of these analytic levels is the middle range: relatively little development has occurred at this level since Merton's conventional sociological formulation of 'theories of the middle range' (Merton 968: 39). The use and development of sociological transformative concepts ('translations', 'strategic interaction', 'unintended consequences', etc.) in the study of social actors' technologies of representation of materials, and for investigating relationships between the contents, contexts, and media involved in the 'transmission' and 'translation' of materials, is in some ways a deceptively familiar sociological rubric: this is because the use of transformative concepts is already well established in microsociology, particularly in symbolic interactionism. In particular, the notion that ideas and practices may alter *during* the intersubjective processes involved in their negotiation and communication among individual actors within local sites is a familiar, long-established conceptual and methodological maxim in symbolic interactionism. Theoretical and empirical relocation of transformational concepts in the study of social processes that include micro-contexts but also 'higher' levels of both spatial and temporal social processes is potentially one of the empirically most productive areas for future development in the sociology of social work. This will need time to develop and will require an initial exploratory phase, largely because these perspectives, despite some movement towards them in the 1980s, are still relatively underdeveloped in sociology: this is reflected in recent conceptual controversies surrounding the development and non-reductionist empirical application of transformative concepts such as 'unintended consequences' (Hindess 1988: 25, 106; Sibeon 1989: 8–11; Baert 1989) and 'strategies' (Crow 1989; Morgan 1989). The currently low level of development in conceptually and empirically relocating these and other analogous transformative concepts had been anticipated in Lidz's observation that 'transformational theory now calls the sociologist to examine such properties of macro-social operations as s/he now routinely does for micro-social processes' (Lidz 1981: 230).

In the remaining pages of the chapter, three briefly described empirical examples will serve to illustrate some applications of the integrated framework described above. The first example is the highly problematic material, 'theory–practice', referred to earlier in the chapter. There are a number of historically documented accounts of conflicts surrounding the construction of this problematic in the first social work education course established at London University under the auspices of the Charity Organisation Society (COS) at the turn of the century (Bosanquet 1900: Loch 1906). An integrated multi-methodological framework, because it is spatially and temporally multi-layered, facilitates understanding of whether and, if so, how and under what conditions the particular phenomenon under investigation – in this illustration, material surrounding the 'theory-practice' problematic – *manifests itself at different levels within and between sites, and also within different historical periods.* An analytic approach of this kind also addresses empirically the theoretical tension between a sociology of transmission and a sociology of translation, by means of directing researchers' attention to the need to search empirically for both continuities (transmissions) and discontinuities (translations) in the space-time 'circulation' of the material under investigation. For instance, the particular *type* of formal academic knowledge involved in the 'theory-practice' problematic is temporally variable. At the time of the COS's first steps, in the late nineteenth century, towards the construction of an academic knowledge base upon which claims to 'professionalism' might be founded, Spencerian sociology was at the forefront of the social work curriculum (Leonard 1966: 4–7). It need hardly be said that the contents of modern social work curricula are far more diverse than at that time (Casson 1982). Nor can it be assumed that the concept 'profession', around which competitive actors' struggles to 'consign' theory–practice have largely centred, has not been 'translated' during its passage through space and time. Tracking down the spatial and temporal 'career' of social work ideas, practices, and concepts is a crucial analytic procedure specified in the integrated framework outlined earlier. The COS's concept of embryonic professionalism was centred on the notion of caseworkers as 'social physicians' (Loch 1906: 81). This construct was resurrected in Flexner's essay 'Is social work a profession?' (Flexner 1915) and more than half a century later Flexner's question featured prominently in the British Association of Social Workers' working party report *The Social Work Task* which contained a section titled 'Social work – a profession?' (BASW 1977: 20).

A problem in the sociology of professions has been the tendency to employ a 'static', unhistorical analytic definition of 'profession' in a way that ignores cultural and historical changes in the *meaning* of the concept (Freidson 1983: 22). The meanings of the terms 'social physician' (Loch 1906) and 'profession' (Flexner 1915) were formulated at a time when 'social work' was a highly diversified, segmented social movement (Wilkinson 1971: 26) with virtually no cognitive, organisational, or practice homogeneity: the context in which these early definitions were formulated and acted upon by aspiring professionals was significantly different from that of the BASW's definitional exercise in 1977 which centred on distinguishing social services work from professional social work in the context of the 'bureau-professional' organisational structures (Parry and Parry 1979: 43) that developed in the local authority social services departments in the 1970s (Billis *et al.* 1980). There are undoubtedly some enduring continuities in the historical career of this concept ('profession') in social work discourse (specifically, a focus on *casework* as the main practice exemplar of professionalism, and a long-standing search for a 'relevant' academic social science knowledge base provided by professional training schools in the higher education sector), but we have seen that there are also important discontinuities in the social work 'career' of the concept and its relation to the 'theory–practice' problematic. The arguments developed earlier also indicate that, though 'theory–practice' is a highly problematic material with a long history, it is not a material that reflects some mysterious 'deep logic' of culture nor is it the unfolding of structural 'necessities' or of a structurally 'given' historical script. It is a material contingently produced largely through the historical dissemination of professional(ising) social work actors' perennial struggles to construct a 'profession' with a formal academic knowledge base (Jones 1979; Armstrong 1980) in the face of simultaneously historically disseminated rejections of 'professionalism' by a variety of actors among whom are included other social work actors. Bailey refers to struggles surrounding 'theory–practice' as an expression of 'deep-seated interests concerning academic study . . . social services structures, and professional associations. We should recognise the competing constituencies engaged in [these struggles]' (Bailey 1982: 12). It is precisely in this sense of *actors'* formulations of particular interests and perspectives that 'struggles over divergent objectives really are struggles' (Hindess 1982: 506) and not an epiphenomenal surface-level effect or 'reflection' of anything 'deeper'.

Significant empirical questions concerning continuities (transmissions) and discontinuities (translations) in the spatial and temporal dissemination and handling of social work materials also arise in the case of a second highly contentious material, viz. 'the politics of social work'. Pearson, though he later moved towards professional social work perspectives (Pearson 1983), was one of many radical critics of professional social work during the era of 'radical social work' in the 1970s (Pearson 1975). North suggested that a psychotherapeutic 'mystique' pervades professional social work which, by providing 'psychic handouts' (North 1972: 81) to clients, is highly conservative by virtue of 'directing the client inward towards himself rather than towards radical change' (North 1972: 87). Similar points were made by Deacon and Bartley. Their micro-empirical case study of professional socialisation in social work education led them to conclude that professional social work lecturers 'cool out' politically radical students through the technique of dismissing critical social science as mere 'theory' or 'intellectualism' and through use of the stratagem of 'channelling . . . social structural or institutional criticism into psychologistic thinking' (Deacon and Bartley 1975: 71).

These expressions of conflict (Clarke 1979) over 'social work politics' are in many respects contemporary re-activations of a long-standing problematic. The COS's proactive efforts to construct a professional casework model were vigorously resisted: the COS's casework model was dismissed as a 'personal pathology' model by the social reformers of that period and some sharp antagonisms developed during the course of the conflict between these two opposed schools of thought (see Young and Ashton 1956; Woodroofe 1962; Stedman Jones 1971). The COS's advocacy of professional casework was opposed by social reformers influenced by the writings of Chadwick, Booth, and, in particular, the Fabians (Alden 1905) who explicitly rejected the COS's casework model (Townsend 1911). The COS's own description of its professional casework model indicated that the model's function was to remedy 'defect in citizen character' (Bosanquet 1909). Jones argues that political continuity between the COS's 'personal inadequacy' casework model is preserved in disguised form in modern professional casework theories which employ quasi-psychotherapeutic jargon that is more culturally acceptable ('genteel') in the modern era; his interpretation is that the harsh language used by the COS in the late nineteenth century in describing the 'undeserving poor' as having defective 'moral character' has in modern professional social work been linguistically modified, 'civilized' (Jones 1983: 90) while still retaining the underlying welfare philosophy of the COS caseworkers rather than the perspectives of the 'social reformers' of that period.

How far Jones's interpretation of historical continuities in the 'transmission' of this particular material ('social work politics') is empirically sustainable is too large a question to enter into here, although it may be briefly noted that some significant *discontinuities* exist. North, Deacon and Bartley, and Jones associate modern casework 'conservatism' with psychodynamic and psychotherapeutic precepts that, however, were not precepts available to the COS advocates of professional casework (Hearn 1982: 22); nor were the early welfare 'anti-professionals' such as the Fabians cognitively equipped with the varieties of radical social work theories and sociological Marxisms that developed in the 1970s as theoretical alternatives to professional casework theory; nor were the early 'social reformers' equipped with the particular practical alternatives to the professional casework model (such as 'community social work') that developed in the 1980s. Rein astutely argues the case that 'social policy is forever debating what appear to be the same issues' (Rein 1976: 24), and this is to some extent also the case in social work; nevertheless, social work and social policy materials are contingently and contextually produced and re-produced, and sometimes re-shaped, by individual actors and by social actors and therefore the theoretical possibilities raised by Latour's performative, processual concept of social action (a sociology of translation rather than transmission) should always remain open for empirical assessment.

The third and last type of social work material to be discussed here concerns social work's long-standing quest for *professional unity*. This quest has generally taken the form of attempts to secure value-consensus and as much cognitive, practical, and organisational commonality as can be achieved in the face of social work's service-delivery diversities. The heterogeneity of social work's service-delivery frameworks arises from the dispersion of professional social workers in diverse organisational contexts, including the local authority social services departments, the probation service, health, education, and other statutory services, and a wide variety of casework, residential, and community work organisations in the voluntary sector. The COS foresaw that the concept 'profession' is unattainable in the absence of at least some identifiable unity and common occupational identity in terms of social work's cognitive knowledge base, practice methods, and service-delivery context. The first recorded use of the term 'social worker' was in Bosanquet's paper of 1893 to the Charity Organisation Society ('Editorial' ATSWE 1984) though this all-encompassing, generic use of the term, given the occupational, cognitive, and service-delivery diversity of 'welfare' activities at that time, was more in the nature of professional intent and aspiration than an accurate empirical description. Twentieth-century progress towards social work 'unity' has been slow; despite the potentially unifying connotations of some post-Seebohm theories of practice such as 'genericism', and social work 'systems' or 'integrated' approaches (Pincus and Minahan 1973), recent social work has been characterised more by internal conflicts over 'theory–practice' and welfare politics.

Organisationally, the degree of professional unification that exists in modern social work is a comparatively recent phenomenon (Seed 1977: 55-6) and organisational unity is still unachieved. Even in professional social work's post-Seebohm organisational heartland (the local authority social services departments), as observed earlier, major conflicts arose in the 1980s from policies to remove the distinction between professional social work ('CQSW work') and social services work ('CSS work'). As noted above, professional unity is also held back by the fact that social work is practised in diverse organisational settings *outside* the social services departments. Some social work writers, for example Young (1979), argue that professional unity is unattainable if it is assumed that unity means that professional social work can be defined independently of *particular* organisational contexts. Many of the 'established' professions have a *primary institutional sphere* within which professional power and autonomy are relatively high (e.g. lawyers in the legal system), and a *secondary institutional sphere* (e.g. lawyers employed in private or public bureaucracies) within which professional autonomy and influence are relatively low (Halliday 1985: 431). Social work is permanently located in secondary or quasi-secondary institutional spheres and lacks a 'primary' organisational sphere. Young makes the point that many and perhaps most social workers holding the CQSW qualification are employed in a wide variety of organisations where *'social work' is not the only or main organisational purpose*: according to Young, there is no identifiable or definable 'professional social work' that floats free of *particular* organisational objectives and purposes in the varied service-delivery contexts in which social workers are employed (Young 1979: viii).

In the face of cognitive and political as well as organisational and service-delivery diversities there have been some professional attempts to construct conceptual frameworks under the rubric 'unity within diversity' (an expression developed in American professional social work literature) where 'unity' is held to rest on social workers' 'common purposes'. These common purposes, however, are usually stated at such a high level of generality and abstraction (e.g. 'people-environment exchanges') that they could apply to a wide range of occupations and services other than social work. The 'unity within diversity' professional conceptual frameworks developed, for instance, by Gross, Murphy, and Steiner (1982) and Germaine (1983) are theoretically and empirically simplistic. Although these frameworks beg far too many questions to be of any serious analytic usefulness, the professional *construction* of such frameworks and the very fact of their existence is an important issue for empirical investigation in sociology of social work. Unresolved questions raised by professional constructions of 'unity within diversity' are analysed by Sainsbury who concludes by posing what some may regard as a professionally outrageous hypothesis: he asks 'On what basis can a collective identity for social work be . . . [established] . . . bearing in mind the various diversities . . . ? More fundamentally, is collective identity necessary or desirable?' (Sainsbury 1985: 10). Non-reductionist sociological empirical analysis of temporal and spatial continuities and discontinuities in the negotiation and dissemination of this particular social work material (the search for 'unity within diversity') rests on a theoretical postulate that the material is contingently produced by professional(ising) actors, and is not an effect of structural 'necessities' or mysterious ('deep') cultural 'imperatives': this seems to be acknowledged in Gross, Murphy, and Steiner's comment that their and others' self-formulated quest for unity within diversity has existed 'ever since . . . social work was first . . . [defined as] . . . an area of *professional* activity' (Gross, Murphy, and Steiner 1982: 79, italics added). Non-reductionist empirical analysis of this particular social work material rests, therefore, on an integrated methodological approach which investigates temporally and spatially the intra- and inter-situational contexts and conditions-of-action surrounding social work actors' assessments and formulation of objectives and actions directed towards 'the profession's perennial search for unity' (Gilbert and Specht 1977: 223).

A larger variety of sociological perspectives exists in the recent history of sociology (Bryant 1989) than it has been possible to review here, and the chapter has mainly concentrated on the major forms of recent sociological theory and upon key theoretical and methodological issues raised by these theories. Also, contemporary anti-reductionist sociology contains diverse strands and cannot accurately be described as a new 'unified' sociological paradigm. There are, though, some discernible common threads that are part and parcel of the recent transitions in sociological theory (Wardell and Turner 1986). These include re-definition of social action and the concept 'actor', rejection of structural theories and of both macro and micro forms of reductionism, and a re-orientation towards a sociology of the middle range: in social theory these developments are reflected in efforts to develop non-reductionist empirical applications of the concepts 'unintended consequences' and 'strategies' together with other transformative concepts (such as the 'enrolment' of actors and the 'consignment' of materials) for investigating the media, contents, and contexts of *interactions between social actors*, rather than confining use of these transformative concepts to the analysis of interactions among individual human actors in particular local places ('sites'). Theoretical tensions between ostensive conceptions of structural system predictability and processual, performative concepts of social processes are becoming important empirical foci in sociologies of transmission and of translation: here, one of the empirically most promising areas for future research in the sociology of social work knowledge is investigation of whether different types of social work knowledge forms ('welfare rights' knowledge, medical or legal knowledge relevant to work with clients, psychotherapeutic concepts, experientially acquired practice-wisdoms, cultural 'common sense', etc.) each have different levels of 'translatability' and different thematisation thresholds (Schwartz 1973) in the ways these knowledge forms (Howe 1987: 164–9) are constructed and applied within and across social work sites through space and time. These sociological re-orientations are reflected in the sociology of knowledge, as in Scott's arguments for 'a middle-range perspective' in the sociology of knowledge (Scott 1988: 52–3). They are also becoming increasingly prominent in the sociology of science (Lynch 1985; Law 1986a; Jacobs 1987) and in urban sociology's theoretical and empirical transition towards the 'new' urban studies (Mellor 1989: 243). Sociology of social work is far less developed than these, or indeed most other, fields of sociological inquiry: to this extent there is a fair amount of leeway to make up and there can be no doubt that some challenging intellectual opportunities face sociology of social work.

CONCLUDING REMARKS

Assessment of possibilities for constructing a non-reductionist sociology *for* social work is not part of the brief for this chapter, nor indeed for the volume as a whole. However, social work perceptions of sociology are a highly relevant research topic in sociology of social work (Heraud 1979: 11–15) and for this reason it is appropriate to conclude with some remarks on the ways in which recent sociology might be perceived and 'received' by social workers. Professional condemnations of the varieties of Marxist sociology that ostensibly 'challenged' professional social work in the 1970s were, in retrospect, wholly unnecessary. As far as mounting a challenge against orthodox professionalism is concerned, Marxist sociology was a chimerical red-herring. Marxist sociology and its partner 'radical social work' in the 1970s formed a *theoretical radicalism* that posed no real threat to professional social work: notably, radical social work contained no identifiably 'radical' proposals for transforming everyday practice and the organisational service-delivery framework surrounding professional practice (Deacon 1981: 46; Simpkin 1982: 94; Hearn 1982; Timms 1983: 97). The 'interests of capitalism' were roundly condemned in the 1970s but in theoretical terms not designed to produce concrete organisational or practice shifts. The radical keyword was 'struggle' against capitalist oppression, but the struggle rarely got beyond analytic formulations of what 'the struggle' – if ever it took place – might consist of (Morris 1975).

It was not surprising that radical theorists 'allowed' professional casework managers, practitioners, and students to pursue their conventional professional tasks without much interruption, rather than attempt the unrealistic task of moving a formidable theoretically constructed mountain of historical 'necessities' embedded in 'the social totality' and in 'objective' structural 'forces' and structural 'needs', objective 'structural contradictions', and the like. Equipped with these reified theoretical rationales, erstwhile 'radical' social workers quickly accommodated to the bureau-professional structure of the social services departments and practised in ways virtually indistinguishable from those of their 'traditional' professional colleagues (Hearn 1982: 25–6).

The 'real' challenge to post-Seebohm professional social work did not arrive until the 1980s. This radical challenge came from two relatively unexpected sources. The first major challenge has been referred to at various points throughout the chapter. This came from social work employers and administrators who, with the Central Council for Education and Training in Social Work, constructed practical proposals to 'reform' social work education and training and the division of labour in social services departments in ways perceived by professional and academic-professional actors as a highly threatening form of de-professionalisation (Carter 1985). The second major challenge, which also laid on the table concrete proposals for reforming professional practice and its supporting organisational service-delivery framework, is emerging in the decentralisation movement (Beresford and Croft 1984) and its prescriptions for 'community social work', service 'democratisation', and 'organic' participatory forms of pluralistic welfare (Hadley and Hatch 1981) based on ideas of client and citizen 'empowerment' (Murray 1983). The proposals for community social work outlined in the Barclay Report (1982) were from the beginning strenuously resisted by professional actors (Cypher 1983; Pinker 1983b; Davies 1983; Pearson 1983). Descriptions and analyses of intense conflicts between professionals and those attempting to give practical effect to local authority decentralisation programmes are provided in David (1983), Weinstein (1986), and Beuret and Stoker (1986). The movement towards 'decentralisation and democracy' (Hoggett and Hambleton 1988) is likely to become an increasingly controversial material in the construction of social work education and training, practice, and organisational policies in the 1990s. In particular, the more radical, far-reaching proposals for decentralisation along, for example, the lines advocated by Rojek, Peacock, and Collins (1988: 175–80) are, if these become influential and are put into effect, likely to challenge established forms of social work in a way that did not happen during the theoretical encounter between Marxist sociology, 'radical social work', and social work professionalism in the 1970s (Jones 1975).

In contemporary British welfare politics the cumulative critiques of statism and professionalism – from right, left, and centre – have reached a 'practical' stage (Lee and Raban 1988: 223). An awareness of social work history, and of social work's recent past, suggests that struggles over radical practical change of professional training, organisational service-delivery frameworks, and forms of practice are far more 'serious' affairs than struggles over theory. Many practitioners and social work students in the 1970s, at a time when the policies and structures of local authority professional social work were seemingly irreversibly 'consigned' and in process of expansion (Webb 1980: 285), sided strongly with critical social and political theories and some even wanted to develop theories designed to 'overthrow the system' (Cohen 1975: 86). Although in real terms, professional actors had very little to fear from radical social work's 'rhetoric of revolution' (Morris 1975: 19), sociology was vigorously condemned by some professionals (Munday 1972; Wilson 1974; Wright 1977) who believed that it was producing a highly dangerous form of intellectualised student radicalism. In contrast, students by the late 1980s were asking for very practical knowledge and professional theories of practice. ('Twelve Students' 1989). Political 'conservatism' among some professional social work students in the 1980s (Webb 1985: 90; Jones 1989: 207–8) is interpreted by Hearn as a response to the failure of radical theoreticians to offer 'radical' practice prescriptions, and as a form of 'radical careerism' (Hearn 1982: 26) in the sense that some students and social workers may perceive that their future occupational interests are wedded to established forms of service delivery (Baker 1983: 4–5) organised along 'bureau-professional' lines (Parry and Parry 1979).

Certainly students and practitioners are correct in suggesting that recent 'alternative' perspectives of social work organisation and practice are 'remote' in the sense that it is difficult to 'insert' these perspectives (often associated with sociology and social policy) into practice: many of these perspectives are very 'practical' (particularly when compared with the abstract Marxisms of the 1970s) but also radical in the sense of *practically* challenging established professional service-delivery systems (Howe 1983) and it is indeed difficult to 'practise' alternative perspectives in terms of the existing deeply rooted cognitions, practice assumptions, and organisational conventions of orthodox social work professionalism. Many of these organisational and practice alternatives are associated with decentralised forms of community social work rather than a casework-led professionalism. The main thrust of the 'de-centralisation' challenge against established professional social work in the 1990s is unlikely to come from professionals: it is far more likely to emerge from an unholy alliance that includes social work employers (Harbert 1985a), voters, clients, and service users (Mishra 1986), politicians and others in the welfare pluralist camp (Hadley and Hatch 1981), and radical community activists associated with decentralisation and with the community politics of class, 'race', and gender nurtured by the 'new urban left' (Weinstein 1986). It is possible that issues of 'race' (Dominelli 1988) and gender (Hanmer and Statham 1988) in professional social work will be professionally negotiated largely outside the 'anti-hierarchical' decentralisation movement; in 'mainstream' professional social work discourse it is more likely that these issues will be defined in conventional 'bureau-professional' hierarchical terms based largely on the notion of increasing the number of black people and women in 'higher levels of decision-making hierarchies in social work' (Hanmer and Statham 1988: 139).

The construction of a contemporary sociology of social work is taking place at a time when its subject matter (social work) is entering a period of major flux and uncertainty that contrasts sharply with the professionally expansionist era of the 1970s. In the circumstances described in this chapter it remains to be seen how recent sociology (of social work) will be perceived and responded to by social workers. In many respects recent anti-reductionist sociology, including sociology of the middle range, is the 'radical' (or 'critical') sociology of the 1990s. This is because, in the terms described earlier in the chapter, social (work) actors are not seen as unculpable cognitive products of some 'deep', humanly uncognisable 'discourse' or as the unwitting tools of 'objective' structural 'needs' or 'objective' interests (e.g. 'the interests of capitalism') enshrined in some overarching social totality against which actors (may claim they) 'struggle' in an attempt to provide relevant services to those actually or prospectively in need. Viewed in non-reductionist terms, social (work) actors are defined sociologically as loci of decision and action; actors make assessments and formulate objectives and employ strategies to 'enrol' other actors and 'consign' materials in ways designed by the actors concerned to achieve as far as possible their own *self-formulated* interests and purposes. This conception of social action is unlikely to erase some existing professional images of the sociologist as a relentless 'critic of the "establishment"' in the form of established institutions and professions' (Heraud 1979: 11). As we have seen, a genuinely reflexive ('self-aware') sociology of social work is intended also to be a critical analysis of sociology itself, in effect a sociology of sociology.

Chapter Three

THE SOCIOLOGY OF WELFARE

Where social work fits in

JOHN OFFER

This chapter will focus on some substantive sociology which, it is argued, is of particular relevance to social work education and practice. The various theoretical and conceptual orientations related to this sociology will be discussed as well as the findings themselves and their utility in social work contexts. It is helpful to use the label 'sociology of welfare' in this respect. The label is used here to make explicit the unity of existing welfare-related sociological research, and to highlight further research needs, rather than to delineate the boundaries of a new specialism in sociology *for its own sake*, which I believe would be fruitless and ill conceived. This label, provided that it is applied in the fairly broad manner envisaged, should also help to locate in a trouble-free way the sociology which is of most immediate relevance to social work. For it encompasses, as it is used here, much of such areas of sociology as the sociology of health and illness, of deviance, of friendship and community, and of gender, as well as studies closely focused on social work itself. Indeed, the list could be expanded considerably. If the label were to gain wider currency it would, I think, help to emphasise that sociology merits a central rather than a marginal place in both the social work training curriculum and the practice of social work.

Sociologists of religion are not concerned to improve religious experience; similarly, the sociology of welfare is defined as such by a concern not with improving welfare, but with understanding welfare relations as social relations. It is, for example, concerned to elucidate the interaction relationships between clients and professionals, and their antecedents and consequences. It is, then, concerned with the explication of all welfare-related social relations, not just those regarded as 'social problems'.

A focus on 'social problems' and how to solve them is characteristic of the studies undertaken within the subject of social administration (or social policy). Sociology of welfare and social administration should thus be seen as complementary, not as in competition. To illustrate the distinction it is worth considering the very important case of those who give and receive informal care (for example, elderly and infirm parents being cared for at home by their adult offspring). For the sociologist of welfare there are important questions to answer about exactly who in the population is involved in front-line care of this type, why they are involved, and how they view their current contact with the agents of 'formal' welfare, for example social workers. Social administration academics would typically be more concerned to identify the 'needs' of carers and how best to meet them through the provision of services. This example indicates the two different kinds of focus which I am trying to expose, but it also shows up as well the desirability of collaboration. The social policy perspective must draw on the sociology of welfare if it is to interpret 'needs' in a way which leads to carers getting what they feel they need rather than what may be seen by them as unhelpful interference.

However, the arguments put forward here for a distinction between the sociological and social administration approaches to welfare, and the need for collaboration, are relatively unfamiliar ones; as a consequence, this chapter is partly about the need *to develop* the sociology of welfare. The distinctively sociological studies often still remain to be done. In particular, more attention needs to be given to the sociology of 'states of welfare' as opposed to 'welfare states'. Room's promisingly titled *The Sociology of Welfare* (1979), for instance, concentrates on the sociology of *ideas* of welfare provision *by the state*. (On the points in this paragraph in general see Warham 1973; Roos 1973; Mishra 1981: 173; Offer 1983, 1985b.)

The arguments of the previous two paragraphs about relationships between social administration and the sociology of welfare apply with only minor changes if 'social administration' is replaced by 'social work education and practice'. However, some additional comments are necessary on how 'the sociology of social work' fits into the picture. It does so best if it is viewed as a sub-area of the sociology of welfare. There are plenty of worthwhile sociological questions and answers about social work in particular, as this book indicates. There are, though, topics where, while a social work presence may be an important constituent feature, a wider perspective is helpful, not least in avoiding our ideas of social work and what impacts it can have becoming ossified or narrowly 'professional'. Clients and carers may interpret their predicaments in ways which are at odds with the views of social workers (see the discussion of Robinson (1978) on pp. 79–80). Material of this sort is clearly relevant to understanding how social work fits into welfare relations in general, and relevant to social work itself, but unlikely to surface in sociology *centred on* social work. Here, then, is an illustration of how the sociology of welfare can provide important contextual perspectives on social work (a role emphasised by Finch (1982)).

I hope I have made the spirit and promise of the sociology of welfare tolerably clear. Provided that its distinctive questions and answers are given adequate acknowledgement, departmental boundaries matter little. Indeed, there have been recent signs that what seemed fixed boundaries are becoming more mobile, if only out of economic necessity. If this process continues, impediments in the way of genuine collaborative research into welfare, involving sociology, must become appreciably fewer.

The task now is to give an impression of what in terms of substance the sociology of welfare is. I begin by criticising some recent conceptions of what might be involved. After all, things social live at the moment in a cold climate. An attempt to expand the contribution of an out-of-fashion subject to a little-favoured profession must endure a rough journey. Vital, then, that the sociology on offer can withstand critical examination. On the whole, unpopular and valid arguments are less easily disposed of than unpopular and invalid ones. In this situation, I wish first to press home the point that not all of the subject's cherished concepts are adequately formed nor all its claims backed by clear logical reasoning: this has been sensed, I think, 'on the outside', with sad consequences for the impact of sociology. It would certainly be disingenuous to continue to blame sociology's lack of input into social work solely on social workers' 'fear' of a 'subversive' subject.

Perhaps I can best illustrate what I have in mind by reference to Sullivan (1987) and Walker (1981). Sullivan, in fact, has aims which are shared by this chapter: to increase the place given to sociology in social work and to stress that sociology itself should take a greater interest in social work: 'Whatever the reasons, sociology has danced coyly at the margins of social work despite the advantages that may accrue to both as a result of closer association' (Sullivan 1987: 173). However, although Sullivan does discuss some of the reasons why sociology and social work have trodden on each other's toes, the possibility that sociology might need to erect clear and convincing defences of some of its concepts and claims to hard-headed potential consumers is not explored. In fact, the contrary is signalled, for he says: 'In the final analysis, I would wish to argue, tests of sociological explanations are not so much tests of abstract truth as tests of social utility. How useful is this or that sociological explanation?' (Sullivan 1987: 175). To elevate 'social utility' (by whom is this defined?) above 'abstract' truth leads down the path to barren and incoherent relativism. More particularly, sociology surely forfeits a claim to be taken seriously as an academic subject. Truth may be difficult to discover, but if we give up trying sincerely to find it we are no better than astrologers *manqué*. Neither social workers nor anyone else need listen. The idea of sociologists being limited to reciting their moral and political convictions to each other with the webs of language occasionally converting a member of 'the caring professions' into a disciple is not an ennobling prospect and would prove unconvincing. It does not have to be the case.

Turning to content, for Sullivan the most fruitful areas of sociology include discussions of 'structure' (1987: 161), and the resultant 'clearer definition of social problem causation' (1987: 174). Elsewhere, Sullivan stresses the need 'to theorize the relationship between opposing social forces as dynamic rather than static' (1987: 135), and the value of the concept of 'class' in analysis (1987: 134). Such concerns are put together when he says

> state welfare and the practice of social work, though constrained, are not completely determined by the interests, values and ideologies of a dominant social class. State social work, it was suggested, operates within a tension between, on the one hand, the requirements of capitalism and, on the other, the capacity of the state to act relatively autonomously from those interests.
>
> (Sullivan 1987: 155)

From the same oven come Walker's comments, in connection with an attempt to broaden the focus of social administration as a subject, partly by urging contributions from sociology. Thus:

> the social construction of 'social policies' is one part of the process of legitimation carried out by the state in furthering the interests of the dominant forces in society (this is *not* to suggest

a conspiracy but rather an inherent process).

(Walker 1981: 231)

Social policies form, says Walker, 'an integral part of the apparatus of the capitalist system' (1981: 232). Once more 'class conflict' is presented as 'a basis of social policy' (1981: 237) and, he adds, the structure of social relations must be considered if we wish adequately to understand social policy.

The statements made by Sullivan and Walker exemplify a style of discourse which has not only been adopted sometimes by sociologists but which is also at the heart of what has been called the 'political economy' approach (see especially Gough 1979). Doubtless such claims were integral to what Pinker has written about ruefully and disparagingly as 'the sociological deluge that swept through social work and social administration in the mid 1970s, shifting the focus of the debate about social welfare from micro to macro issues' (1983a: 154). If the belief cradled within such sociology was that social work was closing its ears to the message, that belief itself was vested with an arrogance which smugly depended upon 'the view that the solution lies in changing the nature of social work in such a way that sociological knowledge will become more relevant' (Pinker 1983a: 155). The 'deluge' was (and remains) unsympathetic to social work; not sociology *for* social work and apparently more *against* it than genuinely *of* it. Writing in a similar context, Kathleen Jones gave a doleful verdict: 'Sociology has been remarkably destructive for the past twenty years' (1983: 227). Pinker is drawn to conclude:

> It would go beyond the limits of tolerance and credibility if a large proportion of social work courses were to be devoted to a sustained critique of the nature of social work itself . . . The first duty of a professional course is to produce capable practitioners. Who would want to be treated by a doctor, most of whose professional training had been taken up with a critique of existing medical knowledge and practice, and with learning a new and untested approach to medical care?

(Pinker 1983a: 160)

Yet it must be unsatisfactory to banish such sociology simply because it seems to be a nuisance from the point of view of life within social work. The sociological criticisms may yet be true, even, to recall Sullivan, if their 'social utility' is minimal. However, I want to draw attention to problems of a fundamental character about some of the concepts and claims given a central place by Sullivan and Walker. Such problems have already been recognised within the subject itself in attempts to ascertain how concepts may be used with most clarity and what claims can logically be made by sociology. The points, then, arise not from a political critique of sociology – though they may sometimes have faint echoes, or pre-echoes, there – but from anxieties within sociology, about the logical strengths and weaknesses of the subject. The result of the necessarily abbreviated discussion here will be that, even if such claims and concepts were being judged likely to make a useful (sociological) contribution to social work, their logical status and the associated epistemological and perhaps also ontological assumptions are altogether too fragile to inspire the confidence which they have sometimes done among sociologists.

In the comments from Sullivan and Walker, references were made to 'social forces' (or 'dominant forces'), 'structure', 'class', 'the capitalist system' and 'social problem causation'. In each case, fundamental problems need identification. Perhaps the idea of 'social force' is the one whose precariousness is most apparent. Is this a metaphorical phrase, deriving from a military analogy? But military forces are *directed* by chiefs and individual members denied autonomy. The analogy breaks down at once. Or is it a reverberation from a source altogether deeper: nineteenth-century physics or biology? This is possible; certainly the concept is to be found in Spencer's sociology (for example, Spencer 1867, ch. 8). Hardly, though, a happy precedent – deterministic and historicist accounts of individual action and social life in general, as envisaged by Spencer, are not thought sustainable nowadays (to characterise the forces as 'dynamic' not 'static' is not a solution any more than is entering the caveat that they are bound up with a mysterious 'inherent process' rather than conspiracy). Basic 'social forces' of this sort have proved stubbornly elusive. Central questions about the logic of the concept are not addressed: there is no definition of 'social force', no clear indication of what sort of relationship such 'forces' have to the doings of social actors and the nature of social relationships. Very few modern analyses of sociological theory find in favour of the concept; it seems as if we have here an idea being used without clarity, which brings with it a dubious conception of social life, and which has been with good reason dispatched to the margins within mainstream sociological theory. It warrants no place in sociology's overtures to social work, for its has no clear place in sociology itself.

Unlike 'social force', 'social structure' has the appearance of being a quintessential concept of sociological discourse. However, this has not always entailed clear and consistent use. Its relationship to the notion of agency in social life is problematic. In particular, fog often afflicts the concept: first, as to the mutability or otherwise of the putative structures and their characteristics; second, as to exactly what properties, causal or in some other sense limiting, are, and also can legitimately be, predicated of them. One of the most commanding comments on the concept of structure comes from Giddens:

> *Structures must not be conceptualized as simply placing constraints upon human agency, but as enabling.* This is what I call the *duality of structure.* Structures can always in principle be examined in terms of their *structuration* as a series of reproduced practices. To enquire into the structuration of social practices is to seek to explain how it comes about that structures are constituted through action, and reciprocally how action is constituted structurally.

(Giddens 1976: 161)

Giddens's *duality* of structure, and the idea of structuration, do not figure in the over-simplistic use of 'structure' in Sullivan and Walker. Evangelical fervour notwithstanding, it seems to be a dubiously mechanical idea of 'structure' which they wish to write into the study of social work and social policy. More must be held out to social work than broken and obsolete gadgetry from which only philosophical or historical scrap merchants can make a profit.

'Class' too is a concept in sociology with a long pedigree. Yet there is sufficient and justified disarray within sociology about the concept for programmes for the development of sociological studies of social work and welfare to invoke it with circumspection rather than advocate it as an essential explanatory ingredient. There is an ambiguity and vagueness about exactly what the expression 'a class' refers to. For example, how important is *consciousness* of a particular putative class position to those to whom it might be imputed, and what are the precise 'criteria' of consciousness and how are they to be applied? And, again, what kind of properties, if any, are, and also can legitimately be, predicated of a particular class? It is not my task here to resolve the ambiguities and contradictions woven into the use of 'class' in sociology. But I would suggest that the aptness of the proverb 'never look a gift-horse in the mouth' might on this occasion be questioned.

I now move on to expressions such as 'the capitalist system' and 'the requirements of capitalism'. No doubt it can be useful to have 'ideal type'-like models of social relations which relate to 'ideal type'-like models of kinds of economic activity and organisation. It is, however, important to remember that logically they are constructed in advance of, rather than following, a full study of the social relations in question. If this is forgotten, complex social reality is liable to be interpreted through taken-for-granted categories and propositions which may in fact be very ill-fitting clothes. As Berger and Kellner comment, 'One . . . "knows" from the beginning what one is going to find; not surprisingly, one then proceeds to find it' (1982: 139). And they continue:

> Against this, it is exceedingly important to insist upon the inevitably limited, 'aspectual' 'perspectival' character of sociological interpretation – and indeed of all sciences. The totalistic or systemic aspiration of Marxism inhibits the interpretation of empirically available meanings, because these are always placed (however arbitrarily) within an *a priori* relevance structure derived from the theoretical system as a whole.
>
> (Berger and Kellner 1982: 139-40)

It follows, then, that references to the alleged *requirements* of capitalism, or to a capitalist *system* and features of it, are much more speculative and provisional in character than Sullivan or Walker present them.

Another problem is that the word 'system' can mislead us into believing that social relations have a life and logic of their own, governed by some kind of irrepressible historicist force (or 'inherent process') beyond the control of, perhaps construed as separate from, the social actors involved. And some of the chief grounds for anxiety about such concepts have already been pinpointed.

There are further difficulties regarding expressions such as the 'requirements' of capitalism. From the conception of them as somehow outside the control of social actors it has proved tempting to go on first to judge them (usually as 'bad') and then, second, to imply that they are in some way *actually so experienced* by people in everyday life. The first move is arguably not itself a matter of social science. The second move is, as it stands, in fact empty assertion. However, regardless of alleged 'requirements', it is an important sociological task to study actual everyday theoretical and moral categories and how they are put into operation; but this cannot of course be faithfully pursued if the categories are imposed from outside, cutting haphazardly across the categories in which life is lived, and the answers in effect assumed. I end this part of the discussion by considering 'social problem causation'. The comments already made should register some reservations about the capacity of sociology as conceived by Sullivan and Walker to give well-grounded answers about causation. There are, though, some other difficulties which need to be raised. One is that the definition of the 'problem' involved can itself be highly problematic. Take the case of 'poverty': for Walker 'the relative nature of poverty' is 'a fact' (1981: 244). Yet Townsend's (1979) influential statement of the case for relative definitions of poverty – in particular one which is bound up with indicators of 'objective' as opposed to 'subjective' deprivation and a 'deprivation threshold' in income terms derived from them – has been widely and effectively criticised. A most powerful objection has been that Townsend's definition of 'poverty' is not constructed by reference to what counts as 'poverty' in everyday life, in other words, its actual social meaning(s). The precise problem, then, for which one can be searching for causes may itself be more a *construct* of social science than of social life in general. This point has been developed in Carrier and Kendall (1973). (See also Offer (1985a) on the criticisms of Townsend.)

Beyond this we encounter a considerable thicket. Many have argued, and I agree with them, that 'causal relations' could only in principle be established concerning, to use Giddens's phrase, 'the reproduced unintended consequences of intended acts' (1976: 154). For in the case of *intended* consequences the presence of conscious agency takes us a very long way indeed from a natural science kind of meaning of cause, which refers to mechanical connections established in nature (Giddens 1976: 153). But even in the area where causal statements are in principle possible it is necessary to recognise a difference compared to the natural sciences. As Giddens says, 'causal conditions that influence human action can in principle be recognized by men, and thus incorporated into that action in such a way as to transform it' (1976: 154).

I shall not venture deeper here into these fundamental and intricate matters. However, there is one further point which it may be useful to raise. Occasionally, statements such as 'low pay causes poverty' are made. But these can involve a misleading, though not infrequent, use of 'cause'. In this case, 'poverty' is usually so construed as *by definition* to include those with income from work below a certain point. Being on the appropriate low income from work is therefore simply to fulfil a *criterion* of being 'in poverty'.

I think ample has now been said on this set of ideas and concepts which ranges from 'social force' to 'social problem causation'. Some of the points are probably familiar. Nevertheless, the comments seemed to be required since the concepts and ideas in question have been promoted as central and with great enthusiasm in some of the recent attempts to articulate a case for the relevance of sociology to social work training and practice. I would add that, while I have aimed to expose the limitations of the raw sociological ideas being proffered, there are matters of profound importance with which they purport to engage, however meagre the returns. I have in mind the production and reproduction of *power* relations in social life. I cannot develop this point here. I do say, in somewhat oblique fashion, more on it below, since systematic asymmetries in respect of both power *over* and power *to*, involving differences in forms of discourse as much as in practical outcomes, are as unavoidable in trying to understand social work/client dealings as they are when other aspects of social life are being studied. Possibly, some of the concepts and ideas discussed above could be so re-worked as to have a genuinely constructive part to play in such studies. Ultimately the principal disappointment arising from the accounts of Walker and Sullivan is that they do not glimpse the need for vital work of conceptual reconstruction.

Let me now turn to some rather different sociology, for the most part not noticed by Sullivan and Walker, which seems to me both sound and of enormous potential relevance to social work training and practice. It is helpful to begin by considering Day's recent book (1987). According to Day:

> Sociological research is . . . of help to social workers in understanding processes of change and development in small groups which are an important setting for practice. Most people are involved in a variety of groups in their daily lives and they are essential to meeting many individual and social needs. Many of the personal needs of individuals are met in an informal way by families and resources in people's neighbourhoods. These informal caring networks often provide a great deal of help, although it has to be recognised that these resources vary greatly. For example, one family may apparently cope well with problems or needs which for another are very stressful or burdensome. Social workers need to have some knowledge of the networks of which people form a part

or of possible networks which they might join. However, the study of sociology suggests a need for caution. In community-based models of social work the most vulnerable, disadvantaged and stigmatised people could be at risk as they offend local norms of behaviour and are often rejected by their local communities.

(Day 1987: 3)

Later, Day reinforces such observations as follows (1987: 125); 'Social workers . . . need to be well informed about the neighbourhoods in which they work and can use this knowledge in the development of relationships in the community and in other ways.'

There is already a body of relevant research, including Bulmer (1985, 1987), Wenger (1984), and Cecil, Offer, and St Leger (1987). Much of it, incidentally, represents a mutually beneficial blurring of the boundary between sociology and social anthropology. These studies also provide a point of rejuvenation for sociological studies more generally, as well as being useful in developing the sociology of welfare (discussed further by Bulmer (1985)). No apology is needed, then, for urging that this work be given much more prominence in the sociology taught to social work students, and in social work research and practice. The research can be a focus for discussions of such central topics as why people become informal carers, and how they care; and also questions about who is excluded from care, from whom care is withdrawn, and why. Other topics too are illuminated, such as the obligations felt by and expectations placed upon women, and the satisfactions and problems in caring, both for the carer and the cared for.

There is a need to plumb deeper, though, without incurring any concomitant loss of relevance to social work. One exceptionally important point has particular relevance to attempts to co-ordinate formal and informal care:

In everyday practice, professionals and informal caregivers have to grapple with different assumptions and expectations about what 'support' means and how it should be provided . . . In many ways, trying to combine the efforts of professional service providers with those of family members, concerned neighbours, and devoted friends, is like trying to link two cultures in which very different beliefs, customs and norms of exchange prevail.

(Froland *et al.* 1981: 260)

Here, surely, are complexities, with manifold ramifications, about which contemporary sociology should have much to say. Indeed, as far back as 1887, the same difference fascinated Tonnies when he drew the contrast between informal and formal social relations in the language of *Gemeinschaft* and *Gesellschaft* (Tonnies 1955), and it may be that the detail which underpins Tonnies's distinction could help in the development of research today. (With founding fathers in mind, it may be noted in passing that it was Spencer who, in the second volume of his *Principles of Ethics* (1893), first distinguished clearly betwen statutory, voluntary, and informal forms of relief. For further discussion see Offer 1983.) The aims and methods of informal caring may thus be quite distinctive. Sociology, provided that it does not seek from the start to impose definitions of its own on the social phenomena involved, should be able to display the meanings and logics embedded in informal care. If the attitude towards informal care, whether on the part of sociology or of social work policy, is one which assumes or superimposes certain meanings in the case of concepts such as 'need' and 'good outcome', then distortion must inevitably result, with social work practice receiving no real benefit.

This 'two cultures' point also furnishes a key to understanding relationships between social workers and their clients. Once the methodological importance for sociology of 'multiple realities' or 'plural meanings' in formal and informal welfare activities and their interactions is grasped and adhered to, sociology has an opportunity to contribute most constructively to a well-grounded understanding of such problems as client 'dissatisfaction' (and 'satisfaction') with social work and the low take-up of some means-tested benefits, as well as to more general but equally important matters such as public attitudes to social provision in general. It is, then, an unhappy paradox that 'one of the few books which stresses this kind of focus has been little noticed. Robinson's *In Worlds Apart* is an essay around the thesis that 'one of the major factors lying behind "troubles" in professional–client relationships is the encapsulation of each in sharply differing subjective worlds' (1978: 2). These differences – and differences in meaning, not inadequacies in communication, are here at stake – are to be uncovered, says Robinson, around at least seven matters: the central or most important feature of a problem; the meaning of time scales; the nature of what is trivial and what is serious; the adequacy of information and advice; the evaluation of costs; the meaning of the terms in which prognoses are made; and the nature of 'progress' (1978: 42).

It seems to me that Robinson is adumbrating an agenda for both teaching and research which is truly sociological in character, of profound relevance to social work practice and policy, and capable of looping back profitably into the concerns of mainstream sociology. Again, though, it must be emphasised, as Robinson does, that whether such dissatisfactions 'are "true" from some outside point of view or from the professional's point of view is not the point'; they must, rather, be studied for themselves – what a client believes 'will affect his relationship with the services' (1978: 16).

This is not all. While 'two cultures' and 'encapsulation in separate worlds' should not be treated as absolutes in the present contexts, their heuristic value is nevertheless not yet exhausted. Robinson suggests that the differences just mentioned may themselves be accounted for by 'deeper' differences, not least between 'lay' theories and 'professional' theories about welfare matters. Thus he observes:

> People rarely seem to make sense of their problems or their encounters with professionals wholly on their own. Before, during or afterwards they may consult other lay people so that there is, in a sense, a filter between the professional and his client even when they meet one-to-one.
>
> (Robinson 1978: 47)

Such consultations produce and reproduce distinctive stocks of 'knowledge' and 'recipes', so that it seems that 'most lay people have common-sense ideas and theories about areas of life that professionals claim expert authority over' (1978: 44). As yet, however, we know little about these matters. One can speculate that questions about who cares for whom and why and how can only be answered adequately when we address the rich stew of language involving ideas of desert, need, responsibility, obligation, and causation at the level of every-day life. At the very least, we should be exploring the claim by Mayer and Timms (1970) that working-class clients adopted a distinctive 'uni-causal' approach to the causation of 'problems' and a 'moralistic' and 'suppressive' approach to action. The interests both of sociology in general and of social work would be well served by extensive research into these matters. Such research might best be described as falling within the sociology of morals. Pinker has urged the growth of such inquiry, suggesting that it would both help us to know 'far more about the preferred and actual forms of reciprocity and obligation which occur between strangers sharing a common citizenship and members of the same kin' and also assist in assessing 'the extent to which the values and assumptions which are implicit in social legislation support, weaken or modify the moral beliefs and practices of ordinary people' (Pinker 1974: 8–9).

Many of the points just touched upon have in a transposed way become significant topics in studies of health and illness. I enter this realm here for two reasons: health and illness matters are themselves of substantial concern to social workers; and the points to be made may serve to reinforce and supplement those made about other aspects of social work practice and theory. To my mind Dingwall (1976) is an important book. Consonant with some of my earlier remarks, Dingwall begins with rejecting what he calls, following J.D. Douglas, a 'moral absolutist' approach to social meanings. 'Moral absolutism', for Dingwall, centrally involves disregarding the fact that concepts such as 'health' and 'illness' – and I am suggesting a range of others, including 'welfare' – can have a plurality of meanings rather than a 'real' single meaning in social life. Once this is recognised, it follows that elucidating and accounting for such meanings becomes a prime sociological task rather than matters which sociology can either ignore or else seek to 'correct'. Thus the sociology of health and illness must have a focus upon 'how both lay persons and "professionals" theorise about the human body and its operations and management', but must remember that from the sociological point of view – understanding rather than judging social life – 'all such theories have an equal epistemological status. Taken in context they are all equally sensible, rational and reasonable' (Dingwall 1976: 27). Dingwall thus describes his position as 'ethnosociological'. Underpinnings can be drawn in general from ethnomethodology and phenomenological sociology, as well as the philosophy of Wittgenstein (on these see Giddens 1976). Such a description could apply to all the sociology reviewed in this ,art of the discussion: it all takes seriously the ways in which the social world is constituted through the meanings of the agents involved.

Healthy flesh is appearing on the skeletal outlines provided by Dingwall as a result of several studies. Williams has shown in a Scottish study (1983) differing concepts of health within a lay population: 'health' as fitness for work; as having strength; and as absence of disease. And a study undertaken in Wales (Pill and Stott 1982) has demonstrated that working-class mothers often lack a conception of health as something for which they themselves have responsibility. A deeply rooted fatalistic attitude, buttressed by a range of lay theories, suggests that it is less ignorance than a counter-logic that health educators may have to confront. (Other relevant sources include Calnan (1987) and Stacey (1988), especially ch. 10.) The actual experiences of patients suffering chronic illness and of the families caring for them at home have been carefully reported in Anderson and Bury (1988). Dingwall himself has also studied (1977) the shifts in meaning which are an integral part of the process of becoming a health professional, in his case a health visitor.

One inescapable theme which emerges from these comments on the sociology of welfare and health is that relationships between professionals and their 'clients' should be seen as special arenas where power is exercised in social relationships (not necessarily always in one direction, *by* the professional). Meanings can be imposed and dissent neutralised in perhaps unintended but profound ways. Recalling Goffman's work in *Asylums* (1961) is helpful in this connection. If *Asylums* now seems a little 'worked out', this is perhaps because it has too often been seen as a book simply about institutions. In fact, though, it is a richly observant study of the exercise, manipulation, and management of power in social relations, in a special set of social circumstances. If we accept that all social relations involve work being done by the participating actors to sustain or modify social life and individual identities, then 'social work' may itself be seen as social work in that kind of sense, where indeed power imbalances may often be lurking.

I hope I have now identified the kind of sociology which may most profitably be taught to social work students and the kind of sociological research, which either has been done or should be done, which can be most helpful in improving the effectiveness and efficiency of social work practice and policy. Naturally, cognate sociological studies in the areas of race relations and deviancy (for example, Rex and Moore 1967; Parker 1974), and of the 'logics' of professionals such as the police (for example Fielding 1988), deserve no less prominence. However, rather than develop these points, I want instead to end by introducing a set of three specific observations which serve in their own way to deepen the case for the relevance to social work practice and policy of the sociology which has been discussed above.

The first of these observations is as follows. Social workers, it can reasonably be assumed, are intending through their work to benefit their clients in some way. Granted sincerity of purpose, monitoring of 'outcomes' should be, it can be argued, an integral part of social work activity, at individual, agency, and national levels (compare Flew 1981: 172–4). Full research projects are not always as necessary in this respect as a sociological imagination informed by the kind of points developed above.

The second observation can be presented in connection with the Barclay Report, already influencing the social work picture in some parts of the country. In advocating a shift in social work organisation and practice towards 'community social work', the Report observes: 'social workers in post will need to be helped to know their own community be it a locality or a group of people with a shared concern' (1982: 209). Might this not legitimately be interpreted as a request for sociology, and sociology of the kind I have been highlighting? It is to be hoped that sociology will make the most of the request and engage in focused, local studies.

The third and final observation is prompted by the Griffiths Report, *Community Care: Agenda for Action* (1988). This report establishes as a central objective of community care policy 'the delivery of packages of care, building first on the available contribution of informal carers and neighbourhood support' (1988: 1). To enable such objectives to be met, Griffiths calls on several occasions for information and training to be available. Again, sociology is an obvious potential contributor. In particular, contributions from sociology could be made on 'how helpful services are perceived to be by consumers' (ibid: 7), to the data needed 'in order to permit decisions as to the cost-effective use of resources' (ibid: viii), and to the training and support of social workers to facilitate 'the transfer of skills from professional staff to informal carers' (ibid: 25). Contributions could be made more generally of course, given the thrust of Griffiths towards providing 'packages of services for individuals *within their own situations*' (ibid: 26) and with specific reference to the significance of differing cultural backgrounds.

Sociology of welfare, then, faces no shortage of opportunities for contributing in positive fashion to social work practice and policy. But furnishing the research is only the beginning; the necessary further objective of the proper incorporation of the results into the policy-making process, whether at national or local level, will be, given present indications (as discussed by, for example, Bulmer 1987), achieved only with difficulty.

© 1991 John Offer

Part Two

SOCIOLOGICAL PERSPECTIVES ON SOCIAL WORK

Chapter Four

SOCIOLOGY, SOCIAL WORK, AND CHILD PROTECTION

BRIAN CORBY

In this chapter I wish to consider how the discipline of sociology has been used (and not used) by the social work profession to construe and respond to the issue of child protection in recent times. While my main focus is, therefore, on sociology *for* social work, I intend to use a sociological perspective to examine this issue and in so doing contribute to the development of a sociology *of* social work. In order to do this, I will initially make some preliminary observations on the relationship between sociology and social work in general. I will then move on to consider the influence of a variety of theories on the way in which the phenomenon of child abuse is first perceived and then responded to in practice.

SOCIOLOGY AND SOCIAL WORK

Social work, as we know it today, is a profession mandated by society to carry out certain prescribed tasks largely in relation to its disadvantaged members. Within and around the social work profession there is considerable disagreement about how these tasks should be accomplished and about what tools are needed to complete them. For instance, there are disagreements both among and between employers and educators. Employers are mainly concerned to get the job done. They are not interested in having a critically aware work-force. Educators are generally committed to a broader-based approach which is less technically specific. There are probably considerable differences in emphasis within both of these groupings, but for the purposes of this paper I will focus on the latter.

While most educators share the liberal democratic values that under-pin our society and profoundly influence the way in which social work is carried out, some will lean more to the views of the employers and focus on the provision of technical training (i.e. knowledge of the law and of the mainstream administrative practices of probation and social services departments), with an additional emphasis on the findings of empirical studies in the social work field. Others will eschew technical training and emphasise the moral/vocational aspects of the work, in particular the person-to-person configuration. Yet others will adopt a critique-of-society approach, casting a broadly questioning eye on the structures of society; their focus is not on what form of intervention might benefit a particular client, but on the social and political forces that have led to her or him becoming subject to the attention of social workers. Two things should be stressed here. First, these emphases are not necessarily mutually exclusive and the teaching offered in most educational institutions will reflect more than one of these approaches. Second, some views and approaches are clearly more acceptable than others given the political framework in which social work is practised.

The social work profession has traditionally looked to the social sciences for its knowledge base. It has always been eclectic, selecting mainly from psychology, sociology, and the study of social policy/administration those theories and approaches that have been thought to be useful to the problems of the day and in tune with the politics of the policy makers. At different periods different knowledge bases have held sway. Thus, for instance, psychoanalysis and psychology were prominent in the two post-war decades, though never to the extent that the term 'psychiatric deluge' implied.[1] Throughout the late sixties and the seventies the developing disciplines of sociology and social policy gained in prominence, influenced partly by the broader remit given to the welfare professions at that time. During the eighties there seemed to be no obvious emphasis, though it is always difficult to be definite about trends close to the time that they are taking place. If anything, the state, through the medium of employing agencies, established firmer control over how social work was practised and taught, and the knowledge base became determined more by the requirements of the job as prescribed by employers, with particular emphasis on whatever was deemed to be technically useful and readily managed.

The way in which social work has made use of sociology is instructive. Sociology is a broad discipline embracing a wide range of perspectives. While it has a general ideology – that human behaviour is influenced and shaped by social forces and institutions such as class, culture, family, community, and religion – there are many differing views about the way in which this happens, the important areas for study, and the ways in which they should be studied. At a general level, one of the key splits in sociological thought has been that between consensus and conflict theories. Consensus theorists are concerned with how societies maintain social cohesion. They do not question the *status quo*. Conflict theorists are more concerned with the issue of power in society and how dominant groups protect that dominance. While the latter have traditionally seen social and economic class as key determinants, much greater emphasis is now being placed on other determinants of disadvantage, such as race and gender. This level of theorising (termed macro-level) is complemented by micro-level approaches which look at the way in which the behaviour of individuals and groups is influenced by social, cultural, and political factors. The most influential of these in social work in recent decades has been that of labelling theory.

Mainstream social work has, according to Bailey (1980), tradition-ally made use of those sociological theories and approaches which do not cast a critical eye on society. It has looked more to the approaches which help explain individual behaviour without addressing larger issues such as the distribution of power and privilege. It has found it difficult to come to terms with the critical theories partly because the criticism includes the role of social work itself and partly because of its limited mandate and apparent powerlessness in the face of this broad critique. Thus, in the early seventies, radical social work, based on orthodox and revisionist Marxist sociological theories, had only limited impact, whereas the more consensus-based systems theory, which had the merit of broadening social work's previously narrow perspective without upsetting the *status quo*, soon became institu-tionalised in social work training.[2] During the 1980s, conflict theories of race and gender gained some ground in social work courses and training, but it is not yet possible to know how they will ultimately influence social work practice.

To some extent this type of relationship between social work and sociology is inevitable. I do not believe that there is the space for the social work profession to embrace a radical perspective fully. The political structure of our society and the function that social work has been given within it (i.e. to act as a service/social control agent with regard to individuals who are disadvantaged) make a radical approach highly problematic, certainly as far as sustained action is concerned. Nevertheless, the more radical sociological perspective, with its emphasis on the power structure and the way in which this creates the problems with which social workers are expected to work at the individual level, provides a credible explanatory theory for many educators and practitioners, the latter of whom daily face immediate problems of human suffering and misery which theories of personal pathology do not seem sufficient to explain. This gap between analysis and allowable action is a key problem for the profession of social work.

SOCIOLOGY AND THE UNDERSTANDING OF CHILD ABUSE

This problem is particularly pertinent to the specific case of child abuse and child protection work because of the public nature of the issue. First, although much of what social workers do is not of particular concern to the public, for a variety of reasons child abuse has excited considerable publicity and public interest.[3] Second, social work does not have sole responsibility for child protection work. It shares that responsibility with a wide range of other health and welfare professions and with the police. Much of the important decision making in child protection work is carried out in 'public' inter-professional meetings such as the case conference. Third, child protection work is very closely monitored at the managerial level in direct response to criticisms arising from the numerous public inquiries over two decades. All these factors have resulted in social workers having far less autonomy in child protection work than they have in other less controversial fields.[4] While the desired degree of freedom of operation in this area of work is in dispute, one clear effect of the factors outlined above is that the contribution of the more critical sociological perspectives to the way in which social workers construe and understand child abuse is even more marginalised than it is in other areas of activity.

Parton (1985) has argued convincingly that child abuse, from its re-emergence as a social problem in 1974, has been seen largely as a consequence of individual (and, to a lesser extent, family) pathology, and that this perspective has been a major determinant of the way in which the problem has been responded to in our society. The work of Henry Kempe and his associates (1962) in the sixties was instrumental in establishing this state of affairs. Briefly, their thesis was that parents who have had psychologically depriving experiences themselves as children are more likely to abuse their own children than parents who have had 'emotionally healthy' childhoods. Such behaviour is seen as likely to escalate unless action is taken to protect the child and unless psychological therapy for the parent or parents is provided. This explanation of child abuse, originally devised with physical abuse in mind, but later applied in a wholesale way to other forms of abuse, has fitted in well with the mainstream political views of our era (and consequently with the philosophies and practices of welfare and medical agencies), namely that good parenting and love for children are the norm, and that deviations from that norm are pathological, individual aberrations and should be treated as such. The cases of serious abuse and killings of children throughout the seventies and eighties which were the subject of public inquiries served to support such views, as virtually all of the abusers in these cases were themselves ill-treated as children. Nelson's study of the way in which child abuse policy was developed in the USA in the sixties and seventies demonstrates the strength of the political appeal of the individualised explanation of child abuse (Nelson 1984). It was an attractive policy issue there because, as it was presented – innocent children at risk and parents in need of help – it was a potential vote winner for election candidates.

While the theories deriving from Kempe's work have been the major influence, because of their compatibility with mainstream political thinking, they have not been the only ones available for understanding child abuse; there has, for instance, been a contribution from sociobiology which has had little direct influence.[5] However, for the purposes of this chapter, I shall concentrate on theories deriving from the sociological perspective. Parton (1985) has identified three such theories, the ecological, the social cultural, and the social structural.

Ecological theories, as exemplified by Garbarino and Gilliam (1980), stress the importance of interaction between people and their environments for healthy development; Garbarino and Gilliam's work points to child abuse being more prevalent in areas where there is greater social stress as a result of a lack of family and community supports. They advocate the need to avoid grouping families at risk in single neighbourhoods and argue for the provision of services which are sensitive to the needs of local communities. This perspective has been influential in practice in Great Britain as demonstrated by the development of family centres. The idea of stress on families as a causative factor in child abuse and attempts to ameliorate it by the provision of community services are politically acceptable. This is because Garbarino and Gilliam's analysis does not seek to offer an explanation of why neighbourhoods have developed in the way that they have. Gelles and his associates (Straus *et al.* 1980; Gelles and Cornell 1985) are exemplars of the social cultural approach. Their argument is that the incidence of abuse is related to cultural support for the use of physical punishment on children. They conducted a general survey of over 1000 families in the USA and found that abusive violence towards children was far more widespread than official reports of abuse suggested. They argue that families are dangerous places and that a wider societal approach to the issue of abuse of all kinds within families is needed. Such views have met with mixed receptions in our society as evidenced by the response to the recent banning of corporal punishment in schools. The implication that family violence is more normal than has generally been believed also challenges two sacred cows: the individual pathological explanation of child abuse and our cosier notions about the nuclear family. Nevertheless, there has been some acceptance of these views, because they hold some common ground with those who endorse a child-saving perspective.

The most challenging of all these sociological perspectives (and thus the least influential) is the social structural causation viewpoint which stems mainly from the work of Gil (1970). In his research into officially recorded abuse in the USA in the late sixties, he found that children on the child protection registers came overwhelmingly from the lowest socio-economic classes. Other studies have supported this finding.[6] Even allowing for the fact that child abuse is more likely to be spotted in lower-class families because they are generally more subject to state surveillance, the statistics are telling. Gil's argument is that the children of the poor are more vulnerable because of the stresses placed on their parents by structural inequalities which result in restricted access to life-enhancing resources. His analysis points to the need for wider structural changes to prevent child abuse. In his later work (Gil 1975), he pursues his argument to its logical end, reasoning that the way in which society caters for the children of the poor is itself an abuse. Further, that if society itself sets the preconditions for child abuse by condoning structural inequalities, then it too must share the blame when a child is abused and such abuse should not be seen to be solely the result of individual pathology.

Not unexpectedly, such views have not been well received other than in radical quarters. Certainly they did not influence policies *vis-à-vis* the children of the poor during the seventies and eighties. The spectre of serious child abuse has been dominant and child care policy has focused more and more on child protection procedures to the exclusion of more positive responses. One of the consequences of this is that the child abuse net has widened and large numbers of marginally at risk children of the poor have entered it.[7] Yet, little has been done to increase financial support or other facilities for low-income families.

In addition to these three perspectives, there are the important contributions of feminist thought to the problem of child abuse and also those of advocates of children's rights.

Although there are many different strands of feminist thinking, a general view deriving from this perspective is that our society is characterised by patriarchy, i.e. it is dominated by male interests and all aspects of social organisation are framed from the male viewpoint. This form of feminist analysis has been applied particularly to child sexual abuse, where abusers are predominantly male and those abused are predominantly female. Put in its simplest terms, the sexual abuse of children is seen by writers such as Rush (1980) and Dominelli (1986) as an extreme example of institutionalised male power. In contrast to the structural perspective referred to before, feminist thought and analysis have been more influential in that they have constituted one of the main reasons why child sexual abuse has been put on the social policy agenda in the face of considerable resistance. However, they still have battles to fight in that the dominant causation theories are individual and family pathology rather than the issues of gender and power.[8]

The feminist perspective has been less prominent in the general child abuse field. One of the difficult issues that feminists have had to face is that, as far as we know, women are equally implicated in the abuse of children with men. A recent account by Gordon (1989) of child abuse work in the USA from 1880 to 1960 demonstrates the importance of applying a broad range of explanatory perspectives, including the much neglected feminist view, to all forms of officially defined child abuse. Her view is that it is important for feminists to look closely at why women, as well as men, abuse children. She argues that class and economic conditions and gender and generational conflicts all need to be taken into consideration when seeking to answer this question. With specific reference to the gender issue, it is clear that notions of natural motherhood, so keenly espoused in the decades after the Second World War, have placed unreal expectations on female carers and added to the stresses that may already be created by having to care for children in impoverished circumstances. One of the main policy implications of the feminist perspective is the need, among other things, to examine and change the way in which males and females are socialised into gender stereotypes. As in the case of the social structural perspective, child abuse is seen as a product of political forces, not of personal pathology, but for feminists the focus is on gender politics rather than (or in some cases, as well as) poverty and class.

In recent years considerable attention has been given to the rights of children, initially by educationalists such as Holt (1975) and Farson (1978) and latterly by those concerned with child care issues such as Freeman (1983), who has identified two main schools of thought in this area, the protectionist and the liberationist. The former view is well entrenched in our legal system and is in line with classical liberal philosophy, namely that of limited intervention into the private domain. From this point of view, children have the right to be protected only when it can be legally proved that they are at risk. Liberationists take a more radical stance. Their view is that, as far as possible, children should have the same rights as adults. Age is seen as irrelevant and self-determination as paramount.[9] Currently, a mid-way position seems to be gaining some favour. A stronger children's rights position has been advocated since the findings of the Cleveland report (Butler-Sloss 1988) and concerns about physical punishment are now firmly on the agenda. The issue of children's rights has an appeal for those who espouse an individual pathology view of child abuse. It also has an appeal for those who are critical of the traditional power relations within the nuclear family. There can be little doubt that in the past too little emphasis has been placed on the child's viewpoint. On the other hand, there seems to be little point in setting high standards for child care without ensuring that poor families in particular are provided with the means to achieve them.

I have argued so far that there are certain theories concerning child abuse that dominate the thinking of policy makers and those practising in this area of work, particularly social workers. The most influential of all the theories has been that of individual pathology. Certainly, it has been used to shape the system that currently exists for responding to child abuse in Great Britain, though it has to be said that Kempe's prescriptions for therapeutic intervention have been implemented in only a few settings (see pp. 98–9). There are other theories deriving from sociology, particularly the ecological approach, that are also acceptable, and some aspects of feminist and children's rights approaches have had and are gaining some influence. However, the viewpoints that more fundamentally challenge the *status quo* – i.e. those theories that emphasise class, access to resources, patriarchy, and paternalism as important factors in considering why child abuse occurs – continue to be marginalised in most quarters. These theories that point to existing power relations as causative factors in child abuse are often seen as fanciful and irrelevant.

In the next section I will look at what theories are influential in social work practice in the field of child protection.

CHILD PROTECTION PRACTICE

Many of the sociological perspectives outlined above may seem to have messages for broader policy, but the social worker in the field of child abuse may well feel as much a victim of policy as some of the families she or he is dealing with. Arguably, the intention and, certainly, the effect of most of the public inquiries into physical child abuse (and this is particularly evident in some of the most recent ones, notably Jasmine Beckford (Brent 1985) and Kimberley Carlile (Greenwich 1987)) has been to ensure that social workers maintain their distance from parents in order to focus more specifically on the protection of the child. To protest that more attention needs to be paid to the social, economic, and political circumstances in which child abuse occurs suggests moving away from that trend and runs the risk of being accused of over-complicating the activity of child protection.

I will return to this issue in the conclusion. First, I will consider what perspectives seem to operate in practice, judging mainly from empirical studies. Most of the studies to be reviewed are concerned with physical child abuse. However, I will also consider child sexual abuse with particular reference to the findings of the Cleveland inquiry.

There are surprisingly few empirical studies of social work practice in the field of child abuse, if we exclude public inquiries.[10] Of the first two that I will refer to, those of Parton (1985) and Dingwall *et al.* (1983), the former is not based on empirical research, but merits inclusion here because it is closely concerned with practice issues.

In fact these two studies provide apparently contrasting, conflicting pictures of practice in the child abuse field. Parton argues that social workers have been forced to adopt a more authoritarian style and that child abuse work has become more intrusive.

It would thus appear that social work practice with children and families has become far more authoritative and decisive and has increasingly come to intervene in ways which can be experienced by families as threats or punishments. Social workers seem to be developing a practice which says to deprived families that they should be able to care for their children without welfare support and that firm, speedy action will follow if they are not able to provide such care adequately.

(Parton 1985: 207)

While these observations are not based on detailed research into practice, they have a ring of truth about them. Parton cites the increase in the use of place of safety orders as evidence of an increase in defensive practice. He paints a picture of social workers working to the requirements of the child protection procedures and having little discretion or freedom to think about what they are doing. The implication is that their work is not theory-led, but a response to agency demands.

Dingwall *et al.*'s research into the work of two social services departments in the late seventies gives a somewhat different impression of social work practice. Their focus was on the way in which cases of suspected physical abuse and neglect were processed from referral through, in some instances, to court action. They concluded that the various professions involved in these child abuse systems used a variety of reasons or theories to account for the allegations of abuse with which they were faced. The most common theories identified were the beliefs a) that parental love of children is natural, b) that standards of care for children are culturally relative, and c) that families have potential for improvement or change (what they term as 'the rule of optimism'). The outcome of intervention on the basis of this theorising was that only the very worst cases went right through the system to care or wardship proceedings.

Thus, a very different picture from that of Parton is painted of the way in which the child protection system operates. Social workers and others are seen to be concerned to minimise abuse rather than respond in an authoritarian way to it. Certainly this view of social work practice has been endorsed in public inquiries. The Jasmine Beckford inquiry was highly critical of the practice of Brent social workers for being unduly optimistic about the potential of Jasmine's parents to provide a safe and secure environment for her.[11] With regard to the specific interest of this chapter, it is not apparent that an individual or family pathology approach was dominant among the practitioners in the areas studied, as this was not a direct concern of the researchers. Yet it is clear that few, if any, social workers adopted an explicit social structural analysis of the cases they were dealing with, even though it is evident that many of the families being investigated were living in impoverished circumstances. Similarly with regard to issues of gender.

My research into child abuse work in one local authority in the early eighties suggested that, at the point of referral, families were dealt with in an authoritative way for the most part (Corby 1987). Social workers followed the child abuse procedures fairly closely even though they did not always wish to. Children suspected of being abused were taken for medical examinations with or without the willing consent of their parents, and, where suspicions persisted, kept away from them until decisions could be reached at case conferences. Parents were not kept well informed of the process in many cases and the small number that were interviewed were largely embittered by what had happened. Up to this point there was much to support Parton's perception of child abuse work. However, decision making at case conferences was a haphazard affair, with a good deal of uncertainty and inconsistency about what factors were important in agreeing on a course of action. At the end of the day, as found in Dingwall's research, court action was the agreed outcome in only a small number of cases. This research suggested that the style of intervention in the early stages is authoritative, but the substance in the longer term fairly liberal. The bulk of child protection work was concerned with monitoring children living with their families. In the area I studied, such monitoring was not standardised, except for periodic reviews of children on the at risk register, and much was left to the discretion of individual social workers. In these circumstances the social workers managed as best they could, ever aware of the climate of fear that surrounds child protection work. There was little evidence of explicit theorising about why child abuse had taken place and this was exacerbated by constant denial on the part of the parents that their children were at risk or had been ill-treated. Some social workers used psychodynamic ideas to understand what was happening within families. Most implicitly employed a general psycho-social explanation, seeing parents as emotionally deprived and living in stressful environments. Intervention was characterised by a belief that over time a friendly supportive type of surveillance was the best or, at the least, the most practical method in all but the most serious cases of abuse. Yet again, it was rare for structural factors, such as class or gender to be referred to as contributory factors.

The work of Rochdale NSPCC demonstrates a very different approach to child abuse work (Dale *et al.* 1986). The social work team there are true to the tenets of Kempe's ideas and explicitly espouse an individual and family pathology causal theory. Their work is different from that of mainstream local authority social services departments in that they mainly specialise in working with families after their children have been made the subject of court orders. They focus on parents and, although they term their work 'therapeutic' and there are elements of individual psychotherapy and family therapy in it, they are in fact assessing the fitness of families to resume care of their children. A basic assumption of their approach is that serious abuse or neglect has occurred and that most of the evidence points to the families being responsible. They expect denial, but argue that unless parents can accept the seriousness of the abuse and their own responsibility for it, then it is unsafe for them to resume care of their children. They expect to work intensively with parents over a period of approximately three months and at the end of that time to be in a position to decide on either rehabilitation or permanent separation of children and parents. They report successful rehabilitation in half the families with whom they work, with no recurrence of abuse two years later on.

This psychological approach is complemented by the use of systems thinking with regard to the roles of the large number of different professionals involved in child abuse cases. They see the inevitable disagreement among such personnel as dangerous for children, allowing parents to escape close scrutiny by 'playing off' different professionals against each other. They advocate the use of techniques developed in the field of family therapy at what they term 'network' meetings of all involved professionals to iron out these problems and to ensure a coherent and co-ordinated approach.

The Rochdale team method is one of the few examples of a theory-led approach to child abuse work. How widespread its application is at present is not clear. What can be said is that its basic assumptions and strategies are in line with mainstream thinking about the causes and the preferred responses to child abuse, if we take the findings of recent inquiries as a yardstick. Certainly the Rochdale approach takes no account of structural factors. It could be argued that, as it is dealing with the more serious cases of abuse, an individual pathology approach is more appropriate. However, there is a tendency for those who espouse this theory to use it as an explanation for all types of child abuse with little regard for other qualifying factors (Corby 1986).

There are other accounts of individual/family based interventions into cases of physical abuse and neglect (e.g. Lynch and Roberts 1982; Reavley and Gilbert 1978; McCauley 1977). All of these focus on psychological factors and on ways of bringing about change. The growing trend in family centre‾ suggests a mixed approach. Some centres, particularly those run by voluntary agencies, adopt a more community-oriented philosophy and aim to relieve social stress for all families in a locality, including those referred to them as being at risk. Others, particularly those administered by the local authorities or the NSPCC, focus on the parenting skills and child care methods of specifically targeted families (see Braye et al. 1987). Ong's research (1985) in an NSPCC centre showed staff using a gender-blind, individual pathology approach and making little headway as a result. From interviews with female parents, it was clear that they required more supportive help based on a realistic appraisal of the problems of bringing up children in a male-oriented impoverished environment.

Social work practice in the field of child sexual abuse is still very much in its infancy and there is little research material as yet to rely on. The work of the Great Ormond Street Children's Hospital team is the best documented, but is not representative of mainstream practice (Mrazek & Ben-Tovim 1981). Their dominant theory base is that of family pathology or dysfunction: i.e. that skewed family dynamics create the conditions in which child sexual abuse is likely to take place. In similar vein to the Rochdale NSPCC team, they work largely with confirmed cases, using family therapy techniques as their main tool of intervention.

With regard to the statutory agencies, the fullest account of work with sexual abuse is provided by the Cleveland inquiry report (Butler-Sloss 1988) and, as far as we know, this may represent an untypical situation. The Cleveland Report is concerned with the early stages of intervention and the detection of abuse. It paints a picture of confusion and conflict between agencies and individuals as a major reason for the crisis which arose. Social workers and paediatricians are depicted as being determinedly zealous to face up to the potential extent of sexual abuse and actively seek it out, while the police and police surgeons are seen as resistant to both this kind of analysis and this form of approach. The report does not delve any deeper into why this state of affairs came about. Campbell's analysis (1988), however, is that the crisis of Cleveland was an issue of competing ideologies and interests. Social workers and paediatricians were prepared to believe that abuse was so widespread, partly because of their professional concerns for children, partly because of a growing literature about the nature and extent of the problem in the USA, and partly because of the influence of feminist views about the causes of physical and sexual violence to women and female children and the traditional response (or non-response) to it by the authorities. Police and police surgeons, largely male-dominated professions, had not accepted the extent of the problem because they did not share the ideology or the concerns of feminism. It has to be said that there are examples of better and more co-operative practices in this field such as reported in Bexley (Metropolitan Police 1987). However, this and other such initiatives mainly reflect a determination to overcome inter-agency communication difficulties. The ideological differences are still around and go largely untackled. Thus, as with physical abuse, individual and family pathology are the main theoretical perspectives influencing practice in child sexual abuse work. However, there can be no doubt that the feminist analysis has done much to get the problem on the agenda and shape some of the principles of intervention (see Macleod and Saraga 1987). How far feminist views will influence practice post-Cleveland is hard to predict. The Butler-Sloss report was notable for its lack of reference to the contribution of feminist thought to the issue of child sexual abuse in general and to the crisis that arose in Cleveland. The official response since the report's publication has been to emphasise the need for better co-operation and training. My analysis is that the family dysfunction approach to the problem is gaining in prominence and that there is a danger that the feminist contribution may be seen to have served its usefulness.

As far as one can generalise, the following picture of social work practice in the field of child protection work emerges. Since 1975, a formal administrative procedure has developed which is intended to place tighter managerial control over an area of work which was previously left more to the discretion of front-line workers. This system, influenced by individual and family pathology causation views of child abuse, has to a large extent moulded and determined practice, pushing it, in the particular case of physical abuse, to a more legalistic, intrusive, and directive type of work with families. This has been a slow and at times bitter process which has gone against the traditional value stances held dear by the social work profession, for example, the belief in human potential for growth and betterment. The key tool in this process has been that of the public inquiry. In this climate there has been little place for social structural theories to have any influence, despite the fact that the period in which all this has happened has been one of major economic recession and restructuring and high unemployment.

Child sexual abuse provides a different kind of picture in that its emergence as a social problem has gained impetus from a radical sociological theory, that of feminism. There is need for closer research into why and how an approach that questions the *status quo* has gained such influence. On the face of it, one could cynically argue that the feminist perspective and the state's needs have temporarily been in agreement, despite the fact that their analyses of the problem are vastly different. The radical feminist perspective sees child sexual abuse as an outcome of male-dominated and male-oriented structures and as a problem to be firmly tackled in the face of expected resistance from all quarters. It does not link the issue to class and poverty. Child sexual abuse is clearly thought to be a classless phenomenon and incidence studies such as those summarised by Finkelhor (1986) support such a view. The state is concerned to tackle child sexual abuse as part of its overall need to ensure that its young are protected. However, the preservation of current family structures is also on its agenda, whereas from the feminist perspective these are a major part of the problem. Thus there is both a division over and a convergence of aims. Hence the rather confusing findings of the Cleveland Report, which, though critical of the apparent crudity of the response there, was at pains to ensure that child sexual abuse should not perish as an important social problem.

CONCLUSION

The focus of this paper has been on the relationship between sociology and social work in the field of child protection. It is clear from the foregoing that social policy in this field has a very constraining influence on the range of theories seen to be admissible and that the dominant perspective is that of individual and family pathology. The result is that social workers, while taking account of the impact of the immediate environment on the behaviours with which they are dealing, largely adopt an individualistic explanation to understand physical abuse and neglect. Reference to more critical social theories is conspicuous by its absence, though in the case of child sexual abuse there is some exception to this rule. This is not to say that all social workers operating in this field lack a critical appraisal (based on sociological theory) of the work that they are doing. For instance, in my research, it was clear that many social workers were aware of the amplificatory effects of processing children through the child protection system and of registering children as at risk (Corby 1987). There was also considerable awareness of the power imbalances operating in the inter-professional decision-making process and of the prevailing climate in child abuse work that constrained a broader analysis of cases. However, there were few examples of such critical analyses being translated into consistent action.

For some educators and trainers, this scenario poses considerable problems. The major issues are twofold: how to build critical sociological perspectives into social work training without being accused of trying to undermine the enterprise of child protection; and how to demonstrate the relevance of these perspectives to employers and practitioners who are daily faced with difficult problems and decisions. There are no easy answers. First, however, it is important to stress the linkages between theories and to emphasise that no theory is all-explanatory to the exclusion of all others. Clearly some theory bases are totally incompatible with each other, and in these cases either/or choices have to be made. For instance, sociobiological theories and the feminist perspective are in direct conflict about the extent to which motherhood is a natural, innate quality or a socially constructed role, and there is little common ground. However, a social structural perspective does not preclude using an individualistic or psychological explanation as well. If it is argued that forms of social and political organisation create the conditions under which families and individuals adapt, this is not of itself a reason for not responding to socially unacceptable behaviour at an individual level. What it does mean is that rather than simply lay the blame at the hands of the individual, consideration should be given at the same time to the conditions in which such behaviour occurs. In other words, a social structural account of behaviour, taking into account a broad range of factors such as class, poverty, race, generation, and gender, can be used to understand how child abuse happens and children can still be protected individually.

However, a major problem within social work is that of polarisation of views, which results in single explanations dominating in different camps. Hence, in the Jasmine Beckford case, it is clear that a social ameliorative response was adopted in a situation which, with hindsight, required greater attention being paid to intra-familial psychological factors. This is not to say, though, that the latter focus is appropriate in every case of child abuse, which seems to be the trend post-Beckford. In our present state of ignorance about the causes and the extent of child abuse, there is need for some modesty about the strength of different claims. Social workers in this field need to be open to a range of explanations and theories among which the contribution of the more critical theories should play an important part. Gordon, in her study of child abuse work over nearly a century, eloquently argues this same point.

> The most helpful caseworkers were those who understood family-violence problems to be simultaneously social/cultural and personal in origin, and who therefore offered help in both dimensions. Good caseworkers might help a family get relief, or medical care, or a better apartment, and build a woman's or child's self-esteem by legitimating their claims and aspirations.
>
> (Gordon 1989: 298)

The difficulty lies in finding the right blend, but this is impossible if critical social theory is not legitimated.

A final pragmatic question is whether such an approach is workable in practice. As has been seen, one of the current concerns of those with influence in policy making in this field is to simplify the issues. At first sight, the more critical sociological contributions do not seem to meet this need. However, certainly in the longer term, pointing to the complexities of child abuse is not necessarily dysfunctional. Regardless of the extent to which child protection work is technicalised by the development of procedures, registers, reviews, and checklists, the validity of which I do not dismiss out of hand, the moral and political problems associated with this area of work will remain. Good practitioners, who can act with some degree of autonomy are an important requirement in this area of work. Such practitioners need a comprehensive knowledge base which includes knowledge of the law, knowledge of a wide range of agency requirements, knowledge of and ability to use intervention skills, *and* understanding of a wide range of theoretical perspectives including critical sociological and political views about the problem. The latter are often seen as obstructive. There is little doubt that they complicate the issues. However, most social workers are aware of the complexity of their role in the field of child protection. Placing this more formally on the agenda in training and in practice should be no bad thing.

© 1991 Brian Corby

NOTES

1 Yelloly (1980) provides a balanced account of the history of the relationship between British social work and psychoanalysis.

2 It should be noted that the systems approach can be applied with radical values to achieve radical objectives (see Bywaters 1982). Nevertheless, the predominant use of systems theory in social work training and practice has been to sensitise students and workers to the influence of immediate environments on individual and family behaviour.

3 See Parton (1985: 63-6).

4 See Howe (1986). He points to the irony of the fact that, while work with children and families is largely allocated to the best qualified social workers, practitioners in other fields, such as work with old people and the disabled, have, for the most part, far more discretion about the way in which they operate.

5 See Barash (1979: 91-131) for a sociobiological perspective on abuse of young animals and children.

6 See Pelton (1978) for an overview and interesting analysis.

7 In 1988 the DHSS collated child protection register statistics for the first time. The number of children on the register was 39,300.

8 See the Cleveland Report (Butler-Sloss 1988) for evidence of this. There is scant reference to the contribution of the feminist perspective to either the discovery of the problem of child sexual abuse in general or to the particular problems that took place in Cleveland.

9 Scarre (1980) provides an interesting counter-argument to the more extreme liberationist views.

10 See Parton (1985), Dingwall *et al.* (1983), Dale *et al.* (1986), and Corby (1986). There are, on the other hand, several accounts of how to practise in this field, the most prominent recent ones being Moore (1985), Jones *et al.* (1987), and Cooper and Ball (1987).

11 Indeed the Report rather misguidedly quoted Dingwall *et al.*'s 'rule of optimism' to criticise social work practice in general. It should be pointed out that, although Dingwall *et al.* concluded their study by

arguing that more needed to be done to protect children, they made it quite clear that the 'rule of optimism' is not a whim on the part of individual social workers or of the profession as a whole, but in line with the requirements of the liberal democratic state placed on those mandated to deal with child abuse.

Chapter Five

SOCIAL WORK, COMMUNITY CARE, AND INFORMAL NETWORKS[1]

GRAHAM ALLAN

In recent years there has been a very strong emphasis on the importance of community care within welfare policies. Moreover, the thrust of state policy has been for care by the community – a form of community care in which the informal provision of unpaid support is taken as paramount. When he was Secretary of State for Social Services, Patrick Jenkin expressed this very clearly in an often quoted statement:

> My colleagues and I have been seeking to argue the case that care in the community must mean care by the community . . . we have stressed the key role of the family, of friends and of neighbours. We have sought to persuade social service departments to try to build partnerships with voluntary agencies and with informal caring networks.

(Sinclair and Thomas 1983)

Though published a year earlier, the main body of the Barclay Report (1982), which examined 'the role and tasks of social workers', reflected this policy drive in arguing that social workers should pay greater heed to developing the capacity of informal carers to provide systematic support. Later the Audit Commission (1985) and the Griffiths Report (1988) also emphasised the need for social services departments to mobilise families, friends, and neighbours to provide support for those in need. This chapter is concerned with the feasibility of such directives.

Because the Barclay Report was designed to be, and indeed has to some extent been taken as, a semi-official blueprint for the development of social work into the 1990s, the ideas the Majority Report contains will be drawn on here in developing the analysis which follows.[2] The aim, however, is not to provide a critique of this Report as a specific document, but rather to use it to highlight the problems that the general initiative for care by the community generates for social workers and other welfare professionals. Precisely because the Report is a semi-official document which reflects and incorporates many currently dominant ideas about the possibility of greater community involvement in caring, it provides an apt vehicle for critical assessment.

THE BARCLAY REPORT

Essentially the Majority Report favoured developing the enabling role of social services departments through encouraging a form of 'community social work' that could effectively utilise the informal caring capacity of local areas. The general arguments it uses to support this stance are now familiar ones. First, it is widely acknowledged that only a small portion of the caring that is done in our society is organised and provided by the state. The greater part is done outside the state's aegis, by what the Report terms 'the informal networks of carers' that exist in every community.

Second, it is impossible – and, furthermore, generally recognised as undesirable – for the state to take over the responsibility for all this informal care, partly because it lacks the resources necessary to do so, but also because of the emotional and affective elements which informal carers bring to the provision of practical support. As a result, the Majority Report of the Barclay Committee concluded that social work should concentrate its resources on developing a 'partnership' with informal carers – be they neighbours, friends, family, volunteers, or what have you – so as to provide a more uniform and systematic service to those in need. The best strategy, in other words, for social work to adopt in future is one that seeks to strengthen the informal networks of carers by developing and harnessing their capacity to care.

At a general level, it is difficult to evaluate the Report's strategy very fully as it actually contains rather little about the way in which community social work should operate, instead claiming rather disingenuously that specific details of policy are best worked out at a local level as circumstances dictate. Even in the section entitled 'What is community social work?', the authors merely suggest that social workers need to broaden their traditional focus on family organisation and consider the client's wider social network – actual and potential. Yet, vague though their advice is, the general position the authors advocate is clear enough. They want to create a modified if not entirely new breed of social workers who will act as 'upholders of networks' and whose main task will be to 'enable, empower, support and encourage, but not usually to take over, from social networks' (Barclay Report 1982: 13.43). In his Minority Report, Pinker (1982) highlights most lucidly many of the professional, organisational, and ethical dilemmas which such a shift creates for social work practice, but this chapter is not concerned with evaluating the overall position that the Majority Report embodies in the way Pinker does. Instead it focuses on the potential there is for developing networks of informal support for those in need, irrespective of the detailed way in which social work is organised. It is the gist of the Barclay Report that matters here rather than its specific implications for the organisation of social work agencies.

SOCIAL NETWORKS AND CARING COMMUNITIES

By definition, formulations of community care are premised on some, albeit often tacit, notion of 'community'. However, as is well-known, the concept of 'community' is one of the most contested in the sociological literature. Among its referents are elements of locality, attachment, social involvement, cohesion, and shared interests, but there is little agreement as to the significance of any of these elements as a criterion of 'community' compared with the others. This ambiguity, together with the degree of normative prescription often evident in the concept, has led to many writers rejecting it as a useful tool for social analysis (Bell and Newby 1971; Bulmer 1987). Instead, recent fashion has been to conceive of the relationships between individuals as the links in a social network. This network analogy overcomes the problems of geographical boundary and evaluative injunction inherent in 'community' and, as importantly, provides a far more promising framework for analysing the consequences for social behaviour of particular constellations of social involvement and attachment, as Bott's (1957) early use of the idea indicated.

At one level, the advantages of the concept of 'social networks' over that of 'community' have been recognised in much of the writing on community care, although only rarely is the idea of 'community' rejected entirely. However, the analytical possibilities of the social network concept are not usually developed with any degree of sophistication in the community care literature (Bulmer 1986). The Barclay Report provides a good illustration of this both in its

108

definition of social networks and in the use made of the concept. Thus, communities are taken to be 'local networks of formal and informal relationships, together with their capacity to mobilise individual and collective responses to adversity' (1982: 13.3). Hence, both in emphasising geographical boundaries and in incorporating a prescriptive potentiality into an otherwise descriptive concept, the Report immediately re-introduces the very analytical dilemmas the notion of 'social network' was meant to overcome. Furthermore, as with other writing in this field, when the Report refers to 'networks' it often does not mean networks in the proper sense, but the collection of first order contacts an individual has irrespective of the further links that exist between these people. So, while the language of social network is used, little concern is given to the actual patterning of relationships – the network structures – which facilitate or hinder informal care provision.

The result of using the network notion in this imprecise, vague fashion is to diminish whatever potential the idea has for overcoming the difficulties inherent in the term 'community'. Indeed it renders it suspect to exactly the same problems and, in particular, rather than revealing the real potential or otherwise of informal relationships in social life, encourages a misleadingly romantic view. While seeming to fit everyday experience, the image produced is sufficiently distorted to mystify and conceal the very reality it is seeking to convey.

Consider for example the following passages from the Barclay Report. In paragraph 13.8, the Report recognises that:

The bulk of social care . . . is provided, not by the statutory or voluntary services agencies, but by ordinary people . . . who may be linked into informal networks in their communities. . . . [A] substantial proportion of those receiving help . . . are largely or entirely dependent upon one caring person – often an unmarried relative and usually a woman.

Five paragraphs later (13.13), they are writing:

We think it essential for the personal social services providing social care on a formal basis to work in close understanding with informal caring networks and not in isolation from them. Social workers . . . need to find ways of developing partnerships between informal carers (including self-help groups), statutory services and voluntary agencies. . . . Caring networks in a community need to have ready access to statutory and voluntary services.

Gradually what starts as a possibility – individual carers who *may* be part of a local caring network – begins to dominate and becomes a main focus for social work effort.

It might be objected that the term 'caring networks' is used in this way as a short-hand. This though is surely the point. Despite the occasional disclaimer, as a short-hand rather than an analytical concept its effect is to conjure up an image of local concern and co-operation in caring for those in need. Just like the notion of community, the continued reference to an unspecified network of carers pervasively envelops the argument in the warm and rosy hue of communal integration.

TRADITIONAL COMMUNITY SOLIDARITY

As with other approaches to community care, the Barclay Report's optimism – implicit and explicit – about the potentiality of local networks to provide resources for informal care seems to be based in some measure on a particular, rather romantic, reading of the traditional urban community studies of the 1950s and early 1960s (Abrams 1980; Clark 1982). In these studies of established working-class areas, individuals appeared to be surrounded by familiars, people who all knew one another, and had done so for years – people whom you went to school with, worked with, or who had once shared a tenement with your mother. In such areas local networks were, in Bott's (1957) terminology, 'close-knit' so that in adversity there were people who could provide support and act as informal carers. In part, recent calls for community care seem to argue that versions of this type of network should be re-created, though, as in the Barclay Report, it may also be recognised that under contemporary urban conditions they need orchestrating by social workers and other professionals.

Such a view seems mistaken on two principal grounds. First, as Philip Abrams (1980) has cogently argued, the social conditions that led to the development of extensive local networks have disappeared, and their passing should not be lamented. In the main the areas were in a marked state of social and economic decline with little mobility into the localities and a good deal of outward migration to new housing estates especially by younger families. Essentially what held these communities together, despite the romantic gloss added, was poverty – insecure and generally low wages, poor housing, shared amenities, and the like. Interdependence was generated by the lack of resources.

The need to co-operate over the use of cooking and washing facilities or over the cleaning of communal halls ensures at least a knowledge – and often an intimate knowledge – of those around you. In settled areas with little inward migration, such knowledge spreads quickly through networks of gossip. As Abrams (1977: 129–35, 1980: 14–15) develops, without access to alternative housing or even to transport, the constraints of locality foster a mutual dependence, one generally based around a necessary yet none the less calculative reciprocity.

But thirty and more years on, such conditions no longer flourish. Poverty certainly still exists, but its form is different. The slum areas studied, and others like them, have been cleared and their populations rehoused. New slums may have emerged, but, even in these, facilities and amenities are not shared in the way they were. In general, people are not so trapped by their locality; nor are they as dependent on their neighbours. Aside from anything else, with the rise in married women's employment, for much of the day there are simply fewer people to be found in residential localities than was the case in the past.

Of course there are exceptions. In their Minority Report (Brown *et al.* 1982), Hadley and his co-authors rightly argue that many social services' clients are especially constrained by geography. Equally, many mothers of young children and many elderly people are effectively tied to their homes and localities, but the conditions they now operate under are distinct from those prevalent two or three generations ago. Certainly, as Holme's (1985) research makes clear, few would choose to swap their present homes for the communal benefits of inadequate housing in Bethnal Green. The point is that with changing material circumstances – increased living standards; improved housing; greater geographical mobility; higher rates of employment for married women; etc. – the basis of the solidarities described in the traditional studies have withered, and cannot in consequence be easily resurrected – even with the aid of fully trained social or other welfare workers.

Second, this view of traditional urban working-class localities is wrong in that it misrepresents the real nature of many of the personal relationships found in them. In particular there is the underlying assumption that because people were known and known about, one was consequently involved with them on an extensive and intimate basis. Yet in the monographs themselves, there is little evidence that this was actually so (Allan 1979). On close reading it is clear that people were differentiated from one another on the basis of whether they were kin. Whereas there was intimacy between family members – interpreted quite broadly – there appears to have been far less between non-kin. Even though the latter may happen to know a good deal about you through contact over time and local gossip, they tended to be treated as familiars – people to chat to and be friendly with – rather than as intimates – people with whom to share feelings, concerns, and problems.

In particular, the studies indicate that non-kin only rarely went into each other's homes. Instead, these relationships tended to be 'public' in that they mainly occurred in non-domestic, open settings – the doorstep, the street, the pub, at work, at the shops, and so on. The home was reserved for family. It was defined as a private arena, providing a shield, albeit often an imperfect one, from the prying eyes of the local gossip networks. At least since the late nineteenth century, restricting access to the home has been a key means by which the working class have attempted to limit local knowledge of personal and family matters and safeguard their respectable status (Daunton 1983; Crow and Allan 1990).

Thus the 'rules' governing non-kin relationships in these traditional working-class localities differed from those governing family and kin ones. The two were neither equivalent nor interchangeable, as the idea of close-knit, but undifferentiated, networks implies. Whereas family formed something of a moral community and could be trusted, non-kin had other loyalties, and consequently relationships with them needed to be controlled more carefully. According to the research literature, the two main strategies used for doing this were, first, developing relationships within well-defined and bounded contexts which did not include the home; and second, maintaining distance by keeping friendly without becoming too close, as is the case with most neighbour relations. Consequently, there seems relatively little evidence to support the idea that non-kin played a major part in informal caring, except in crises. Given the way relationships were organised, long-term, systematic caring was predominantly seen as being a family obligation.

THE CONTENT OF RELATIONSHIPS

If nothing else, this highlights the inappropriateness of assuming that social networks are undifferentiated wholes and that the individual relationships of which they are comprised are all equally able to be mobilised for support in times of need. This tendency to treat all links in a network as equivalent is not uncommon, and quite understandable in that the strands of a seemingly analogous physical net are all the same. But in any social analysis this position is clearly problematic. Indeed a case can be made that the failure of the network perspective to generate adequate explanations of social phenomena is in part a result of the tendency of most studies to ignore 'content' and assume, in analysing network structure, that there is equivalence between the different links mapped.

Equally, in creating appropriate strategies for fostering informal caring, it seems essential to consider the organisation and content of different categories of relationship for only then can their potential for providing particular forms of informal support be gauged. In practice, individual social workers who are attempting to develop supportive informal networks for particular clients no doubt make such judgements, though of course in some cases their efforts may none the less be based on inappropriate conceptions about relational obligations. However, at a policy level, there is generally little recognition of the different capacity different relationships have for providing systematic care and support. Usually, as in Patrick Jenkin's quoted comment at the beginning of this chapter and in the Barclay Report, the implication is that any relationship an individual maintains has potential for becoming incorporated into a network of informal caring. But social engineering is not this simple. As will become apparent in what follows, studies that have examined the normative patterning and exchange content of different informal relationships, and, in particular, friend, neighbour, and kin ties, indicate that they are not all as suitable for care provision as is often imagined.

NEIGHBOURS

Incorporating neighbours into informal networks of carers seems an obvious strategy as they are so readily on hand to provide support. Yet the research literature on neighbouring suggests that this is rarely the case in practice, at least if those kin who happen also to live nearby are excluded (Bulmer 1986). The dominant form of neighbouring relationship in contemporary society is not one which includes an element of caring. Indeed, it is better characterised by friendly distance. That is, most people aim, without always succeeding, to maintain friendly and cordial relations with those they live near to but do not seek to be highly involved with them. Simply because of proximity, the potential for neighbours to irritate and come into conflict with each other is quite high. Equally, most people value their privacy and do not want their neighbours interfering in their way of life or forever being on top of them. What is called for is a reciprocal respect for each other's personal space and the exercise of control over behaviour likely to cause disturbance (Abrams 1977, 1980; Bulmer 1986; Cecil *et al.* 1987).

Within this pattern, the contingencies of everyday living often result in more active co-operation between particular neighbours with each helping the other out in small ways – taking in parcels, letting in repair men, keeping an eye on the house, or watering the flowers while the other is on holiday, and so on. As these services are relatively minor, they are easily reciprocated and do not normally escalate to involve either side in extensive inconvenience. Nor do they necessarily lead to a high degree of social involvement, though this is likely to depend on the extent to which the home is normally used for socialising and the degree to which individuals are tied to the home. However, apart from the minority who become friends, the essence of good neighbouring lies in maintaining the tension between co-operation and privacy, helpfulness and non-interference, between friendliness and distance.

So in these respects the predominant organisation of neighbouring does not seem particularly suited to providing the sort of support that models of 'informal caring networks' imply. Consistent caring is not an extension of neighbour relations but a break from their routine patterning. It would create a greater dependence, a reduction of privacy, and of course the public recognition of one's private troubles. While many people profess in the abstract to be willing to provide support for neighbours, in practice this is only rarely forthcoming (Glastonbury 1979; Wilkin 1979). Moreover, issues of status and respectability generally pattern neighbourhood interaction. As Pinker (1982) suggests, a proportion of social services' clients will be thought disreputable by their neighbours and stigmatised rather than considered worthy of help. So too, for similar reasons to do with respectability, not everyone would be willing to receive support from their neighbours unless there was a more secure basis of solidarity than neighbouring alone.

The one exception probably concerns the provision of very practical services for elderly neighbours. Because of the legitimacy accorded their incapacity, doing such things as cutting their lawn, replacing light bulbs, helping with their shopping is feasible without the need for reciprocity (Rossiter and Wicks 1982). Even here though, more personal forms of caring become problematic because they involve a degree of intrusion into personal life that lies well outside the normal 'rules' of neighbouring. To the extent that such aid is given, it is unlikely to be between people who are *just* neighbours, as the neighbour bond is usually defined in far too limited a fashion. It is also worth noting here that the more informal support the elderly person already receives from family or others, the less likely neighbours are to become involved in providing care, in part through not wanting to interfere. As a consequence, informal caring *networks* which involve neighbours along with other carers rarely occur in as straightforward a manner as policy initiatives would have it.

FRIENDS

On the surface it might also seem that friends are well suited for providing support and being part of effective caring networks. However here again there is very little evidence in the research literature that friends actually do figure significantly in care provision of the sort that concerns policy makers. On reflection, the reasons for this are not hard to fathom and stem from the way friendship is routinely organised. Apart from the fact that friendships are not all equally close, most are as much focused on sociability and enjoyment as they are on giving or receiving practical or even emotional support. None the less, in general friends do care about one another and are concerned for each other's welfare. However, as Parker (1981) has argued, there is an important distinction between caring *about* someone and caring *for* them. Friendship typically involves the former but not normally the latter: caring for someone, looking after them, and providing for their needs, especially on a systematic or long-term basis, is not usually an element inherent in the routine patterning of friendship. Despite quasi-philosophical rhetoric to the contrary, providing this type of support is as much a contradiction as an extension of the principles under-lying friendship.[3]

To see this, it is worth examining the social characteristics of friend-ship more fully. A preliminary point to make is that many of those in need of care and support are actually likely to have relatively few friends to draw on. Principally this is because they tend to be excluded from the organisations and contexts which act for most of us as sources of friendship, be these employment, leisure and voluntary associations, the neighbourhood, or whatever. For example, handicap and infirmity often structure people's day-to-day lives in ways which restrict the opportunities available for developing and servicing friendship ties. Often the same applies to those who act as primary carers. They too are likely to find that the fragmentary and privatised character of caring restricts their opportunities for social involvement with the result that their friendship circles often tend to become depleted.

Even assuming the existence of some friendships, it remains questionable how suitable these are for significant levels of care provision. A central issue here is the degree of equality that lies at the heart of most friendships. Aside from the tendency for friends to occupy broadly similar positions in the social structure, friendships are generally premised upon a broad equivalence of exchange. Because friends are defined as socially equal, the organisation of the tie emphasises reciprocity and a balance of exchange in the services and favours which over time each side provides and receives. This reciprocity usually takes quite a casual form, so that a rough balance of exchange is maintained without its basis being made fully explicit or negotiated in great detail. It is manifest though in some of the rituals which attend friendship – buying rounds of drinks in turn, alternating visits to each other's home, and so on.

From the standpoint of incorporating friends into informal care provision, the crucial issue is that, by its nature, friendship is undermined if for any reason the equality and equivalence of exchange on which the relationship is premised breaks down. Yet this is precisely what the realisation of the community care model would entail. It calls for one side in a friendship to receive unilateral support and care from the other, thereby over the long run placing the individual in a disproportionately dependent position. Under such circumstances, sustaining the balance that defines the relationship becomes extremely difficult and the friendship itself is likely to become strained.

As a result, the majority of friendships can be expected to fade slowly, notwithstanding the concern and good will expressed and genuinely felt within them. In some part this will be because the friend who is unable to reciprocate may discourage interaction so as not to make his or her dependence on the other evident. But equally over time, in the majority of friendships the advantaged friend is likely to find the relationship hard to maintain because of the increased effort needed to show continually that the friend is not making undue demands – in the face of contrary evidence – or because the demands are indeed too high. In such ways all but the strongest friendships are likely to dissipate and become that much less active, that much less close.

It is not being argued here that friends never provide help or care for one another. Clearly they do and clearly this expectation is built into our everyday notions of what friendship means (Willmott 1987). This is particularly apparent at times of crisis when friends can generally be relied on to provide a good deal of help. Rather the argument is that this is difficult to sustain in the long run because the provision of care undermines the equality on which friendships are based. In other words, the social organisation of most friendships is such as to discourage systematic caring, in the tending sense (Parker 1981), because such care would disrupt the balance of exchange inherent in the relationship. However willing friends are initially to help each other, it is likely that most friendships will die away if the need for support continues indefinitely.

KIN

Even if friend and neighbour relationships are not necessarily well patterned for providing long-term and consistent support, kin relationships at least seem better suited. They also have the advantage that the genealogical links usually generate a network of interlocking social relationships. Yet, of course, kin relationships do not comprise a single, uniform category. The moral obligation and responsibility that kin feel for one another clearly varies depending, in part, on the closeness of the genealogical connection that exists between them. In this respect Parsons (1943) was essentially correct in arguing that the distinguishing feature of contemporary western kinship systems is the structural isolation of what he terms the conjugal family. Despite frequent misunderstanding, Parsons is simply pointing out that the characteristics of industrial societies – individual wage labour, comparatively high levels of social and geographical mobility, and the like – discourage the creation of extensive obligations to any wider kin (Harris 1969; Allan 1985).

If the somewhat ambiguous term 'conjugal family' is interpreted broadly so as to include for present purposes all primary kin, i.e.

117

parents, siblings, and children, there can be little disagreement with this claim. While secondary kin, at least up to first cousins but often more removed, usually know about one another and meet on occasion, there is little evidence from either kinship studies or research on informal caring to indicate that this involves any extensive obligation to one another, or consequently any great potential for systematic caring. The relationships are normally too shallow, especially in adult life, and too dependent on the servicing of intermediary kin to provide the basis for long-term care (Allan 1979; Finch 1989). Of course there are exceptions. Individually a particular grandchild, living locally, may be a very significant social contact for an ageing grandparent. Equally a nephew or niece may take responsibility for a childless aunt or uncle. More significantly, different patterns exist among some of the ethnic minorities who have migrated to Britain since the 1950s. Here ties to some secondary kin may be much stronger and result in a greater commitment to providing them with care and support (Anwar 1985; Finch 1989). For most of the population, though, secondary kin ties are predominantly 'social' and are maintained largely through formal and informal family ceremonies.

The 'rules' of primary kinship are structured quite differently. They routinely involve a relatively active, long-term commitment to each other's welfare, a feature long recognised and built on by the state in its social policies. Such a commitment is taken to be the natural outcome of the genealogical bond that by definition exists between primary kin. Two aspects are important within this. First, these relationships typically endure irrespective of the changes there might be in either side's circumstances or of the actual level of social contact at any time. Second, being secure in the long term, there is far less pressure for any short-term reciprocity in these ties than is the case with most non-kin relationships.

The extent to which the moral obligations that primary kin have for each other's welfare are translated into active caring will clearly depend on the specific circumstances of both parties and the competing domestic and other responsibilities of the potential carers. The greatest commitment is normally between parents and children, and undoubtedly it is here that the major components of familial caring are enacted, though in different directions at different stages in the family course. Overall, the nature of primary kin ties is well characterised by Adams's (1967) concept of 'positive concern'. The very vagueness of this term is significant because, at least in adult life, the obligations these kin have to one another are both broad and imprecise. There are no formal principles that govern the type of support or care that is considered appropriate. As Litwak's arguments imply, it is this which allows the flexibility which is necessary if the individual contingencies that result in people needing informal caring are to be catered for (Litwak 1965; Harris 1969; Allan 1985).

While these principles apply to primary kin generally, in practice the active caring they entail affects females far more than males, as a result of the standard division of responsibilities within domestic life. With the exception of care provided for spouses (Briggs and Oliver 1985; Ungerson 1987; Arber and Gilbert 1989), the predominant burden falls on mothers, sisters, and daughters, supplemented by their equivalent female in-laws. In this sense to talk about family care is as much a myth as talking about community care. The caring is not done by communities or families as such but by females whose social and economic opportunities may be affected quite significantly as a consequence. While this point is now well established in the research literature (Land 1978; Finch and Groves 1980, 1983; Nissel and Bonnerjea 1982; Glendinning 1983; Cecil *et al.* 1987), it still warrants emphasising as it so easily gets lost in general discussions of 'community' care.

Given recent demographic and social trends, these issues will become more rather than less salient. In essence, not only will relatively fewer daughters be looking after increasing numbers of elderly parents over the next twenty-five years or so, but, given the relevant child-bearing patterns, many of these daughters will themselves be of late middle age and established in employment. Increasingly too, some of those looking after very elderly parents will themselves be of an age where they might need some form of support. Sufficient research has been done on the consequences of these patterns of caring for the point not to need developing further here (Rossiter and Wicks 1982; Walker 1982; Rimmer and Wicks 1983; Green 1988).

One final issue to emphasise is that caring is not usually spread equally throughout even the primary kin network, but normally falls most heavily on particular *individuals*. It is not just that tending is gendered, but also that in many cases a primary carer emerges who generally appears to receive little support from other kin. Thus, even kinship, with its genealogical web, does not usually generate a *network* of carers. Instead responsibility for tending is frequently left to individual females who bear most of the burden alone (Allan 1988).

CONCLUSION

Clearly the discussion here has been couched in very general terms. This applies not just to the broadness of the categories of relationship considered but also to the whole concept of 'caring' (Finch and Groves 1983). Individuals' needs differ, as do the specific relationships that they construct with others. None the less considering the basis of relationships in these general terms does allow us to gauge the feasibility of attempting to construct a public policy around them. The conclusion that is inevitably reached is that the great majority of these relationships do not normally entail a sustained caring element, and that generating one within them is unlikely to work in the long run because it would require such a radical alteration to their exchange basis. The only routine relationships in which the majority of people are, as it were, 'naturally' involved that do include a practical caring element are primary kin ones, as is so clearly indicated by the fact that the enormous bulk of informal caring is done by such kin, principally female ones.

The 'failure' of other relationships to provide a basis for caring does not mean that they are in some sense pathological or lacking. The organisation of informal relationships which has developed historically to meet the requirements of a society whose major institutions emphasise social independence and individuality cannot be modified on demand to produce a range of ties that can provide extensive care. The error lies in the assumption that all forms of relationship contained within informal networks can readily be converted into caring ones. This is simply not so. Even those which entail an element of 'caring *about*' are not easily transformed into 'caring *for*' ones. In normal, routine life, these relationships are not created for this sort of work. Any failure on their part to act as 'caring for' relationships is not an indication of their deficiency; rather it is a consequence of their following social 'rules' in which 'caring for' plays little or no part.

If these arguments are valid, social workers would have a most difficult task in meeting the sorts of recommendation for interweaving formal and informal care made in the Barclay Report and other recent policy documents with a similar emphasis. Leaving aside the many other problems involved in interweaving formal and informal services (Abrams 1980; Pinker 1982; Bulmer 1986, 1987; Twigg 1989), any attempt to influence networks of neighbours, friends, and kin so as to encourage greater support and caring for members in need would not be so much an extension of 'natural' networks as a wholly artificial manipulation of them. The extra requirement of 'caring for', in the absence of reciprocity, would be experienced as contradictory to their nature.

Such arguments, though, do not mean that social workers should pay no heed to the possibility of improving the effectiveness of patterns of informal caring – far from it. What they do mean is that workers need to be clearer than the Barclay Report was about the ways in which this can be achieved. For example, rather than trying to use existing networks to increase the number of informal carers involved in supporting someone, a more realistic strategy would be to use the agency's resources to assist those who normally do the routine caring. In other words, if it is recognised that the great bulk of caring is done by single individuals, more often than not by female primary kin, then ways need to be found to relieve the burden they bear, not by sharing it among friends and neighbours but by making more readily available services – such as day centres, short-stay homes, sitting services, financial assistance – that provide some relief from the demands of caring.

Similarly, where social workers seek to generate new relationships that would enable individuals and families to cope better with their troubles, then the (potential) exchange basis of these relationships needs considering. It would be extremely difficult, for instance, for social workers to foster friendships between people in the absence of any foundation in the relationships for equivalence and reciprocity, factors which tend to be undermined when there is unilateral need for care. On the other hand, they are likely to be more successful in generating informal solidarity between people who are in similar circumstances and share similar problems. Thus, for example, despite the obvious logistical difficulties facing individual carers, there is likely to be more mileage in facilitating 'self-help' groups and associations for those providing informal care than in trying to foster less focused friendship networks. Not only will those involved have a greater awareness of the difficulties they face and the resources they need but, as importantly, there could be a flow of support and help that would not leave one party continually indebted to the other.

To conclude, this paper rests on the idea that social policies aiming to encourage and facilitate particular practices need to consider quite carefully the existing structure of relevant social activity if they are to prove successful. Thus in the present context, social workers, and other practitioners, concerned with developing more effective forms of community care should be aware of the implicit 'rules' that different types of informal relationships commonly follow. Here, as in other areas, the policies they promote are likely to be successful only if their basis is compatible with the social world they are attempting to influence and modify. Within this, sociological research can clearly be of much assistance to practitioners and policy makers who would otherwise have to rely on common sense or intuitive knowledge – neither of which is likely to prove satisfactory. In contrast, sociological research can play a key role in generating effective social intervention by providing a more systematic analysis of the sets of relationships and the social structures to which policy initiatives need to be accommodated. Without such a grounding, efforts at developing appropriate policies, however well-meaning, will, like the recommendations of the Barclay Report, generally be flawed.

© 1991 Graham Allan

NOTES

1 This chapter is a revised version of a paper entitled 'Informal networks of care: issues raised by Barclay' which first appeared in *British Journal of Social Work* (1983) 13: 417–33.
2 The full Barclay Report contains a Majority Report and two Minority Reports. In what follows references to the Barclay Report refer to the Majority Report unless stated otherwise.
3 Some of the arguments used in this section are developed more fully in Allan (1986) and Allan (1989).

Chapter Six

STUDYING TALK IN PROBATION INTERVIEWS

STEPHEN STANLEY

In this continuing debate about social work's effectiveness there is a tendency to ignore the question of how work is routinely accomplished at present. There is all too often the assumption that work is somehow inchoate and unspecifiable yet this clearly neglects the way that practitioners presently construct a meaningful work setting that, for all intents and purposes, makes practice an orderly and creditable endeavour. . . the daily setting will be revealed as the authentic and purposeful construction of members who competently employ their own assumptions and 'theories' of what constitutes good work.

(Pithouse 1987: 46)

In this chapter I propose to show the value of one particular sociological approach to the study of social work; the approach is a branch of ethnomethodology called conversation analysis. First, I shall argue both positive and negative reasons for using conversation analysis and, second, I shall use data drawn by me from probation officers' interviews with clients to show aspects of their construction and to illustrate issues that arise out of the methodological approach.

WHY CONVERSATION ANALYSIS?

The central activity of social work is talk, whether this is described as therapeutic intervention, negotiation, elicitation, advice, or just passing the time. What social workers spend most of their time doing is talking to clients and other people involved with their clients.

Yet if you look into the literature of social work research you will find that it relies very largely on accounts of social work; accounts that are derived from records, interviews with clients, and interviews with practitioners. Studies of effectiveness rely additionally on various control devices such as experimental design and triangulation and on the generation of presumably relevant and objective measures of outcome. A consequence of this is that the object of study, social work intervention, seems to disappear, being either fragmented or rarefied into general statements about the nature of social control. The question that has to be faced, therefore, is whether these accounts constitute an adequate description of social work? Are they a resource from which it is possible to study social work as a topic? More widely, is it possible to imagine a different resource which would enable such study to take place?

One answer is perhaps now a commonplace: there is no reason to suppose that accounts of an event provide a definitive 'history' of it (Gilbert and Mulkay 1984: 33–4). This is as true of social work as of other human activities. On the other hand, these accounts often do provide a coherent story which appears credible by comparison with stories from other sources; they are typically used as a basis for evaluation yet their relationship to the activities they purport to describe may be tenuous.

By contrast, conversation analysis uses the interview material itself as the topic for analysis. The central concern is thus not what is meant by the interview but what occurs in the interview and what is the order to which that interview relates.

A BRIEF DESCRIPTION OF PROBATION RESEARCH

If we look at the key characteristics of probation research we see that a major one is a concern with outcomes – does probation work? What are its results? What are the effects of preparing social inquiry reports for courts, and of making recommendations in them? Examples of this are descriptive studies of the 'results' of probation in terms of termination of orders (Radzinowicz 1958), of re-conviction rates (Folkard *et al.* 1976; Home Office 1986b), and of changes induced in individual probationers (Folkard *et al.* 1976; Goldberg and Stanley 1985). Similarly in the field of social inquiry reports Davies examined the proposition that social inquiry reports improve the effectiveness of sentencing (1974), Roberts and Roberts (1982) the effect of social inquiry report production on courts' use of custodial sentences, and Thorpe (1979) and Stanley and Murphy (1984) the association between social inquiry report recommendations and the sentences imposed by the courts.

On the other hand, a common feature of these studies has been their failure to produce evidence that probation 'works' better than realistic alternative disposals (Brody 1976), that improvements in probation practice (e.g. intensive supervision, task-centred casework) make any overall difference to outcomes as measured by reconviction (Folkard *et al*. 1976; Goldberg and Stanley 1985), or that the provision of social inquiry reports improves courts' sentencing (Roberts and Roberts 1982; Davies 1974). While the methodologies of some of these studies, such as IMPACT (Folkard *et al*. 1974, 1976), may be criticised for failing to specify clearly the difference between alternative methods of intervention and for expecting unreasonably large effects from these differences, the consistency of their results suggests that they have accurately represented the ineffectiveness of intervention in achieving the outcome measures used in these studies. This may be seen as an example of a general truth – that intervention in a complex system at the individual level is unlikely to affect the operation of that system. A corollary of this is that individualised intervention is better studied on its own terms.

I have already referred to the reliance of research on accounts, including reports, case records, and probation officers' reflexive descriptions in interviews and questionnaires. Garfinkel (1967) has commented on the problem of using case records to evaluate practice. Some studies, such as the NISW research on task-centred casework (Goldberg and Stanley 1985), Willis's small scale study of supervision practice (1986), Day's (1981) study of probation officers' and clients' perceptions of supervision, and the ILPS study of parole (Maitland 1983), have incorporated what is called 'consumer feedback' into the research design, and this seems likely to be an increasingly important component in probation research. Nevertheless these methods give us at best what Agar (1986) describes as level two discourse – reflections on the activity – and while it is at times helpful and often salutary to know what probation officers and clients believed to have happened during the supervision of a probation order or parole licence, we still lack knowledge of how those beliefs were formed – what *did* happen?

In recent years a few researchers have attempted to fill the hole at the centre of probation research. Baldock and Prior (1981) included several probation interviews in their study based on recordings of interviews of social workers talking to clients. Willis (1986) observed and recorded supervision interviews between probation officers and clients and Sheppard (1980) also observed probation interviews, while Day (1985) recorded social work interviews.

The results of these studies have however been somewhat imprecise, due in part to the analytical techniques employed. Baldock and Prior attempted a replication of Byrne and Long's study (1976) of doctors talking to patients. While they were able to point to certain important gross characteristics of social work interviews with long-term clients that distinguished them from doctor–patient consultations, their conclusions about the skills displayed by social workers and their apparent approval of their deduction that the goals of these interviews were opaque to clients were both criticised by Clifton (1981).

Willis (1986), in his work, was more concerned with a general characterisation of the probation interviews he observed and with collecting clients' responses to them – in particular with establishing how concordant clients' perceptions of interview goals were with those of the probation officers. He found a high degree of agreement between clients and probation officers over goals, but characterised the interviews themselves as lacking the obvious paraphernalia of enforcement and offence focus that might have been expected from some of the theoretical commentaries on the subject. He linked this to the collapse of the treatment ideal and suggested that probation officers' work had been pre-adapted to the general critique of treatment set out by Bottoms and McWilliams (1979).

Sheppard's observational research (1980) produced results similar to Willis's – an apparent lack of concern with offending, enforcement, or 'treatment', and a concentration on specific welfare problems.

From the corpus of research we can obtain the following statements about probation practice.

On the one hand, Willis (1986) argued that the evidence supported the proposition that treatment has been replaced by an eclectic and contingent practice, responsive to clients' material needs. Fielding (1984) also showed the eclecticism of probation officers' thinking about their practice.

On the other hand, Hardiker (1977) noted how probation officers' treatment ideologies were contingent on their perceptions of the client's need and offending behaviour, and not universally applied to all clients referred to them, an observation seemingly echoed for social workers by Day (1985).

Third, to complicate matters still further, Baldock and Prior (1981) described probation officers' interviews with clients in terms more reminiscent of 'treatment' – getting a person to talk about his motorbike because this is related to his offending – than of the welfare-dominated practice described by Willis.

While it may be sufficient to regard these findings as evidence of the variety of practice, these variant descriptions may also be seen as evidence of the consequence of using interviews studied through observations and recordings as a resource rather than a topic in their own right.

STUDYING INTERACTION IN PROBATION INTERVIEWS

Probation interviews are occasions for interaction between probation officer and client. As Kirwin (1985) pointed out, while not all the interaction that takes place need be verbal, talk is likely to be the major form of interaction, and it is the one on which this study focuses. The probation officer may talk to the client both to elicit information and to give advice, counselling, criticism, or encouragement. The client may be expected to participate in this talk, even if only as a listener. How then can probation officers' talk with clients be studied?

Studying talk requires two things, collecting data and analysing them. In theory, collecting data about talk is simple; tape and video-recorders are familiar tools in many probation areas, particularly for training purposes, and it should need little adaptation, if considerable negotiation of access, to use them for data collection, as indeed was done by Willis and Baldock and Prior. Analysis is more problematic. The work that has been reported on to date has been informed by ethnographic methods and by content analysis. The talk recorded appears to be treated as a resource for generalisations about practice rather than, as is the intention here, a topic in its own right. Because of this, the interaction between speakers and the sequential character of talk has been de-emphasised by comparison with an emphasis on the content of the utterances of probation officers and social workers. Thus Baldock and Prior (1981) focused on what social workers said, not on clients' replies, and used the contents of social workers' utterances as a basis for an argument about their skill in, for example, topic initiation that might or might not have been borne out by a sequential analysis of the relevant fragments of conversation. Willis (1986) used his recordings to generate generalisations about practice which he then investigated by interviews with the participants, thus giving their reflections on the interviews primacy over what had occurred. The characterisation that Willis gave to practice was in turn based on the presence or absence of certain types of statement (such as serving a probation order) in the interviews he recorded rather than on the interaction between probation officer and client.

Neither of these approaches appears to have given sufficient weight to the fact that talk is an activity that is done jointly by its participants, nor to the proposition that the creation or production of this talk is at least as important for study as is participants' interpretations of their actions. Furthermore, without the benefit of analytic descriptions of how talk is done in probation interviews, it is difficult to see how theoretical discussions of probation practice can be grounded in any reality beyond the discussants' own experiences.

Atkinson and Drew (1979) made the same general observation about research in other social settings: that without such material the findings of survey research and ethnographic studies may become increasingly problematic to use, outside certain boundaries. Their criticism of studies of courtroom proceedings seems applicable to much of social work research and probation research, including these otherwise valuable attempts to look behind the curtain of official records and reflexive accounts:

> the general point is first that, having outlined 'noticeables', their analyses move too quickly towards imposing an order on them with reference to theories (both lay and professional) derived from outside the settings, thereby leaving open the question of what specific problems of the setting such 'special' procedures might resolve.
>
> (Atkinson and Drew 1979: 17)

Sacks (1984) pointed out that the strength of 'order' in society is such that in well-attested areas of study quite crudely designed pieces of research (e.g. polls of voting intention) will produce 'accurate' results, but these must depend on the correct elicitation of appropriate concepts to study or measure. Conversely, it may be argued that when little is known or agreed about social concepts or processes – which is demonstrably the case with probation interviews – 'traditional' approaches to researching society may produce problematic or inaccurate results, regardless of the quality of their design, because they do not properly respond to the 'order' they are supposed to be studying. Conversation analysis, on the other hand, is reliant on the description of normatively attested and produced items of behaviour in talk. If, as Sacks suggests, behaviour is grounded in order it follows that the order itself is recoverable from an analysis of this behaviour. As conversation analysis is concerned with sequences of behaviour (i.e. talk and its reception) so it is possible to analyse not necessarily the full intent but certainly the effect of any utterance by studying where it is placed in any sequence of talk and how it is received. Since the analysis uses an objective and replayable (that is mechanical) record of the behaviour in question, it is relatively unaffected by the problems noted above. As the analysis uses some of the very skills that participants display in a conversation (i.e. hearing talk and responding to talk), it is demonstrably concordant with the order that is being studied.

The project that is described in this chapter was conceived as a descriptive study of probation officers' interviews with clients through an analysis of the talk that took place in such interviews. It was hoped that such a study would serve as a pilot of the methods of both data collection and analysis to show their applicability to the problem of describing what probation officers did with clients and to suggest how such descriptions of practice linked with other forms of discourse about the work of probation officers.

BASICS OF CONVERSATION ANALYSIS

The objective in this study is to analyse aspects of talk between probation officers and clients. As a preliminary to this, a brief résumé of the principles of conversation analysis is appropriate.

The central goal of conversation analysis is the description and explication of the ordinary competences of the participants in a piece of interaction. A basic assumption of this is that the activities that take place are accountable between the participants as the products of a commonly held and understood set of procedures. It follows therefore that the order of the analysis of the data will reflect the order of the analysis that is carried out in the conversation. A further assumption is that regular forms of conversational organisation are produced and oriented to by participants as normative grounds for inference and action. This is done in a sequential form so that the force of a particular utterance can be determined by its position in a sequence of talk. To restate this more clearly, one speaker talks, another speaker hears the talk in relation to prior activities within the conversation, or in relation to another context, and replies accordingly. If the conversation is recorded, as in this research, participants' actions are accountable to each other and can be accounted for by any other hearer or viewer. While it is true that participants may decide not to notice particular utterances (and so how an action is treated is not an absolutely reliable guide to its intent), nevertheless it should be possible to reconstruct how the different utterances in the conversation are projected and understood.

The technique of conversation analysis itself therefore is not an arcane discipline but simply the systematic application of a common accomplishment, an accomplishment characteristic of human beings in general.

A consequence of the assumption that conversational forms are regular is that breakdowns in conversation can be perceived and are routinely indicated by pauses, restatements, etc.

The regulation of conversation can be described in terms of systematics and preference systems governing both basic and complex forms. For example, Sacks, Schegloff, and Jefferson (1978) have developed a systematic governing the application of speaker turns within conversation. Button and Casey (1984) have described a common approach to topic elicitation in ordinary conversation. A central presumption of the analysis is that such systematics, although developed for ordinary conversations, can be applied to interaction in institutional settings. Atkinson and Drew (1979), for example, showed how legal procedures in courtrooms are based on the turn-taking systematic and some of its correlates, and in general, Sacks, Schegloff, and Jefferson say, in relation to the general applicability of the turn-taking systematic, 'it appears likely that conversation should be considered the basic form of speech-exchange system, with other systems. . . representing a variety of *transformations* in conversation's turn taking systems' (1978: 47, emphasis added).

THE METHOD

Initially two probation officers were recruited who agreed to video some of their interviews for the researcher. The number of probation officers was limited because the researcher wished to be able to demonstrate that both similarities and differences between interviews were not simply quirks of individual style but were responsive to specific situations. Providing equipment to record the interviews was anticipated to be a problem, and this was another reason for initially recruiting only two officers – anticipated logistical difficulties would be minimised.

The two officers initially recruited were both familiar with video equipment and had made video recordings of client interviews already. Thus they had experience of persuading clients to be videoed.

Originally both officers agreed to video a quota of interviews of varying types, including social inquiry report interviews and different kinds of supervision interviews. The researcher visited each of their offices and established fixed camera positions that would normally keep both participants in full shot. Sound levels were also checked at the same time.

A consent form had been agreed already and the general procedure was that each subject would be asked to give his/her consent to be videoed before the start of the interview. The camera was in plain view, either on its own tripod or on top of a filing cabinet or bookcase but some distance (around 12 to 15 feet) from the participants. The camera would be started by the probation officer, and the researcher would not be present at the interview.

In the event, changes were made to the method. During the period of research the two probation officers changed their role from being generic workers to being specialists in writing social inquiry reports. For this reason, and because the flow of interviews recorded was slower than had been expected, a third officer was recruited to record (audio only) some interviews in current supervision cases.

THE CHARACTERISTICS OF THE SAMPLE

Before discussing the analysis of the interviews it is necessary to look briefly at the participants. All the three probation officers who agreed to take part in this study were male, which introduces one obvious bias into the results, one that would need correcting in any replication or extension of this research.

A total of nineteen interviews were recorded for the project, but only fifteen were used – three videos were rejected because no sound had been recorded, and one audio-tape was rejected because the sound quality was too poor.

The fifteen interviews included sixteen clients (two co-defendants were interviewed in one session). Two of the interviews (one supervision, one social inquiry report) were attended by a third party – probation officer and social worker respectively. Four of the fifteen interviews were in ongoing cases and eleven (with twelve clients) in social inquiry reports. Of the eleven social inquiry reports, six were for the Crown Court (one pre-trial) and five for Magistrates Courts. The offences concerned were thefts (four cases), burglary, dishonest handling, assault, criminal damage, shoplifting, and driving; in one social inquiry report interview (for day training centre assessment) the offence was not discussed.

Of the sixteen clients, thirteen were male, three female; five were black, eight white, and the ethnic origin of three (all audio-tapes) not known. Of the twelve clients who were social inquiry report subjects ten were male, two female, and five were black, seven white.

While there were more Crown Court social inquiry reports than one would normally expect (about one social inquiry report in three is prepared for the Crown Court according to Inner London Probation Service statistics), the sample of clients, and particularly social inquiry report clients, is not obviously untypical of those referred to the probation service. For example, Stanley and Murphy found that a fifth of the subjects of social inquiry reports included in their 1980 sample were female; the main offences were thefts (48 per cent), burglary (13 per cent), violence (12 per cent), and taking and driving away (8 per cent) (1984: 76). The main difference between this (local) sample and that 1980 sample (which covered the whole of Inner London) is in the proportion of black clients – five out of twelve in this sample, only 15 per cent in 1980 (Stanley and Murphy 1984: 10).

THE RESULTS OF THE ANALYSIS: INTRODUCTION

As an example of the structures of probation practice that the conversation analytic approach can illuminate I am going to discuss the establishment of topic in probation interviews, and particularly in interviews for social inquiry reports.

In the data extracts on which this discussion is founded I use a version of the transcription system developed by Gail Jefferson. The full set of transcription conventions is given in Atkinson and Heritage (1984: ix-xvi). The key features are as follows:

Numbers in brackets (1), (.5) denote pauses timed in seconds; (.) denotes a pause of one-tenth of a second. Words in brackets (agree to be videoed) denote transcriptions that are not entirely certain; (. . . .) denotes a passage of talk that is too unclear or quiet to be transcribed.

Phrases in double brackets ((forename surname)) ((kick)) are literal descriptions of phrases of talk, or sounds on the tape that cannot, or for reasons of confidentiality should not, be transcribed phonetically.

Punctuation marks are used as follows:

a ? denotes a rising (interrogative) tone
a , denotes a pause
a : denotes an extended sound of the preceding letter or phoneme
a . denotes a sharp pause, with an emphasis on the immediately preceding letter

The = sign is used to join two passages of talk which follow without a noticeable break between them.

Square brackets [ ] are used to denote the beginning or ending of overlapping utterances.

The tilde ~ denotes the beginning and ending of a quieter passage of talk.

The logical operators > < are used to denote the beginning and end of an utterance that is faster than the surrounding talk.

Emphasis indicates a louder utterance.

An immediate observation of probation interviews is that a topic is established very early on and that in a high proportion of the social inquiry report interviews studied the first main topic to be established was the offence. Sacks is quoted in Atkinson and Heritage (1984: 165) as arguing that there are two kinds of topic movement, boundaried and stepwise; boundaried topics appear in conversation without necessarily referring to earlier topics and following an explicit closure of any previous topic; stepwise topics are characterised by a relationship with a prior aspect of conversation. Button and Casey (1984) have produced an analysis of topic initiation which applies particularly to boundaried topics. They identified a species of topic initial elicitors which are linked to the request by the elicitor for the 'news' and the offering by the topic proposer of a news item which may be suitable for adoption as a topic of conversation. They characterise topic initial elicitors as providing 'an open though bounded domain from which events may be selected and offered as possible topic initials' (Button and Casey 1984: 170). A topic initiation procedure of the type that they describe occurs once in the data that I have collected; this is in a long-term case and it is given in more detail below; it has to be observed that even this example presents deviant features in that the topic proposed takes a long time to be established.

In social inquiry report interviews three main devices are used: a reference to information already known to the probation officer; an explanation of the purpose of the social inquiry report; and a reference to prior contact. A common characteristic is the segmentation of the talk in the interview to allow the topic of the offence to be distinguished from other passages of talk.

A possible explanation of these observations is that in probation interviews in general, and social inquiry report interviews in particular, the boundaries of the topic domain are highly restricted, and are controlled by probation officers. It may indeed be the case that we are dealing, not with a narrowly boundaried but open topic domain, but with a set of one or more closed domains. This would in turn have implications not only for the forms of topic initiation and movement that are preferred but also for the interactional consequences of attempting topic initiation in a way that is not responsive to the nature of the topic domain(s) in probation interviews.

The following sections examine topic initiation in detail, focusing separately on clients' and probation officers' initiations of topic.

CLIENTS' PROPOSALS OF TOPIC

The analysis begins with the clearest example in the data of a client's proposal of topic in response to an invitation by the probation officer at the start of a probation interview being consequently accepted as a topic by the officer.

Extract 1

P: An' now all I godda do is fin:d (1) find the file?, (1) 's ~ (. . . .) ((forename surname)) ~?,
C: Uh hu
      (2)   ((Searching noises in background))
C: hhhe hhe yeahh
      (2)
P: 't it migh' be an idea 'f you just: (.) first talk about (.) wha'

134

you been doing in the last, I mean even tho' I saw you not
very long ago =
C: = I-I go' ass*ess*ed yisterday.
P: You di:d.
C: Yeah (.) 's good.
P: Wha' happen'd
C: I go' really good ((kick)) goo' mark (.) ~erm
     [hhh ~
P: [w' how do they grade it?,
C: Well: I don' know w' exac'ly my mark was bu' (I) I'w' d'
     the *guy* who team:ches on Mon'day(.) he say' it's *good* I
     def'nitely (.) y' kno' go' really done really well

This fragment comes from the beginning of an interview in a long-term case. The first utterance by the probation officer is linked to his looking for (and presumably finding – this interview was on audiotape only) the client's file. Topic initiation begins with a request for 'news' directed by the probation officer to the client. This request is separated from previous talk by a two-second pause, but is not otherwise marked off by any transition. The client responds with a piece of 'news' and this is subsequently adopted as a topic. In this outline it can be seen that the form of topic initiation and adoption used here is similar to the invitation/proposal/response sequence described by Button and Casey (1984). There are however deviant aspects to this fragment which are worth considering in more detail.

In extract 1 the initial invitation to propose a topic is in fact expressed in an unusual form. Whereas Button and Casey found that a common form of invitation/elicitation was 'Wha' you been doing in the last?', in the quoted extract this clause is preceded by a proposition that this might be a possible (but not the only possible) next action, and succeeded by an account or excuse for this proposal.

P: 't it migh' be an idea 'f you just: (.) firs' talk abou'˙(.) wha'
     you been doing in the last, I mean even tho' I saw you not
     very long ago =

The inclusion of the latter serves to reduce the force of the invitation as a proposed first half of an adjacency pair. The invitation to propose a topic is made conditional, being presented as one, not necessarily the preferred, course of action and followed by an utterance that delays the client's response – and would make a refusal to propose a topic less problematic.

Second, the probation officer's utterance in the response position ('you di:d.') is not treated by the client as a full response leading on to an elaboration of the topic but as an occasion for an assessment ('Yeah (.) 's good.'), so that the actual production of the topic has to be restarted and maintained by the probation officer asking a series of questions.

As is established by the probation officer's first utterance in this fragment, this interview is one of a series of at least two; no other purpose for it is proposed here except the telling and receiving of recent news and so it is noteworthy to find the elicitation and confirmation of topic taking several turns of talk. Arguably this is a consequence of the conditional nature of the initial invitation and the neutral character of the response.

The data also contain examples where the client proposed a topic to the probation officer without waiting for an invitation:

Extract 2

> C: Been in 'ere before
> (.)
> P: Hav' you?
> (1)
> C: Mnher
> P: Wha' (.) see me?,
> C: Mno: s'erm 's'm else 'bou' fthree years ago
> P: Yeah (.) can you jus sign that t'say you ~(agree to be videoed)~
> (2)
> C: Cert'ly
> P: 's fine

The client's first utterance is made after he has stepped into the office – accompanied by the probation officer who has been to collect him from reception – and briefly looked around. The probation officer's response is followed by a one-second pause and an indistinct confirmation from the client. The probation officer then attempts to restart the proposed topic by asking for a particular elaboration – had the client been to see *him* on his prior visit. On receiving a negative response he closes off the topic and asks the client to sign the research consent form.

In this sequence, while the probation officer's first response ('Hav' you?') is in the place and form of a 'topicalizer' (Button and Casey 1984: 182), it is not received as such by the client. The probation officer can be seen then to be re-proposing the topic, with special reference to any past contact between him and the client, and having established that the topic would not include that contact he moves to another topic – signing the consent form.

In both these examples, topic was proposed by the client. The probation officer's next utterances after the proposal of topic were capable of being taken as 'topicalizers'. In extract 1 extra 'moves' were required to establish the topic proposed, while in extract 2 the proposed topic was rejected in subsequent utterances.

It appears therefore, from these examples, that clients' proposals of topic are accepted at best conditionally by probation officers, and that further moves are required to establish what may provisionally be regarded as the 'appropriateness' of the topic before it is confirmed (as in extract 1) or rejected (as in extract 2).

PROBATION OFFICERS' PROPOSALS OF TOPIC

The need for probation officers to propose topic stems from the fact that certain kinds of work have to be done in social inquiry report interviews. Specifically, information has to be elicited from the client for re-presentation to the court. In addition, the process of eliciting that information has to be marked off from any antecedent talk. The next two fragments illustrate approaches by probation officers to achieving this.

Extract 3

P: Right, (.) one o' things 'partic-larly wanted
    to talk about today, wus the this Day Training
    Cent[re business.
C: [yeh cos I'm I think I've (.) I go' the training bit but
    what does it involve?
P: Ri:gh (1) ((Phone rings)) I'm sorry, excuse me. (2) ((Picking
    up phone)) Hello its ((name)) (1) . . .

Extract 4

P: I jo thanks very much (2) Ok:ay can I check (.) that the
    information I've got is ri:gh'

C: ~(mm)~
P: Wu wu We had your name down as ((forename1 surname1))   (1)
C: ~(mm)~
P: Wh Wh Which: which is: >your real name< o' of y'no which is the name tha' you use?
C: ~((forename1 surname2))~

The common features of these two fragments are that the probation officer produces an utterance – 'Righ', 'Ok:ay' – marking the move to the topic proposal, then provides a reference or rationale to the proposal before specifying the topic itself.

The difference between them is in the reference used. In extract 3, which is taken from the very beginning of the interview, the proposal of topic is accomplished with reference to previous contact. The utterance 'one o' things 'partic-larly wanted to talk about today' implies both that the probation officer has an agenda for the interview and that this agenda, being for 'today', arises from an earlier interview. The elaboration of the client's response goes beyond the simple assent that might be expected in this position. This is arguably a consequence not simply of his interest in the topic itself, but also of its presentation as deriving from earlier talk in which he was involved. In extract 3, then, the design of the probation officer's utterance has the following characteristics. First, it is marked off from earlier talk. Second, the topic proposal is referred to prior contact with the client.

Three things can be noted here, contrasting extracts 3 and 4. First, the officer's reference to 'information' in extract 4 stands in the same place as the reference to 'today' in extract 3. It may be seen as topicalising the agenda proposed. Second, although the sequences of the probation officer utterances in the two fragments are in parallel, the client responses are not. The enthusiastic response in extract 3 can be contrasted with the minimal one in extract 4. Arguably this is, in part at least, a consequence of the difference between 'information' and 'today'; the reference to prior contact – known to both officer and client – is more 'powerful' in establishing topic than is the reference to information held only by the probation officer.

Third, it can be seen that, although the information being checked appears relatively straightforward – the client's name – its elicitation is in fact problematic. The fragment in extract 4 presented here follows a 20-second pause after the probation officer has obtained the client's consent to the interview being recorded, during which the client has signed the consent form. The probation officer first thanks the client for doing so, then achieves the shift to the topic of checking basic information about the client. After the provision of thanks, three stages can be observed:

a) 'Ok:ay' marks the move to next topic proposal;
b) 'Can I check' specifies the proposed activity in general;
c) 'that the information I've got is ri:gh'' objectifies this by referring to information that the probation officer already has.

The client's utterances in this fragment are minimal except in response to direct questions. This first utterance is taken as assent to the proposed topic but the second, which is delayed, is taken as an insufficient response to the probation officer's statement about his name (as recorded), and is treated as such by the probation officer from the start – both his first two utterances are marked by false starts and the question in his second utterance is repaired before being answered. In the data the initiation of topic can be seen as having two major components – a marker or separator from previous talk, and a reference (to time or information) accounting for the introduction of topic.

The existence of separating utterances preceding topic initiation proposals by probation officers suggests certain things about these sections of the interviews. It can be seen that clients do not find it necessary to use such transitional utterances and their use by probation officers can be seen as a form of segmentation similar to that reported by Turner (1972) when discussing the segmentation of therapy sessions. Turner particularly refers to the initiation of such sessions and the beginning of a topic in these sessions. It may be argued therefore that the use of such utterances serves to mark a move from one part of the interview to another and to break the interview into distinct parts. The need to break the interviews into parts may be linked to the need to do particular pieces of work during the interview. In this, topic initiation by probation officers may be seen as different from topic initiation by clients. Client topic initiation does not appear to need segment markers of this type, arguably because it is proposed as a part of 'normal conversation' where the topic domain is seen as open, but is not necessarily relevant to what might be seen as the purpose of the interview. The probation officers' conditional acceptances of client proposals of topic may be explained by the consideration, referred to above, that the topic domain is *not* open – only certain topics are admissible or topics are only *conditionally* admissible for acceptance. By contrast, the probation officer proposals of topic do appear to be linked to the function of the interview, whether it is to elicit news about the client or to collect certain kinds of information which can be used in preparing a social inquiry report.

The power of topic initiation in this setting can be inferred from the observation that the officer's proposal was initially if minimally accepted in the majority of cases (only one obvious failure). Also in five interviews the client's response to the proposal was presumed by the probation officer, and that presumption was accepted by the client.

The 'success' of topic initiation by probation officers is apparent in that clients participate by responding to probation officers' utterances. However, it must be noted that in most cases this participation is minimal. It is notable that the cases where the client produces a fuller response are, first, those where the probation officer initiates topic with a reference to prior contact (and where the topic proposed is not the offence), and those fragments where the probation officer initiates topic in the context of 'checking' information and follows this by a request couched as the first part of an adjacency pair for particular information. One fact that must be considered here is that the clients' responses to the topic proposals are in part affected by their understanding of what is expected of them. Where the proposal takes the form of a direct question or where the proposal refers to prior contact, the response appears to be fuller than where the proposal is simply one of topic without any explication either of its place in the interview or of what is being required. Thus, the client response to the topic proposal is in these circumstances conditional and may be seen as deferring a fuller reply until a particular formulation is indicated.

To summarise this and the preceding section, we have seen that the normative structure for topic elicitation in conversation, described by Button and Casey (1984), does occur in the early stages of the recorded probation interviews, if only rarely. Closer and more distant variations of this structure have been described, that rely on references to previous contact or to information received.

Topics initiated by clients are met initially with responses that do not signify immediate acceptance; their elicitation or response by probation officers appears to give the probation officer rights over the continuation of talk on that topic, including rights to terminate the topic and move on to another.

Topic initiation by probation officers is generally preceded by a short transitional phrase that serves to terminate or mark off the new topic from preceding utterances.

Clients respond to topic proposals but their responses are often minimal; the exceptions to this appear to be situations where the client knows from the precise form of the proposal, or from references that it contains, what kind of response is specifically appropriate.

All these observations would seem to be common to both social inquiry report and supervision interviews, and there appear to be no absolute situational or contextual constraints that make the practice of topic initiation, in general, radically different in social inquiry report interviews from supervision interviews.

On the other hand, there are obvious constraints according to whether or not there had been any recent contact between client and probation officer. Button and Casey's (1984) model of topic initiation seems on the face of it to work best when the participants to a conversation already know each other. Clearly there will be interactional situations where a request for 'news' is inappropriate, and social inquiry report interviews between strangers may be one of these. It is also a priori unlikely that requests for 'news' would be common *after* other forms of topic initiation. It is notable that probation officers initiating topic typically took care to locate these sequences in the context of their previous and recent contact with the same client, where such contact had been made. When there was no prior contact probation officers related topic initiation to information they had received. It is clear to a third party when there had been *no* previous contact, if only from the basic nature of the information (typically name, date of birth, address) elicited from the client as an early topic in most of these interviews.

Topic initiation in interviews can therefore be seen as a process which relies on the establishment of some pointers to the client of the appropriateness of particular responses and/or topics. These pointers can be directly achieved through probation officer reference to prior contact or through direct questioning. Reference to prior knowledge which is used alone as a device does not appear to elicit more than a conditional response. These specific situational factors suggest preferences, responsive to them, for different approaches to topic initiation. Above these, however, appears to be an overriding consideration that the topics established should be relevant to what may be regarded as the purpose of the interview. The reason for adducing the existence of purpose is that if the domain for topic were entirely open then topic initiation would tend to be more responsive to such factors as prior contact, and client topic proposals would be less dispreferred than they appear to be from this data. The explanation for the difficulty of operating the 'news' form of topic initiation, and the preference for other segmented structures may well be that the topic domain is *not* open. The nature of the conditional responses by probation officers to clients' proposals of topic and the nature of the topics proposed by probation officers suggest that the topic domain is restricted to topics that are relevant to the agency function reflected in a specific (if unstated) purpose for the interview.

It may also be argued that probation officers' use of approaches to topic initiation that are not sufficiently responsive to the restriction of the topic domain will tend to lead to interactional difficulties in the generation of topic.

DISCUSSION

The traditional approach to studying the effectiveness of social work appears to have two main problems (apart from the problem of establishing effectiveness): the disappearance of the topic and the problem of establishing 'what really happened'; both of these stem from a reliance on accounts of social work by practitioner or client and from the relationship between the methods of analysis and the theoretical approaches of the researchers. Thus, while we may be able to say something about the relationship between the outcomes of task-centred casework and re-offending, we have problems in saying precisely what happened in task-centred casework that led to the production of these outcomes rather than others and we have difficulty in saying what the production of task-centred casework itself really entailed.

The limited value of caseworkers' accounts in answering questions of effectiveness was of course illustrated in Garfinkel (1967). The point is further made by Pithouse, who stressed two specific observations: the contingent and variable relationship of accounts to practice and the fact that within the context of an organisation the account *is* the practice in that members' competence is defined by accounts that they produce rather than by anything they may have done.

In this respect the details of family life are forever hostage to the selective views and understandings of the worker and her occupational requirements. Thus accounts are never about what 'actually' occurred between worker and client whatever that might be. Instead accounts are an occupational reality, they are an ex post facto construction assembled around negotiable understandings, identities and relationships within the work world.

(Pithouse 1987: 113)

The research that has been described in this paper is an attempt to go beyond accounts into practice itself and specifically that area of practice that is described by probation officer/client interviews. Within this territory I have focused on one aspect of interviews – topic initiation, specifically at the beginning.

The question that has to be faced is whether this form of analysis has any value. Does it take us any further in understanding social work practice and particularly any relationship that there might be between actions and results? To answer this question we need to ask some subsidiary ones: first of all, what is practice? Is it the contact between social worker and the client, the account of that contact in records and supervision, or some combination of the two? If the accounts are the topic then we have to ask what the status of the action is. Is it, for example, a trivial process by which the agency record of the client's problem is converted to an account? If the topic is the action then is the account itself irrelevant but a part of some other process of agency functioning? If both accounts and action are topics and are to be brought into the same frame then we need to look at the links between them.

If we regard action as a primary topic in the study of social work, a consequence of this is to undermine the accounts themselves. Logically one might say this is tending to undermine the profession of social work as it is currently organised, given that professional competence is shown through the presentation of accounts rather than through specific activities. Obviously this is not a position which is peculiar to social work agencies; many other forms of professional and quasi-professional competence appear to have similar characteristics. Clearly this is an extreme position, but it illustrates the point that the adoption of one particular methodological approach to the study of social work does involve some kind of statement about the nature of social work practice and what this consists of.

So what light do the data that I have presented throw on this issue?

Is the hole in the mint missing material or an integral part of the structure of social work? It is worth noting that probation officers, in initiating topics in interviews made reference to the existence of written accounts – in case files or in documents ('information') received from the court or other agencies – and that therefore the activity of talk in probation interviews is situated within a context of accounts and procedures and proceeds by reference to them as well as to the client's history of contact with the interviewing probation officer.

Topic generation in probation interviews shows a preference for what may be described as a segmented structure. Arguably this is because only certain topics are allowable at any one time so that the domain of talk is regulated by the probation officer. A consequence of this is that client proposals of topic are treated conditionally at best, and that topic initiation sequences which appear to presume an open conversational domain run into interactional difficulties. As the social inquiry report interviews studied also appeared to be oriented to the production of the offence as an early topic it is probable that the regulation of the domain of talk is an aspect of the function of the probation service and its primary concern with offenders and offending. Talk in probation interviews therefore exhibits some key differences from 'ordinary talk' – and more may be found – and may also be both similar to and different from talk in other institutional settings.

Thus these data produce two hints of an order that relates to accounts both of practice and of procedures specific to that practice. It is not intended to suggest that conversation analysis is the only means of researching this order; the existence of accounts, and their use as resources in talk, implies that the accounts themselves are an important topic for study. It is, however, worth stressing that other forms of analysis of the same data, such as content analysis, would not necessarily have produced these results because these findings are gained from examination of the structures of passages of talk in the light of comparisons with other structural forms and in the light of topics embedded in them. The converse however may also be true, that certain theoretical constructions of social work, e.g. symbolic interactionism, treatment orientation, law enforcement, may be difficult to recover from the data.

So what next? Obviously the range of data available at the moment is too narrow to support general conclusions and only hints at the possibilities available. If more data were available I think we would need to have a more rigorous addressing of the relationship between accounts and action and the order that may be seen as underlying both, if only for the good practical reason that assessments of social workers' competence are likely to rely on some form of accounting. This has been presented as a problem. Gilbert and Mulkay say 'social action is not "directly observable" . . . which of these or other actions is being observed on any particular occasion can only be established by reference to the statements, either written or spoken, of participants' (1984: 8).

My response to this would be that participants' statements about social action do not have any necessary primacy over third-party observation as evidence for that action; conflicts between statements and observation should not necessarily be resolved in favour of the former. Participants may be self-deluded or incompetent to be doing what they claim to do. Talk (to which Gilbert and Mulkay were not explicitly referring) is a form of social action which is jointly constructed by its participants through the process by which each piece of talk can be held to account by the next action. This means that each actor is perceived by fellow participants as doing *something*; co-participants' actions are responsive to this perception and will in turn be 'answered', as appropriate, by the first actor. As this process demonstrably operates within a set of normative procedures that can be seen as being 'tailored' to a particular setting, it should be possible to recover what is achieved by the observation and analysis of that episode of talk.

If we can do this then we will have developed a form of analysis that provides material on topics that are not otherwise accessible and that are necessary for our understanding of social work.

© 1991 Stephen Stanley

A NOTE ON TERMINOLOGY

In this paper I have used the term 'client' to denote people subject to the intervention of the probation service. The contemporary Home Office preference is to use the term 'offender'. There are two reasons for not conforming to this preference. The first is that not all probation service clients are convicted offenders, and even in the study presented here one client had not been convicted of the offences alleged when the social inquiry report was prepared. The second reason is that this paper is presented as a contribution to the sociology of social work in the hope that its theme will be seen as applicable beyond the boundaries of probation, and there seemed no reason to use language that would emphasise differences that are not relevant to the material presented here.

Chapter Seven

THE FAMILY AND
THE THERAPIST

Towards a sociology of social work method

DAVID HOWE

Fashions and fads breeze through occupations every bit as much as they blow through the world of clothes, music, and cars. At one level fashion is viewed as no more than froth and fancy, short-lived tastes that flavour the substance. But dive below and fashion reveals the mood of the times; it says something about the style and outlook of those who are in fashion. Plotting the rise and fall of particular social work methods tells us a lot about movements in the underlying state of social work. Practices are embedded in a matrix of laws and budgets, public concerns and private emotions, technological innovations and personal values, organisational structures and professional aspirations. So, with curiosity raised about the appearances and disappearances of different social work practices, we might ask questions such as: Why was there a 'psychiatric deluge' in the 1930s? Why are psychodynamic caseworkers an endangered species today? How do we account for the ubiquitous and obligatory case conference? Does anybody still write process recordings? And is it still true, as Wright Mills once barracked, that social workers are constitutionally incapable of rising above the case?

Of course, social work's critics have always recognised that prevailing practices say something about what social work is really about. Radical social workers (in their day) spotted the conservative and coercive nature of practices that diagnosed people to be at fault and not the system in which they had to live. In the opposing camp, Brewer and Lait (1980) dismissed social workers as woolly and muddled. They advised them to take a leaf out of medicine's book and embrace the sciences. Their fervent wish was that welfare workers would become behaviourists and adopt an objective, causative view of human action, allowing them to treat people clinically and purposefully. But, though these critics are right to examine the relationship between a practice and its ideological implications, sociologically they miss the point when they merely regret matters, insisting that things should be different. Much more rewarding are questions which ask 'Why are things like they are? Why is this practice so prevalent? And why do the recommendations of the critics appear to fall on deaf ears?'

We need a sociology of social work method. We need to consider the relationship between a particular practice, the times in which it lives and dies, and the context in which it does well. The comings and goings of different methods will then seem less random as we discover that methods are shaped by, and themselves shape, the ideological currents of the time.

Family therapy, currently enjoying considerable popularity among practitioners, is a good example of a method that has swept into social work. In fact, in one form or another, family therapy has been around for over thirty years, attracting a small, but significant band of enthusiasts. But why should it have begun to flourish in social work in the last decade? Whose needs does it meet? Answers to these questions, though specifically about family therapy, help provide general pointers to a sociology of social work method.

Family therapy carries two meanings, though, as we shall see, there is an intimate relationship between them. The first suggests an *object* of treatment, in this case the family, implying that there is something wrong with the family that needs to be fixed in order to return it to a healthy state. The second, more usual effect of the descriptor, is to identify a particular *method* of treatment. So, for example, we have chemo-therapy and radio-therapy in which cancer is treated by the use of drugs and high energy radiations. Family therapy, in analogous fashion, is a way of treating a problem by using the family; the family effects a cure of itself. Psychotherapy (treating the mind by using the mind) and behaviour therapy (treating behaviours by modifying behaviours) are two other examples in which the object and method of treatment are the same. But in whatever way they are qualified, words like therapy, cure, and treatment suggest that there is something wrong which has to be returned to normal and healthy functioning. Family therapy offers a disease model of family performance in which families are diagnosed as dysfunctional and their way of doing things is seen as pathological. However, I have said that the method of treatment does not involve the use of some external agent requiring, for example, the removal of an alleged faulty part (usually a wayward child) or remedying the behaviour of the disruptive member by the administration of some drug. Treatment is effected by manipulating the workings of the family itself. This unusual state of affairs, in which the family has become an entity which is both the site of the problem and the method by which the problem is treated, needs further consideration. Looking at the ideas of the post-structuralists gives us a route into this topic.

FORMING A SOCIAL DISCOURSE

Interest in the disobedient, the disruptive, and the difficult has become an increasingly refined activity. Politically, great efforts have been made to establish the performance levels of individuals in the general population in order to recover or isolate those who are in danger of becoming a social and economic liability. People's abilities and conduct are matters that cannot be ignored by those who wish to run a well-ordered and productive state. As the powerful gave thought to the whys and wherefores of people's behaviour, knowledge was acquired which in turn gave power to those who said they understood, could control, and could harness human potential. The political and the personal began to meet and define an area which Donzelot (1979) calls 'the social'. In the domain of the social, the public face of personal behaviour is identified, classified, and explained by experts and administrators who act, think, and speak within the language of the 'social discourse'. Historically, there has been a shift from simply inflicting personal penalties on wrongdoers and poor performers to demanding their return, both body and soul, to the path of social righteousness. For example, for those who had committed a crime, it was no longer the body that was the object of punishment but the quality of the mind that needed attention; a move from simple vindictiveness to humanism with a scientific face (Cohen and Scull 1983: 6). According to the new paradigm, all nature was malleable; people could be re-programmed to function once again as competent members of society (Ingleby 1983: 152). It was the person and not the deed that had to be treated:

> By the end of the eighteenth century, the move from body to mind was well under way. The 'social' had been constituted as a special domain in which people could be scrutinised, supervised and changed. This transformation incorporated and facilitated the

victory of positivism. As the mind rather than the body became the object of penal repression, so the actor rather than the act became the object of criminological attention. Those developments, seen as specific products of the twentieth century – rehabilitation, the treatment ideal, the 'therapeutic state', the medical model, the whole baggage of progressive penology – are fully continuous and consistent with that original transformation.

(Cohen 1985: 139–40)

To help cultivate these practices and to discourse in the language of the 'social', to replace old ways of punishing with new techniques of treatment, to render obedient the social miscreant, to care for the helpless and the hopeless, a 'new army of technicians' – doctors, social workers, wardens, psychiatrists, psychologists – emerged to educate the promising, to train the worthwhile, and to cure the bad. Their interventions are legitimated and made efficient by appeal to the 'human sciences', 'methods of surveillance and theories that extend into every nook and cranny of social life' (Ingleby 1983: 161). In their maturity, these developments create what has been called the 'therapeutic state' in which vast areas of social and personal difficulties fall under the category of 'malfunction' which receive 'treatment', 'the whole operation being seen as apolitical, value-free, and nothing more than the application of technical expertise' (Ingleby 1983: 161). The existence of these disciplines, to a large extent, creates the domain of 'the social'; it is not that central powers spot social problems and then ask the professions to treat them, but rather that these occupations and their knowledge of human affairs tell the authorities that a social problem exists, defining both its character and the manner of its treatment (Ingleby 1983: 171).

SOCIAL POLICY AND THE FAMILY

The family has been defined as one of the most important sites where social behaviours are either learned or not learned. The quality of parenting and family life is said to determine the social performance of children. It is hardly surprising, then, that if the family is defined as the place where children learn to think and act, the state has become very interested in the family. Much social policy is shaped around the idea that the family is a critical group in the socialisation of children. But, as social policy takes its shape, as experts pronounce on family matters, so the family becomes defined and constructed, less on the basis of its inherent qualities and more to do with the power of external agents to say how families should function. Even though many policies do not formally recognise the family as the direct object of official attention, it is the vehicle by which such policies are applied (Parker 1982). According to Fogarty and Rodgers, the family performs a number of roles and functions.

> [The family] has a spatial dimension, and needs in terms of housing, community design, transport and communications. It is an economic unit whose composition and functioning affects the distribution of incomes, expenditure patterns, the supply of workers to the labour market and the accumulation and transfer between generations of economic assets such as homes, capital, economic know-how and networks of contacts for opportunities of employment and enterprise. Unpaid service and mutual aid within the family constitute a major addition to the real national income, and often are or may be a substitute for public expenditure. Families are social and psychological units, which influence their members' personality, impose roles on them, and provide them with more or less free space for social interaction. They are cultural and educational units, with an influence extending across generations.
>
> (Fogarty and Rodgers 1982: 3–4)

This formidable list of responsibilities shows the vital part the family plays for the state. It is little wonder that the way these roles are performed is of critical social concern, witnessed in the legislation that surrounds the family and the effort that is put into supporting, obliging, and encouraging the family in pursuit of its economic and social functions. Yet the state walks a fine line between leaving the family alone and intruding on its affairs. Privacy, independence, self-discipline, and looking after oneself are prized values which have to be sponsored. Failure to promote these virtues sees the state and its agents moving into educate, mend, control, and remonstrate with the family and its members. But such interventions themselves are always in danger of going too far, undermining the very qualities that are being sought. The trick is to teach the family to regulate its own affairs, to learn to judge itself by external social standards, and to value the art of behaving in socially useful ways. Nowhere is this more so than in the sphere of child rearing.

A century ago, children could still be regarded as the exclusive

property of their parents. There was little outside interest or interference in the relationship between parent and child. Gradually,
however, the idea grew that there should be explicit limits on parental
power and that children should be protected in their own homes
(Behlmer 1982). The sovereignty of the family was being eroded.
Arguments, literature, and expertise began to flourish on the theme
of the 'preservation of children' (Donzelot 1979: 9). A dual focus
emerged. On the one hand there was the wish to free the child from
unhealthy constraints to allow the maximum growth of his or her potential. On the other, there was a desire to control and prevent the neglect,
abuse, and misuse of the child, particularly within the home, as well
as to shepherd those who were given 'excessive freedom' to roam the
streets and get up to mischief back to the family, back to school, back
on the straight and narrow (Donzelot 1979: 47). By the early twentieth century the family was no longer beyond the purview of the state
and its regulations. Throughout Europe, parental authority was turned
into a contestable right. It became possible for parents to lose their
authority. Today there exists much law on the rearing and the conduct
of children. Thus, relationships between parents and their children
which were 'exploitative and authoritative' were required to become
'affectionate and nurturant' (Freeman 1983: 13).

In the United Kingdom, by the 1960s, various government working
parties were increasingly of the opinion that the family was the key
group in leading the fight against delinquency, in the protection of
children, and in the promotion of socially acceptable behaviour. The
Seebohm Committee reported that the personal social services should
be reorganised into a 'unified family service'. It envisaged that the
service would be delivered by social workers who were experts in family
matters. A critical association between the family and the maintenance
of the state was sensed. The family helped socialise children, fostering
ideas about the importance of obedience, conformity, and discipline
(Morgan 1985: 750). Things which upset these functions concern the
state. Increases in the rate of divorce, the neglect and abuse of babies,
and the inability to control adolescents adversely affect the social
behaviour of children. The family is held responsible for the children
it produces and so it becomes a legitimate target for those agents
charged with promoting social well-being, public morality, and good
political order. And though 'the sanctity of the family' is upheld, 'it
is a family carefully monitored and controlled from the outside; while
the human sciences exhaustively scrutinize its inner life, medicine,

social work, the "psy-professions" and the courts set firm limits to its autonomy' (Ingleby 1983: 170).

Foucault (1975) insists that social agencies do not arise simply in response to a pre-existing problem; such agencies help constitute the existence of the problem and our understanding of it. But having defined it in terms of their skills and knowledge, only they know how to treat it. In order to understand the family and help it perform to standard, experts analyse its workings. Out of this analysis, the concept, purpose, and expectations of family life are constructed. The family takes on its meaning in relation to the theories that the experts create to explain and treat family life. Surrounding these 'technicians in human relations' is the domain of the social, where the political penetrates the personal and the private erupts into the public (Donzelot 1979). Two acts are performed simultaneously by these technicians as they deal with the family: they judge and they treat. A hybrid emerges made up of the judicial and the therapeutic, where law and medicine compose the social discourse. The family is judged to be the cause of the problem and it is also the place where the problem must be returned and resolved. The parent, argues Donzelot (1979: 225), is continually called upon to fight an enemy that is none other than himself. The statutory control of children and the therapeutic interventions of experts arise out of the same understanding: some behaviours are judged unacceptable (in acts of surveillance) and those behaviours have to be changed (in acts of education and treatment). The independent authority of the family gives way to a form of social management in which the expert manipulates the family itself to return the child to the moral community without ever removing him or her from the relationships that allegedly spawned the problem. All this supervision and intervention, direction and education Donzelot calls the 'tutelary complex'.

Cohen adds that parents are now taught that they cannot meet the needs of their children without the advice and scrutiny of experts – social workers, health visitors, psychologists. The private space of the family is politicised. But the ultimate ploy, having taught the parents how to be good parents and run an effective family, is for the experts to bow out: 'there is no need for the state to act as parent and teacher if parent and teacher can be made to act like the state' (Cohen 1985: 136). Good illustrations of how far things have gone along this road are provided by Morgan (1985) in his examination of marriage and the family. He quotes from the Working Party on Marriage Guidance (1980):

We have come to the view, which we think is shared by many informed people in the educational and caring services, that the part which marital disharmony plays in the creation of social problems is a frequently neglected cause of personal and social distress. Similarly we consider that, in marital relationships, the potential for the development of the couple and their children is too often overlooked in the current climate.

(Morgan 1985: 23)

The important point, made repeatedly by Morgan, is that there is a growing emphasis on interpersonal relationships in defining and understanding marital and family life, a shift from viewing marriage as an institution to seeing it as a relationship. With this move from duty to personal interaction, men and women who experience difficulties in being spouses or parents find that the failure is explained in terms of the quality of their relationships and so they turn away from the priest and seek the doctor, the therapist, Donzelot's 'technicians in human relations'. Couples now want counselling and not guidance. The medical model of marriage that underpins this approach implies that there is a class of problems called 'marital problems' related to the condition of the marital relationship. These problems can be isolated, examined, and treated. Marital problems are seen as problems which arise out of the complex pattern of emotional, interpersonal, and sexual relationships that constitute marriage (Morgan 1985: 34–5). As this way of understanding marital and family life takes hold of the professional imagination, we find a growing body of knowledge about the way families work and, based on this knowledge, we see a rush of techniques which help the experts treat failing marriages and faltering relationships. Family therapy is one such technique.

FAMILY THERAPY

There are many varieties of family therapy. Most, however, derive their inspiration from systems theory. Systems theory recognises that natural and mechanical systems are more than the sum of their parts. Moreover, the parts themselves can make sense only as constituents of the whole. All parts interact and are interdependent on one another. The scientific observer can examine any system and analyse the patterns, regularities, and relationships within it and so describe that system's operating characteristics. For example, the world's climate is maintained naturally in a state of balance. Energy in the form of sunlight enters the earth's atmosphere. Some is retained as it is absorbed by land, oceans, air, and life, and some is reflected back into space. But if some external event interferes with this balance, things can go awry. If the proportion of carbon dioxide in the atmosphere increases through burning fossil fuels and trees, the system can cope at first by, for example, the oceans absorbing more of the gas, or plant life growing more luxuriant as photosynthesis takes advantage of the enriched atmosphere of carbon dioxide. But should the increase continue, the atmosphere retains more of the sun's energy and less is reflected back into space. There are fewer forests to convert the gas into organic matter. The earth's temperature rises in what is known as the 'greenhouse' effect. The oceans warm and expand, ice caps melt, and sea level rises. Weather patterns change drastically, and one way or another the world becomes a very different place.

Initially applied to biological and engineering systems it was not long before social and behavioural scientists applied the model to human affairs. The family was quickly identified as a significant social system in which:

1. the parts of the family are inter-related;
2. one part of the family cannot be understood in isolation from the rest of the system;
3. family functioning cannot be fully understood by simply understanding each of the parts;
4. a family's structure and organisation are important factors determining the behaviour of family members;
5. transactional patterns of the family system shape the behaviour of family members.

(Epstein and Bishop 1981: 447)

With the emphasis on the properties of the system in relation to the performance of each part, there was a major shift in focus from the individual and his or her internal psychological state to the social nature of psychic life. Individual psychologies exist only in the pattern of inter-relationships. What goes on *between* people is more important than what goes on *within* them. This kind of thinking led a number of psychiatrists and psychologists to recognise the possibility of treating families along systemic lines. Where husbands and wives were in conflict or teenagers were up to no good, the family system could be analysed so that it might become clear who was doing what to whom and with what consequence. True to the tenets of systems theory, therapists who worked with difficult family members insisted that the only effective way of helping was to deal with the whole family for it was within its interactions that the problem appeared. The problem behaviour itself makes no sense outside the operations of the family.

Family therapists no longer diagnose relationships in simple linear cause and effect terms but prefer the idea of circular causality. A husband says he withdraws because his wife nags and she says she nags because her husband withdraws. An anxious daughter stays away from school to keep an eye on her mother who says she has no interest in living since her partner started an affair, though he explains that he finds life at home oppressive with a watchful daughter and her moping mother – he needs to get out. The therapist requires all members of the family to be present to explore and identify the patterns of interaction and their effect. The aim is to alter what members say and do to each other, to break old patterns of behaviour and substitute new. In this way sounder relationships appear, communications are less distorted, and the family returns to healthier functioning. Treatments usually take place over a prescribed number of sessions and typically each session lasts about an hour.

THE MEDICAL ORIGINS OF FAMILY THERAPY

Most of family therapy's founding figures were trained in the natural and medical sciences. It was in the early 1950s that the ground plans for a systemic approach to working with families were first drawn. Post-war developments in cybernetics, ecology, communications theory as well as systems theory all influenced the early models of family therapy. Communication was intelligible only in the context of a relation. Therefore the notion that one member of a family could be labelled as 'sick' had to be rejected in favour of recognising a dysfunctional system. Problem behaviour was not the result of an individual's psychopathology but the product of distorted interactions; generally speaking, a disturbed psyche emerged out of a disturbed social environment. In 1956, Bateson and his colleagues attempted to explain schizophrenia in these terms. As the fault did not lie with the psychic condition of the individual, personal therapy was not appropriate and the thing to be doing was to work with the whole family, paying particular attention to the patterns of communication that circulated between members.

It was not long before the exciting potential of this way of thinking and working spread to the treatment of delinquency, marital conflict, and disturbed children. By the 1960s family therapy was in full stride. Although the intellectual centre remained in psychiatry and psychology, family therapy rapidly settled in social work and counselling. Today it is practised in child guidance clinics and social services departments, it is to be found in the offices of the NSPCC and the probation service, and it is rife in voluntary family welfare agencies.

The scientific and medical origins of family therapy are still very much in evidence today. Families are diagnosed by experts in objective terms. Explanations about what is wrong rest with the therapist who possesses a specialised body of knowledge to help him or her make sense of the family. Families may be described as functioning healthily or unhealthily. There are techniques to treat the problems which families are said to suffer. Therapists choose the course of treatment and direct its administration. Therapeutic interventions tend to be purposeful; they focus on particular problems and run for relatively short prescribed periods of time. These are important characteristics which tell us something about the success of family therapy in modern welfare agencies.

However, there is one more aspect which needs highlighting. Earlier it was mentioned that there had been a historical switch in emphasis from punishing the act to treating the actor. But Cohen recognises that one more step has been taken in the history of social control. There has been a return to dealing with the offending act, but not in a visible, physical way through brutalisations of the body conducted in full gaze of the public. The emphasis is now on demanding that the actor change his or her act, not by treating the mind and changing the person, but by directly addressing the behaviour and its consequences. 'Rehabilitation', observes Cohen (1985: 144), 'was to be given another turn – not change through internal insight this time but change through external compliance. . . . You can observe behaviour in a way that you cannot observe insights. . . .' The disruptive and the disobedient, people who have not learned the rules of the social game, are not asked to change, they are simply asked to conform. They are taught new skills and social behaviours. Treating what you can see, what is before you, and what you can measure is the hallmark of much modern practice. Only the observable act matters and not the workings of the mind that produced it. It can be seen in behaviour modification, task-centred approaches, social skills training, and family therapy. People are taught how to behave. There is no exploration of the reasons for their behaviour. What you see is all you need to know in order to redesign what is said and done. Progress can be reported in quantifiable terms to families, fellow therapists, and managers. The characteristics of family therapy and its stable-mates are peculiarly suited to the style of the modern welfare bureaucracy.

MANAGERIAL SOCIAL WORK

As organisations, the personal social services have been getting steadily larger. Prior to 1969 in Scotland and 1971 in England and Wales, social workers practised in relatively small, specialist departments. The Social Work Act in Scotland (1968) and the Local Authority Social Services Act in England and Wales (1970) brought into existence much larger, generic social work units made up of the old children's, welfare, and mental health departments. With the 1974 local government reorganisations, these new social work and social services departments became even bigger, employing thousands of people and serving large administrative districts.

Such large departments could not be run along the lines of their small-scale forebears. Size and demands for efficiency meant that welfare managers had to leave behind their social work knowledge base and learn new managerial skills. Although public agencies were not businesses, they had to behave in a business-like manner in which case there was much to be learned from commerce and industry. Top managers were sent on high-powered training courses which were saturated with the wisdoms gained from running successful businesses. New concepts and skills were picked up, objectives were identified, service production systems were designed. Managers became cost conscious and resource minded. Indeed, throughout the health and welfare services of the 1970s, the emphasis was on achieving managerial control through administrative rationality using ideas derived from business management.

Uncertainty is anathema to all occupational groups. There is a need to control materials and predict the outcome of one's efforts whether you are a carpenter, a doctor, or a product manager. If you are unable to work directly on the things which your organisation tackles, your work-force, as well as the 'raw materials', represent potential uncertainty. On the whole, managerial strategies are designed to minimise reliance on the skills and actions of other groups. Whenever possible, systems and routines are established in which the work is conducted in a prescribed, invariant fashion. Workers know what to do, they know the basis on which situations are to be assessed, and what resources are available to meet needs or achieve purposes. In the case of social workers, actions are prescribed by procedure manuals, access to resources, and managerial command. Practices become regularised and standardised. Managers do not have to treat each new situation as unique and unknown. This way, the organisation can operate in a steady, predictable fashion.

On the face of it, it might seem that social work clients present welfare organisations with many idiosyncrasies and unique features. But much of the inherent complexity and uncertainty that clients possess can be ignored and filtered out so that they are assessed only in terms of what the organisation sees as relevant to its purposes and resources. Clients can be standardised according to the statutory obligations of the agency (particularly in the case of child protection work) or the resources and provisions that the department is required to offer (particularly in the care of old people and the handicapped). Clients, then, are made to fit the organisation and its practices, and not, as is often imagined, the organisation made to fit the varied and subtle needs of each client. The power to define this 'task environment' (the clients of the social services) lies with managers (Howe 1986).

PROFESSIONAL WORKERS AND AWKWARD CLIENTS

The control of the manager, though, is not absolute. Not all clients and their behaviour submit themselves so easily to the tight grip of statutes and resources. In these cases, the skills of the manager are incapable of anticipating the key characteristics of the work in advance; some uncertainty remains to trouble the organisation, and control at a distance – the skill of all good managers – becomes threatened. For example, parents may insist that the social services department takes their unruly children into care, seven-year-old boys do not appear to be going to school, fourteen-year-old girls get pregnant; social workers, thinking on their feet in such situations, may commit the organisation to actions and the use of resources that are not to its liking. If practitioners were completely autonomous, running welfare organisations would be difficult and hazardous. Generally, the solution lies in training practitioners to think and act as the organisation would like them to in situations where the worker is on her own without the safety and constraints of procedural guidance; as a result the practitioner is made ideologically compatible with the department's values and purposes, so that she can safely be handed discretion allowing her to act flexibly but acceptably in volatile situations.

Family work is a particularly awkward area for managers. It is not easy to regularise what matters each family presents to the department. Routine prescriptions and administrative formulae do not always work. The appearance of family therapy could hardly be better timed. All its working characteristics fit beautifully with the values and administrative style of welfare bureaucracies. There is a theory to explain the functioning and malfunctioning of families. The inherent complexity of family life, particularly troubled family life, is explained and systematised as a pattern of interpersonal exchanges. This understanding is the creation of the therapist. To the outside world, which may view the family and its behaviours as puzzling and exasperating, anyone who claims to make sense of what is going on and to be able to do something about it will be received with relief and probably left to get on with things in their own way. Problems are blamed on the family system rather than on the political environment or some inaccessible, untreatable individual psychology. Families and their behaviour 'make sense' but only in terms of a medical and pathological framework of understanding. Again, it has to be emphasised that those who are in positions of power control what situations mean and it is they who determine what knowledge is to be brought to bear (Howe 1989a: 95). The family therapist does not respond to the immediate experience of the family; she reacts only to the situation as she defines it. It is her meaning that is imposed on the family. She has the power to control both what the problem means and how it is to be tackled (Howe 1989a: 91). The therapist is not revealing the 'real' world of the family, rather the language she uses, the concepts she holds structure the experience of others and give them meaning to suit her purposes. She assembles a 'reality' with which she can work and that maintains her authority (Rojek *et al.* 1988: 137). In this way, the therapist establishes the family as a suitable case for treatment.

Sophisticated techniques are used which are able to treat the malfunction using the family itself as the major resource. The problem (usually a difficult or disturbed child) is kept within the family and is not allowed to detach itself to threaten the resources of the department. Aims are clearly identified, entailing the return of the family to a healthy interpersonal performance. Treatments are relatively short, purposeful, and couched in terms of behaviours which are observable. A social worker knows where she is, where she is going, and how long she will be involved with the family. This is wonderful news for the administratively tidy manager. No longer is the worker involved with a family on an open-ended, indefinite basis. Family therapy, as a service response, can be packaged into discrete envelopes of activity. It also parcels families into definable, intelligible, and manageable social work entities. The commitment of personnel, time, and resources is predictable.

Family therapy has the added bonus of being very popular with social workers. There is freedom to deploy and develop skills which are personally demanding. Intellectual stimulation is high. Few of the constraints that bedevil so much of social services work are present. Social workers, as therapists, get to meet other interesting folk of high prestige value – psychiatrists, psychologists, people who specialise in family therapy. Books are written about the technique. And what other method in social work has its own reputable journal (*The Journal of Family Therapy*), runs major conferences and training workshops, and travels well internationally? In some social services departments the method is so highly valued that social workers can practise it only under departmental licence, a sure sign that the activity is well into its first step towards professionalisation. No matter if some families are not keen on family therapy; as long as social workers are enthusiastic and their morale is kept high, the technique is likely to earn the support of workers and managers alike, if for no other reason than, as one manager put it, 'A happy worker is an effective worker' (Howe 1989a, 1989b).

A METHOD OF THE TIMES FOR THE TIMES

The conjunction of managerialism and family therapy is a happy one, but hardly accidental. What managerial social work wants and family therapy supplies is curiously well matched. It is not that family therapy happened to be around and just happened to fit the style of large social services departments. These are times when there is a common outlook on material and social life. The ideas and the logic that produced rational management techniques also produced the intellectual climate that led to systemic family therapy.

As the domain of the social emerged, both experts and agencies formed to define, judge, and treat the family. Professional expertise and the organisation of welfare agencies followed parallel technological careers. Experts developed knowledge about human behaviour and the quality of relationships between people. Their skills and interventions employed a rational, systematic approach in the assessment and treatment of the individual and his or her family. Managers of welfare agencies also needed to devise systems which could monitor as well as respond to the social consequences of personal behaviour, and, like their professional counterparts, they too developed a knowledge base which was systematic, rational, and scientific in its attitude to people and their management. Derived from the same intellectual sources, possessed of a similar ability to hold both a judicial and a welfare perspective, and constructed with equal subtlety to operate in the domain of the social, experts and those who manage social agents have a common outlook on the family and its difficulties.

Ideas have their time and place; they are shaped by whatever intellectual currents prevail. Particular styles of thought, knowledge, and concepts cannot be entertained by anyone at any time. They form because the time is right and their time has come, and in a broad sense we all think in a particular way at a certain time. At some deeper level, then, these are times which generate ideas which, when they surface, look superficially unconnected. This is not so. Scientific management and the systemic understanding of family behaviour tap the same deep discourse. That is why, when they meet, they fit.

© 1991 David Howe

Chapter Eight

THE SOCIOLOGY OF SIZE IN RESIDENTIAL CARE

PETER HUXLEY

'Four is a magic number, but then again, so is five'
(Loudon Wainwright III)

This chapter examines the nature of the relationship between a particular piece of social policy and the factors which gave rise to it. The policy statement is one contained within a draft policy document on mental health services, produced by a social services department. The statement is as follows:

> It is proposed that housing should be provided in as ordinary and dispersed units as possible to afford privacy, personal space and enhance the dignity and independence of the individual. No more than 6 people should be accommodated in one building be that hostel, sheltered flat or house.

The primary area of interest is why the limit is six people and not seven people or five. This is the 'material interest'. The authority decided to limit residential developments to six people and refused to register (under the Registered Homes Act, 1984) any provision which was larger. This decision brought protests from the voluntary sector, and an appeal to the Registered Homes Tribunal was suggested by one voluntary body which was trying to register a home for twelve people.

Our primary 'material interest' is size, but the consideration of this issue will take us into the realm of ideas and beliefs; that is, into an examination of the extent to which the policy is based upon or influenced by accepted beliefs and 'publicly acceptable shared representations' (Barnes 1977) or, in other words, 'knowledge'. Webb (1988) has said that the study of 'consonance between the trajectory of ideas and material interests' is part of the domain of the sociology of knowledge, and the material presented in this chapter clearly falls within this field.

Although the struggle for and the exercise of power do play a major part in the processes which will be described and could therefore be the basis of a further analysis of the material interest, using the concept 'power' is, according to Lukes (1977), 'likely to involve further particular and contestable judgements'. As such complication is avoidable, it is avoided in what follows. The relevance of the concept of 'power' lies in its utility in understanding the process which occurs when ideas, knowledge, values, and interests are brought to bear on a social policy issue. Latour (1986) shows that when a person 'has' power, nothing happens; it is only when the person chooses to 'exert' power that something happens, and this something is enacted by *other people*. He points out that there are two models for understanding what happens when commands are given and action ensues. The first model is the *diffusion* model, in which a successful command moves under an impetus given to it from a central source. In this model, when an order is faithfully executed, the explanation is that the 'commander' has a 'lot of power'. When an order is not executed, the explanation is that the 'commander's' power has met with a lot of resistance.

The second model is the *translation* model. A successful command results from the actions of a chain of agents, each of whom 'translates' it in accordance with his/her own projects. In this model, the faithful transmission of a command is a rarity (and if it occurs, it requires explanation). People in the chain act in different ways to modify, ignore, add to, or appropriate the command. In the first model what happens is transmission; what happens in the second model is translation.

For our present purpose we propose to treat the impact of ideas, values, and knowledge in the same way as Latour treats commands. Some commands in social work are literally that, mandated by legislation; in fact, a lot of work in social services departments is made up of the attempt by workers to 'translate' legislation into practice. Other 'commands', which are in relevant academic literature, in social work teaching, in social work principles, and in social work policy statements, are not mandatory and are therefore much weaker in their impact or their degree of penetration than legislative 'commands'. In these instances the influence is more subtle than that of a command, not least because any individual is subject to a unique set of influences, some of which constitute shared representations while others do not. When making policy, managers and administrators use a combination of ideas, personal knowledge, research evidence, previous experience, or practice wisdom. In my view, most workers and managers in the field currently hold to the diffusion model of the process of the influence of ideas and commands. In this chapter I shall examine the extent to which the translation model is appropriate, by using a single policy example.

The arguments are limited in a number of ways. Theoretical writings in the sociology of knowledge are usually about the relationship between systems of thought and their particular socio-cultural environment. They are less frequently *used*, as they are here, in a consideration of one very specific product of the thought-system. If the attempt fails it may be due to the inappropriateness of the chosen method.

I am not concerned with tracing a 'main' origin or foundation of the policy, which would be a 'difficult and fruitless' endeavour (Jones and Fowles 1984) and would possibly be construed as 'idealist' by some writers (Mepham and Ruben 1979). 'Idealism' in this context means that one assumes one has explained an event, such as this policy, when one has traced it to an agent, for instance the local authority (implementing legislation).

Nor am I concerned with broad philosophical questions, such as 'how can we tell that what we claim to know is genuine knowledge?', or with an attempt to demonstrate that knowledge has a 'foundation'. Williams (1977) has argued that there is in any event no need for a foundational justification of knowledge, and he offers a philosopher's view of the subject which brings him close to the position of 'sociologist of knowledge', when he says:

> Instead of the picture of knowledge as an edifice resting on fixed and immutable foundations, I want to offer the picture of human knowledge as an evolving social phenomenon. At any time, we will have a solid core of unquestioned perceptual reports, and the like, against which more marginal and less certain beliefs can be checked. But even this solid core may come in for drastic revision in the interests of deeper insight or theoretical advance. Any belief can be questioned, though not all at once. In this way, the pursuit of empirical knowledge can be seen as a *rational* pursuit not because empirical knowledge rests on a foundation but because . . . it is a self-correcting enterprise.
>
> (Williams 1977: 180)

An interesting way of considering the material interest in this chapter would have been to look at it as an example of Weberian 'rationality' at work. According to Habermas, the fourth stage in Weber's idea of practical rationality is 'action which is guided by generalised value-principles', a description applicable to the kind of action considered here.

Before considering various social influences on the policy, we will describe the extent to which the policy is reflected elsewhere in current social work thinking. Further examples of the empirical evidence concerning the influence of size on aspects of residential care will be reviewed. From the social work literature, in particular that on residential care, and from policy statements in the field, it is clear that one or two writers have had enormous influence. Their views will be examined, and the extent to which their writing tends to embody the diffusion or translation model will be considered.

THE MATERIAL INTEREST

The social services department policy which is the primary material interest of this chapter is one example of many similar policy statements, found in social services documents, health service and central government statements, as well as in the wider literature. A number of the examples come from the field of mental handicap. Several questions arise in this regard. The first is the extent to which policies generated in mental handicap are applicable more widely; the second is whether, and if so why, policy changes have been proposed more frequently, consistently, or with greater urgency in the mental handicap field, than in relation to other client groups. Both of these questions are worthy of attention in their own right, but there is no scope here to consider either of them in any detail.

Among the policy documents which make statements very similar to the one in the material example is the All Wales Strategy for the development of services for mentally handicapped people. This document argues the case for care in ordinary homes, not purpose-built hostels. The report of the All Wales Advisory Panel on the development of services for mentally handicapped people, *A Home of Their Choice* (Welsh Office 1986), says that 'normally groups of no more than four or five should be accommodated, and even in special circumstances determined by local need, groups should never be more than six' (para 2.5.7).

Ward (1984) makes similar points less specifically, and the Wagner Report (1988) quotes from the evidence of several agencies which argue for fewer than ten places in residential settings. Evidence about registration practice under the Registered Homes Act (1984) shows continuing disagreement in Wales concerning maximum numbers in residential settings (Vyvyan 1987). Vyvyan says, and Table 8.1 shows, that 'not all authorities appear to have sorted out policies on the maximum size of establishments, and those which have show little agreement'.

Table 8.1 Maximum numbers specified for residential homes in Welsh authorities

Client group	Clwyd	Dyfed	Gwent	Gwynedd	Mid Glam.	Powys	Sth Glam.	West Glam.
Elderly	54	–	36	(homely)	40	50	40	–
Physically handicapped	54	–	36	(homely)	30	50	40	–
Mentally handicapped	12	dom.	–	6	24	12	40	–
Mentally ill	24	–	–	12	24	14	40	–

Source: Vyvyan 1987

The Code of Practice which accompanied the Registered Homes Act, *Home Life*, argues for care to be based on the principles of privacy, autonomy, individuality, esteem, choice, and responsible risk taking; while Wagner's principles were that: care should be personal; there should be choice, continuity, and opportunity for change; and that services should be based on common values. In these publications, and in the social services statement in which the material example occurs, there are considerations other than mere size. Two of the most important of these considerations are that the housing used as residential accommodation should be 'ordinary' and that it should be located in the individual's own community. Ward (1984) reports on the rejection of a 50-room house on the grounds that it was neither 'ordinary' nor 'local'. Wagner says that accommodation should be of a 'domestic size' which, for the National Autistic Society, means too big if it requires the use of something other than 'ordinary domestic' size equipment, such as a fridge.

There are three examples of the translation model at work in these writings.

First, size becomes wedded to a conception of a small 'domestic environment', with the idea that this is best achieved in 'ordinary' housing (never defined) and that this will enhance integration into the community. The fusion of these ideas tends to occur imperceptibly in many policy statements, although the ideas have separate origins which are present in earlier writings and which can be critically examined separately.

Second, there is a strong presumption that the articulation of the values and principles underlying policy makes for a better policy. In fact, the translation of the principles into practice is often left to others, who may have problems when the practical consequences of the principles (as translated into practice) conflict with one or more policy principles. In the material example this arises when the individual chooses to live with seven or eight other people. Although, as we shall see later, a primary purpose of principles and values is to enable policy evaluation to take place, this is rarely done by seeking evidence about the efficacy of the policy and then critically examining the principles or values espoused in the first place. It is far more common to retain the principles and critically examine the 'service'.

In fact, those who have to operate the principles-in-practice are likely to translate them when faced with contradictions, inconsistencies, and other unrealities which make their practice tasks difficult or impossible without such 'rule-bending' behaviour. Freidson points out that:

> Just as they are likely to take liberties with the formal knowledge they learned in school and read about in professional journals, so are they likely to take liberties with the guidelines promulgated by their supervisors and managers.
>
> (Freidson 1986: 217)

Third, there is a strong tendency to wish to avoid the negative effects of institutional living – loss of liberty, loss of autonomy, depersonalisation, low material standards, stigma – which are clearly seen as the antithesis of the aims of the new services: giving residents autonomy, privacy, and choice. There is usually no reference to any potential benefits of institutional living – it is always regarded as a 'last resort' service – and there is little attempt to consider the specific causes of 'institutionalisation'. For some writers the chances of developing 'institutionalisation' are directly associated with the size of the institution; as the size increases so do the chances of its becoming an 'institutionalising' environment. Much of this writing is simply 'anti-institution'. As we shall see from the next section, the writing on the harmful effects of institutional care does not substantiate the case that size is the major contributory factor, but shows that other factors are more important. Nevertheless, the writing has been translated into policy statements on the assumption that size is a major factor.

DIRECT WORK ON THE RELATIONSHIP BETWEEN SIZE, RESIDENT BEHAVIOUR, QUALITY OF CARE, AND COMMUNITY INTEGRATION

There is a considerable amount of work in the field of mental handicap and some in child care. Dalgleish's study (1983) of residential provision for people with a mental handicap in Sheffield included nineteen institutions ranging in size from fourteen to 183 places. This showed that they did not differ in terms of the measures of community involvement used, nor in terms of the management of 'daily events' in the institution, but that smaller institutions were 'more homely'. Hill and Lakin (1986) argue that small size does appear to be related to superior developmental achievement, but the large institutions to which they refer had the least favourable staff:resident ratios. Llandesman and Butterfield (1987) conclude that 'place and size of residence probably are not as important to friendship as are the stability and social characteristics of the environments in which individuals find themselves'.

Balla (1976) concluded that care is more adequate in smaller community-based institutions, especially in those with 'under 100 residents', but he reports considerable variation in the standards of care given in smaller institutions, a finding repeated in other studies and in residential child care (Berry 1975; McCormick *et al.* 1975). King *et al.* (1971) found that there was essentially no relationship between size and the degree to which care practices were individually or institutionally oriented. In only three of the reports of the quality of care cited in the Wagner Report was the size of the institution given in the text. The examples of good practice came from institutions of forty and 103 places, and the examples of bad practice from an institution with twelve places. Edgerton (1975) reported that 'little institutions appear to be no better than the ones from which . . . [residents] . . . came and some are manifestly worse'.

Large institutions may, of course, have much smaller 'living units' within them, and this would contribute to better individualisation possibilities (Baroff 1980). Large institutions are typically built away from centres of population, making community integration, in the sense of the residents going out, more problematic (Balla 1976), but clearly making it more likely that the community may have to come in – for employment, if nothing else. Large institutions may have worse staff:resident ratios, and this, together with the dependency levels of residents, needs to be taken into account in any comparison between small and large institutions.

Wagner reports on several aspects of the question of the size of institutions and the effects of size. Table 8.2 shows the range of size advocated in the evidence to the committee.

Table 8.2 Size of residential establishments advocated in Wagner evidence

Size	Source
6–8	Dyfed SSD
< 10	Association of Directors of Social Services
10–12	Children's Family Trust
10–20	Soroptomists

All those offering evidence agreed that the level of staffing was a crucial factor in the quality of care provided. Christian Concern for Mental Handicap pointed out some of the dangers of being too small, and the financial and staffing implications of small units were raised by several bodies, mostly in the voluntary sector. On the subject of community integration, the National Schizophrenia Fellowship pointed out that 'a house in an ordinary street can be more of a stigmatised ghetto than an open community that provides plenty of interaction with the wider community'.

The issues which Wagner says matter – choice, quality of care, material standards, independence, autonomy, contact with the community, staff:resident ratios, and staff attitudes – are clearly not unrelated to size. But small size *per se* is not the primary determinant of good standards and good practice. Even in the face of substantial evidence to the contrary, people still believe that size is responsible. The same conclusion, that size is not the major factor, occurs in several settings and fields, but it does not appear to be transmitted from one to another. In contrast, the idea that large institutions lead to bad practices is easily transmitted from one field to another. Why this should be the case lies outside our present concerns.

The two writers whose work is most frequently cited in support of the adverse effects of size are Goffman and Wolfensberger. Interestingly, Jones and Fowles do not refer at all to the latter in their book *Ideas on Institutions* (1984), giving, as do most writers (including Wolfensberger), an important place to Goffman. In most policy statements and literature and in practice, pride of place is usually given to Wolfensberger. Jones and Fowles selected writers 'in terms of what they had to say', (which could conceivably have been a reason for excluding Wolfensberger) or in terms of their 'impact on the reading public' (which clearly could not have excluded him, unless the authors meant to exclude human service professionals from the realms of 'the reading public'; they do suggest that 'people who run institutions seldom have much background in sociological theory').

GOFFMAN AND WOLFENSBERGER ON SIZE

It has been said that Goffman (1961) is cited by many and yet examined by few (Ditton 1980), and Jones and Fowles point out that there is little in the way of serious analysis of what he said. What he said about size was precious little. In his definition of a *total institution* as a place of residence and work he simply says that this applies to 'a large number of like-situated individuals'. He describes the 'key fact' of total institutions as the 'handling of many human needs by the bureaucratic organisation of *whole blocks of people*'. He implies that a small number of supervisory staff for a large number of people is part of the essence of a total institution, but dismisses any further consideration ('not here at issue') of which comes first, or what would happen if the ratio of the former to the latter were to be altered.

His main point – the 'central feature' of total institutions – is the 'breakdown of the barriers ordinarily separating those spheres of life normally kept separate; sleep, play and work'. He says that those who eat and sleep at work can hardly sustain a meaningful 'domestic existence' but then admits in a footnote that the Israeli kibbutz is 'an interesting marginal case'. He argues that households and total institutions are incompatible forms of social organisation, because the latter 'suppress a whole circle of actual or potential households'. Clearly this is an exaggeration, since his own example of the kibbutz, some forms of communal living, and even some large institutions with smaller (sometimes called 'family') units within them can permit a 'meaningful' domestic existence, in this limited organisational sense.

This idea of the 'meaningful domestic existence' finds its way directly into Wolfensberger's work (1972), and influences workers in the field (viz., the 'domestic' fridge example). But in the writings which I have reviewed, Goffman's original distinction between work and other contexts is not included. In Wolfensberger's work this question becomes translated in the following way. Wolfensberger wishes to limit *domestic size*, because of the size limits on *the normal family*. He also contends that small domestic units are outward looking and not inward looking (and implicitly that this is a good thing). He is of the opinion that 'a person in a large group may find too many of his social needs met *too conveniently* to motivate him to reach out for "normalising socialisation" ' (Wolfensberger 1972).

This passage illustrates some of the difficulties involved in translating Goffman's original conception into one involving 'culturally normative' behaviours and experiences. Do members of large families find their conducive social experiences more conveniently within the family? If they do, is this a good thing or a bad thing? Is the experience of the social life of a community achieved only by 'outward-looking' families? Are not small families at risk of becoming isolated from the community? Wolfensberger believes that the size of residential establishments is partly determined by the number of residents that 'the surrounding community can readily "absorb" in terms of recreation, transportation, shopping, socialisation, and tolerance of perceived deviancy' (Wolfensberger 1972).

(Of course it is not abnormal for communities to resist increases in population where this threat comes from non-deviant sources, or even where it is expected to follow from some other form of development, perhaps industrial; nor is it unusual for some areas to encourage these changes, usually in the economic interests of an area.) Wolfensberger gives no clear indication of the exact relationship between community levels of tolerance and numbers of deviant individuals within the community, nor of the mechanisms which might be in operation. One has the impression that his views are more unsophisticated than our present understanding of community responses to mental illness (Link *et al.* 1987).

An interesting example of the way in which Wolfensberger's writing has been translated is that, unlike many subsequent writers on normalisation, he clearly recognises that different types (and sizes?) of accommodation will be needed. He says that:

a continuum of living facilities will provide many more options.
. . . The vast majority of chronically and severely impaired persons
. . . are ideal candidates for sheltered community hostel living.
Some require the services of hostels that function much like nursing
homes. . . . In some fields . . . (mental health is one) . . . more
than a dozen types are needed.

(Wolfensberger 1972)

Again, unlike some subsequent writers on normalisation, he makes
the distinction, emphasised by Wagner, between the need for accommodation and the need for support services. He argues that 'a system
of dispersed and specialised residential services works best if it is
supported by an adequate back up system' (Wolfensberger 1972).

He also recognises that, under certain circumstances, the
domiciliary function has to be merged with others, for example when
individuals require major medical services or detention. He is, rightly,
concerned to keep people with similar needs together, to encourage
specialist residential accommodation, and to keep separate people
whose needs are predominantly social, medical, or for detention.

His 'theory' of normalisation is the main theory which informs the
social services document, the evidence to Wagner, and other policy
documents. His theory and the motives of the policy makers are
themselves in turn heavily influenced by a desire to avoid the harmful
effects of institutionalisation, which has been translated into 'anti-
institutionism'. However the size, *per se*, of institutions is not a major
contributory factor in the quality of care, the separation of the
domiciliary function, the nature and extent of support services, or the
degree of community integration. The question of the nature of
beneficial 'community integration' and how it varies with the size and
location of units could usefully be the subject of further empirical
investigation. There is some evidence about this in studies in mental
retardation (Campbell 1971; Rosen 1972; Kushlick 1972), and some
recent work has been published in the mental illness field (Smith and
Giggs 1988). Locally based accommodation was valuable for adults
with mental handicap, if they still had interested relatives. Kushlick
found that the differences in quality of care between hospital services
and small hostels for children with a mental handicap were not directly
associated with being locally based. Of more importance in the development of community services were the number of staff needed to provide
care in a domestic environment and the need for decision-making

powers to be located at 'living-unit' level. One could argue that this last example illustrates the need for freedom to translate policy at the practice level. The benefits to be gained by front-line workers controlling their own budgets could also be seen as an example of the freedom to translate policy into practice.

THE SOCIOLOGY OF KNOWLEDGE AND THE MATERIAL INTEREST

A brief review of social policy theory shows that the concepts of values and of interests are frequently used to explain social influences on the creation of social policy. To what extent do values and interests actually become involved in the translation of the policy into practice? We will look at the present example, but first consider the role of values and interests in a more general sense.

VALUES

Most, if not all, of the policy documents that we have considered contain statements of the values or principles underlying the policy. Commonly they chastise service providers (particularly in the health service) who do not make their values explicit. The material document states that services should be based on 'explicit values generated by the principle of normalisation' (translated from principles into values) and 'normalisation can help create a vision of a service which appeals to fundamental human values'. Services can be evaluated by judging the extent to which they espouse these principles in practice. This process is universally seen as unproblematic; there is no mention of any possible difficulties which may arise because of conflicting or self-contradictory principles, nor any prediction of problems in their translation into practice.

Hindess has argued that:

> to analyse social policies solely in terms of the realisation of some general principle is to ignore the unavoidable complexity . . . of . . . social conditions and of attempts to change them. Principles do indeed play a part in political life, but they do so always in conjunction with a variety of other concerns, *interests* and objectives. . . . Some of these conditions may well be changeable as a result of political action, but many have to be regarded as more or less

174

fixed in the short term. It makes no sense to analyse societies, or parts of them, in terms of the realisation of general principles.

(Hindess 1987)

He goes on to say that the evaluation of a social policy is a complex matter in which considerations of equity or freedom or individual liberty (or normalisation) are only one element. We will look at some of these other elements in a moment.

The term 'value' is used in a loose and fluctuating way in policy statements. Rescher (1969) asks how we could detect when a value is in operation in any situation. There are two ways. First, the value may be taken into account in a rationalisation (defence, justification, recommendation, or critique) of aspects of a way of life. Second, it may be manifest in overt action. Rescher says that a value 'represents a slogan capable of providing for the rationalisation of action by encapsulating a positive attitude towards a purportedly beneficial state of affairs' (1969).

So the fundamental role of a person's values is, not surprisingly, to underwrite the evaluation of his actions (justifying the translation of policy into particular actions), to support 'practical reasoning'. In the case of the material policy a 'purportedly beneficial state of affairs exists' which involves a better quality of life for the residents in the accommodation. The need to restrict the number of places is purported to be consistent with this 'beneficial state of affairs' and the values which derive from the normalisation principle 'underwrite the evaluation of the policy' and support the 'practical reasoning' behind it. In fact, as we have seen, not only have the principles of normalisation themselves been translated from Wolfensberger's original conception, the beneficial state of affairs which is purported to exist is itself a translation of the evidence from practice and research.

Other problems arise in the translation of the policy into practice. To take one concrete example, the policy will be judged a success in so far as it manages to increase the active participation of residents in community settings. It runs into one of Hindess's 'other concerns' when the resident does not wish to have such contact but wishes to minimise social contacts because he suffers from schizophrenia and knows that such contacts are overstimulating and likely to lead to the return of symptoms. Another such concern is that the policy wishes for the people's voice to be heard, but effectively removes from the people any choice between different types of housing or of household.

Rescher suggests that, because values and their realisation are bound up with a *vision* of a *good life* (for self or others), values are fundamentally ideological in character. In terms of Mannheim's distinction one might legitimately consider them utopian rather than ideological because they orient conduct towards elements which the present situation does not contain.

INTERESTS

Hindess points out that *interests* are used to provide justification for actions said to be performed on behalf of others. They may be used to justify or evaluate some aspect of policy; consequently

> they belong to that broad class of entities that have been supposed, by social scientists and others, to provide actors with *ends*, and therefore with reasons for action. Other members of that class include values, preferences, wants, fears, dislikes, desires, needs, habits and impulses.
>
> (Hindess 1986b)

In other words, the 'stuff' of social work.

Hindess feels that most people would follow Weber in suggesting that an actor's values are, or may be, freely chosen, but no one would suggest that interests are a matter of choice in the same sense.

Barnes (1977) regards the development of knowledge as a function of two great interests: an interest in prediction and control, and an interest in rationalisation and persuasion. Knowledge generated under the auspices of the second is 'ideologically determined' but not necessarily false. The same point can be made even if one uses the term 'determined by utopian motives'; this does not automatically confer truth or falsehood upon the ideas in question.

Barnes argues that what is central to the sociology of knowledge is the investigation of the processes whereby knowledge is generated and sustained in the light of particular situated *interests*, by the use of available cultural resources. We do not, he says, 'impute beliefs on the grounds of social location, but rather on the basis of the "functioning" of beliefs in the life of sections of society which claim and utilise them' (Barnes 1977).

So, to say that the policy is in the *interests* of the patients, the social workers, or the managers is to say that these people would benefit from its implementation, and, moreover, would be likely to translate a policy so that it is more consistent with these interests. What the actor's interests are in any case is open to dispute.

One of the major interests is in the manipulation, prediction, and control of the environment. The relationship between knowledge and the real world is a process in which knowledge affects *activity*:

> knowledge is related to activity which consists precisely in men attempting to manipulate, predict and control the real world in which they exist. . . . [It] arises out of our encounters with reality and is continually subject to feedback correction from these encounters, as failures of prediction and control occur. . . . It is the utility of certain types of knowledge in furthering a wide range of objectives, which results in their widespread use and sustains their credibility as knowledge.
>
> (Barnes 1977: 10)

In the material example, one can see that the use of the principle of normalisation is furthering a range of objectives, resulting in widespread use, which is *itself* sustaining the credibility of the principle. Wolfensberger himself, in accounting for his failure to change the name (which he never liked), uses the fact that the idea had gained its *own momentum* through widespread use (1988a). The same point could be made about the 'anti-institutional' position.

The principle has been subject to feedback correction and hence to major revision (Wolfensberger 1988a). One could postulate that one of the reasons why the principle has been the subject of major revisions and various statements of dissociation or refinement (Mansell *et al.* 1987; Brown and Alcoe 1987) is that it does not give an adequate level of prediction and control in practice. In other words, it is difficult to operate. This in turn may be related to its fundamentally utopian thinking, which sets objectives which are unachievable in the short term, because of the other constraints on their achievement, identified by Hindess. It starts from the proposition that handicaps and disabilities *should not be handicapping and disabling* and attempts to move the present realities of services towards this view.

Utopian views, instead of corresponding strictly to the environment, arise in opposition to prevailing belief structures and stress varying degrees of 'wish fulfilment'. One might ask whether the changes from normalisation to social role valorisation (SRV) represent a shift from more utopian to more ideological thinking. However, one can already detect in the use of SRV by practitioners translations similar to those which led some practitioners to understand normalisation as regarding people with handicaps as 'normal'. Valorisation – the conferring of value on to people – is being interpreted in policy statements and elsewhere as 'valuing' individuals (equally; in terms of their inherent capacities, etc.). Brown and Alcoe (1987) speak of 'people [whom] society values', and of a value-based training which will ensure the 'just and appropriate application of practical skills'. (An appeal to the values of social justice, but in effect enhancing the ability of the workers' prediction, control, and manipulation of the client.)

This view is specifically ruled out by Wolfensberger who says:

we can only speak in terms of the valorisation of the *role* of a person. When we speak of 'valuing' the person we step outside a theoretical framework that is profoundly anchored to empiricism, and into the realm of 'supra-natural' value systems (or utopian thinking?).

(Wolfensberger 1988b)

How do the various values and interests at work in relation to the size of residential institutions affect the translation of the policy into practice? There are many possibilities but there is space here only for a consideration of some of the more obvious ones. In the material example there are professional interests, economic interests, and administrative or bureaucratic interests, among others.

For example, in terms of professional interests, the use of small facilities means that there will have to be a lot of them, and more support staff will be needed. The same policy statement translates the need for more support into a case for a further eighty-eight social workers. This increases the establishment of the welfare bureaucracy and enhances prediction and control. In economic terms the provision of a large number of small local authority units and the associated revenue costs add weight to the argument for the transfer of funds from the health authority, and, if this transfer takes place, it releases other local authority resources for spending on other client groups. The policy is translated into a means for achieving additional revenue for client groups which have a higher priority.

Also in economic terms, the interests of the voluntary organisations are not served by the policy for smaller units, because of the cost implications. In Table 8.2 it is the statutory authority which proposes the smaller numbers, and the voluntary bodies (which already operate large units) who favour the larger sizes.

Another, perhaps more doubtful argument is that by selecting small units, which are more costly and more difficult to achieve, often because health and voluntary bodies are happier to set up units which are slightly larger, the local authority delays *any* policy implementation. This has the effect of saving local authority investment of time and money in these schemes, enabling money to be spent elsewhere, and saving on the future costs incurred by residents in the community who are encouraged to make use of existing local authority facilities in use by this or another client group. Finally, the difficulty of implementation has political effects, in that it can be used by local politicians to blame central politicians for the failure to produce sufficient resources for policy implementation. The policy is translated into an effective argument against central government.

A clear interest in normalisation is the maintenance of family-like accommodation. Anything which strays away from the idea of domestic existence in a four-person household is deviating from culturally accepted patterns. The policy is appropriated by those who have an interest in sustaining this conception of 'family life'.

Returning to professional interests, one of the effects of the policy is to add weight to the argument for social services control of the arena of community care for mentally ill people. This contributes to a professional anti-medical ethos. A conflicting interest which might also sustain the idea that the policy is worthwhile arises from the desire of some workers to de-professionalise welfare services. They wish to enhance the care of people in the community through voluntary or natural care networks – a view consistent with central political interests.

Wolfensberger confirms that this is one of the interests of SRV. He is of the opinion that 'retarded people are likely to be vastly better off if their needs are met outside the structured human service system. Thus, being a "client" ranks much higher among the things that are now "dangerous" to mentally retarded people' (Wolfensberger 1988a).

An associated reason for the desire to eliminate their need for a structured welfare system is the fate of the present economic system. He goes on:

> the true – though hidden – major function (of the human service system) is to fuel the economy by employing workers displaced out of agriculture, manufacture and similar primary production work . . . it is in human service where the jobs are and increasingly will be until the present economic model collapses – as it inevitably must.
>
> (Wolfensberger 1988a)

So the policy is sustained by an interest in doing away with, or at least reducing the size of, the very agency which is proposing the policy. Wolfensberger is clearly aware of the way in which knowledge is translated across time and space:

> the entire professional and agency structure of mental retardation surrendered itself to falsehoods and atrocities of the eugenic era – the mentally retarded population was viewed as a sinister menace . . . indeed for about half a century it was extremely rare to hear anything good of any sort said by any workers in the field about retarded people. Many of these workers were 'good people' . . . but their minds were benighted by the larger social context.
>
> (Wolfensberger 1988a)

Much, one is tempted to add, in the same way that some workers are benighted by the translation of normalisation.

CONCLUSION

The material interest was a particular piece of local authority policy, to restrict the registration of homes for mentally ill people to no more than six residents. The policy document outlined the principles upon which it was based, and these were heavily influenced by normalisation.

Hindess has said that to use a general principle to attempt to justify a policy is to ignore the complexity of social conditions and the attempts to change them. The thinking behind normalisation could be said to be utopian in character. Barnes suggests that the main interests at work in the creation and support of knowledge are rationalisation, prediction, and control. Rescher also suggests that values are used to rationalise and defend actions. Both writers see the importance of the testing of knowledge in practice and its modification in the light of feedback. Latour suggests that there are two models of the process by which commands are carried out in practice by a chain of actors, the diffusion model and the translation model.

We have examined the policy in question from the point of view of the translation of ideas and values into practice. Several different aspects of translation have been identified. The translation of policy into practice is influenced by values and interests, and by what Freidson calls the 'primacy of experience over theoretical knowledge'. Empirical findings and academic writings are amended when used in the creation of policy and in practice. There are various ways in which the actors in the chain of events amend the original material. Latour gives us a number of possible methods of translation: appropriation; modification; deflection; betrayal; or simply letting it drop!

In the example given here one might argue that selective inattention plays a part, but whether this or the other methods of translation can be shown to be systematic is a question for another paper, and empirical testing.

What, then, are the implications of this sociological contribution to the question of size of residential establishments for managers and practitioners?

First, the quality of care in a residential environment is almost certainly not a feature of size alone. Managers and workers who are concerned to monitor and improve the quality of residential care will be better (more effectively and efficiently) employed in attending to the nature of the relationships between residents, staff, and the wider community.

Second, the quality of the experience of a user of residential services will be enhanced in so far as the individual has real choice between alternative resources. The main problem for managers and practitioners is to ensure that the choice is a genuine one, and that it is not ignored simply because it is not in accordance with the values and interests of the organisation. An additional difficulty for managers is making a real choice available, while at the same time not producing inefficient services which are sometimes underused. To put the same dilemma more positively, they have to learn to justify the provision of a wider range of flexible facilities than is strictly necessary in terms of the ratio of those in need to 'places available'.

Finally, the sociological literature, and some social policy writing, would suggest that the quality of the residential experience is improved for the user when the worker in that setting is also given greater choice and responsibility. In other words, the further down the line decisions are made (or the greater amount of freedom there is for front-line workers to translate policy into practice) the better the quality of the experience for all concerned. A wider implication, perhaps not justified by the discussion in this chapter, is that better services require greater responsiveness to user and front-line worker opinion, or more 'bottom-up' planning.

Chapter Nine

'RACE', GENDER, AND SOCIAL WORK

LENA DOMINELLI

'Race'[1] and gender as sites of oppression and discrimination represent two of the most critical social divisions with which social workers currently have to contend. The handling of the issues encompassed by these divisions is fraught with controversy, making the resolution of the questions they pose difficult. But not confronting the problems encompassed by them results in poor practice which renders a disservice to black people and women. Hence, notwithstanding the obstacles which must be overcome, social work has little option but to respond to the challenge of 'race' and gender if its practice is to enhance the well-being of women and black people.[2]

Two pressing matters which must be addressed are: providing services which respond appropriately to the needs of women and black people; and countering their poor prospects as employees. Attending to these issues requires differential handling, for 'race' and gender occupy dissimilar positions within the profession. For example, their starting points are different. Black people are conspicuous by their absence; while the presence of women makes gender inconspicuous.

Black people are seldom found in positions of power in social work, particularly in the higher decision-making echelons of management or in structures determining resource allocation (Durrant 1989). Posts created for black people under Section 11 of the 1966 Local Government Act and the advent of specialist ethnic minority units staffed mainly by black workers have reinforced their marginalisation by keeping them out of mainstream grades and in provisions more vulnerable to cuts. The low status accorded black workers has contributed to the perception of black people as service users rather than service providers (Devine 1985). Consequently, black workers are often subjected to the indignity of being taken as clients by white workers and white clients in their initial encounters. The quickly masked look of surprise when white people meet black workers in positions of relative authority is also symptomatic of the racism prevalent in social work.

Racism is 'the belief in the inherent superiority of one race over all others and thereby the right to dominance' (Lorde 1984: 115). Racism oppresses black people and is reproduced by and through social relations. It comes in three forms: cultural, institutional, and personal (Bromley and Longino 1972). Cultural racism is reflected in the values, beliefs, and ideas endorsing the supremacy of white culture. It operates as the thread stitching institutional and personal racism together. Institutional racism is enshrined in public power and authority as the customary routines which ration power and resources by excluding groups defined as racially inferior. It draws upon personal racism for its implementation. Personal racism consists of those attitudes and behaviours which result in a negative prejudgement of racial groups. Without institutional backing, personal racism rests at the level of individual prejudice (Dominelli 1988).

Black people are rarely evident as users of services connected with the positive delivery of provisions, for example, home helps. As clients, they are over-represented in arenas linked to the more controlling and punitive aspects of service delivery such as prisons and stigmatised provisions in residential establishments (Durrant 1989). The pathologising of black people, their lifestyles, cultures, traditions, and relationships accounts for this trend to a large extent (Dominelli 1988). The position of black people in social work, both as clients and as workers, is therefore defined by racist dynamics.

Gender issues have also become marginalised in social work. The assumption is that gender issues are addressed by virtue of the presence of a predominantly female work-force and clientele. The fact that women form the majority in these roles obscures their location in low-status jobs confronting issues derived from direct contact with clients, while men occupy crucial decision-making posts dealing with resource allocation and management (Howe 1986; Coyle and Skinner 1988), and the reinforcement of traditional gender roles through social work practice (Brook and Davis 1985; Dominelli and McLeod 1989).

Gender oppression is vested in sexism, or the belief in the inherent superiority of one gender over the other, thus according it the right to subjugate the other (Lorde 1984). Like racism, sexism is the product of social relations which both reproduce and reinforce it. It also exists in three forms, cultural, institutional, and personal. Cultural sexism centres on those values, beliefs, and ideas endorsing male culture, and provides the glue holding institutional and personal sexism together. Institutional sexism consists of routine policies and practices which consign women to inferior positions. It derives its power and authority from being socially sanctioned and is used to pathologise women and hold them responsible for their failure within the system. It draws on personal sexism for its maintenance and reproduction. Personal sexism is made up of those attitudes and behaviours whereby individuals prejudge women and cast them in a negative light.

The advent of large numbers of men in British social work following the Seebohm reorganisation (Howe 1986; Coyle and Skinner 1988) and the imposition of corporate management techniques (Ginsburg 1979) has strengthened professionalism in it. This has raised its status, caused a decline in the number of senior positions held by women and shifted social work's values (Skinner and Robinson 1988). Primary among these shifts has been the concern of managers, usually men, with resource allocation rather than service delivery. Another important aspect of these changes has been the replacement of 'expressive' values with 'instrumentalist' ones. Expressive values are connected with caring, an activity socially ascribed to women and accorded low status. Instrumentalist values are given high status and held by men (Parsons 1954). These are usually linked to action, particularly the allocation of resources and the husbanding of organisational personnel.

The supremacy of instrumentalist values in social work has facilitated a process of de-feminisation (Dressel 1984) leading to tighter definitions of the social work task and a reduction in workers' autonomy in decision making regarding their work with individual clients. Managerial directives and inadequate resourcing have exacerbated this process. It has also: heightened the controlling elements of social work; become the means whereby the proletarianisation of social work is enhanced (Joyce et al. 1988); and augmented men's control over women's labour (Hearn 1982). The outcome of these changes is most evident in the ministerial and managerial guidance governing the handling of child abuse and neglect. Men, often appointed for their managerial expertise rather than their knowledge of social work practice, create the procedures and guidelines governing such intervention, while women implement them (Skinner and Robinson 1988).

The ascendancy of male values in social work is reinforced through gendered power relations and dynamics which undervalue women's experience and ensure that women get progressively squeezed out of management. Gender bias leads to a negative evaluation of women's skills and qualifications, deeming them irrelevant to the management of resources and people, while favouring men's. This interpretation of women's capabilities relegates their skills of managing caseloads and family matters to the realms of irrelevance despite their being a form of managerial experience (Skinner and Robinson 1988). Its enactment becomes prejudicial to women's employment in senior positions when women appear before interviewing panels which assess applicants on the basis of values, belief systems, and managerial traditions already in place. This has been dubbed the 'cloning' theory of management (WMDG 1982). Adhering to this theory enables employers to ignore the unattractiveness of managerial positions to women. Instead of questioning the appropriateness of the current system of management, the lack of career structures which would enable women to rise to senior positions while maintaining their contact with clients, and the dynamics of men replacing women previously in management posts, employers pathologise women for their lack of drive.

Similar problems hold for black people who also fail to meet the expectations of those on selection boards. They are deemed unsuitable for managerial posts for actively rejecting racism and being community oriented (Rooney 1987). Black people are further marginalised in the work-place in so far as they are appointed at managerial level in specialist units outside mainstream career grades, thus making it difficult for the majority of them to proceed up the social services managerial ladder.

Black women are in a different position from white women because they experience their subjugation on both 'race' and gender lines. They find fewer employment opportunities available to them (Bruegel 1989), and can usually be found in the lowest paid jobs servicing other professionals or locked into the low-status residential sector. As Howe says:

> there is a strong suspicion . . . that black women, when employed at all, are highly likely to be working with old people and the disabled, particularly as manual workers in jobs such as care assistants and domestic labour in residential homes, home-helps out in the community and cleaners in the local area teams.
>
> (Howe 1986: 25)

In other words, work with low-status client groups as well as low-status work is the lot meted out to black women.

As clients, black women seldom receive services specifically geared to their needs (Mama 1989). For example, black women leaving violent men find that in refuges offering them succour white women subject them to racist abuse (Guru 1987). Refuges catering specifically for the needs of black women are few. In 1986, only four women's refuges in London were specifically for Asian women (GLC-WEG 1986). Such provisions have been cut during the post-Greater London Council era (Mama 1989). Black women's contact with social services leaves much to be desired. They are usually at the receiving end of a system which pathologises them, passes negative judgements on their child care activities, and splits their families (Carby 1982; Dominelli 1988; Wilson 1986).

The stratification of the work-force and service delivery on both 'race' and gender axes has resulted in social work being a site reproducing and reinforcing racist and sexist relations, despite its commitment to providing for people's welfare. How can a sociological analysis informed by an anti-racist feminist perspective help us understand the failure of social work to promote the well-being of women and black people and their relegation to low-status jobs? This chapter examines this question by focusing on 'race' and gender in social work,[3] the roles women and black people occupy in it, and the contribution women and black people have made to the welfare enterprise. Hopefully, this analysis will enable us to understand better the management of the tension between care and control in social work and how the lives of women and black people are affected by it.

FEMINIST SOCIOLOGY: AN ANTI-RACIST FEMINIST PERSPECTIVE

Feminist sociology is a developing subject drawing on the contribution of feminist writing in a variety of disciplines including philosophy, politics, education, and economics. The analysis developed in this paper is marked by features which are typical of theoretical thought still in the making. Its application to practice is also limited by relying on work engaging with the process of creating new forms of intervention consistent with its theoretical analysis. Fortunately, feminists have undertaken sufficient work in the welfare arena for a sizeable pool of material relevant to the purposes of this chapter to exist. The particular sociological approach used is an anti-racist feminist one. This aims to integrate anti-racist and feminist perspectives on the theoretical level and apply them to social work policies and practice.

This approach focuses overtly on the social relations through which 'race' and gender are articulated and mediated. Concentrating on these two social divisions also brings into relief other social divisions which interact with them, including class, age, sexual orientation, and disability. Moreover, since feminist and anti-racist perspectives are concerned with changing existing social relations so as to eradicate the oppression of women (Gordon 1976) and black people (Gilroy 1987) respectively, an anti-racist feminist approach is also committed to challenging the *status quo* and replacing it with one embodying non-oppressive egalitarian relationship between women and men regardless of their 'race', age, disability, or other social division. This commitment to ending oppression also orients an anti-racist feminist perspective in the direction of improving the welfare of all.

Thus, it takes a moral position which directly aims at promoting everyone's well-being rather than endorsing mechanisms excluding people from eligibility. As Mama puts it:

> [existing] public services were never intended to reach particular groups of the public . . . . The 'deserving' and 'reputable' groups earmarked for good welfare services and provisions exclude women who are not in traditional nuclear families and Black people.
>
> (Mama 1989: 34–5)

An anti-racist feminist perspective does not overlook the scarcity of social resources. But it demands that equality should permeate their formation and distribution. This requires changing the current allocation system, making the basis of distribution visible, using resources efficiently and empowering users.

Fostering people's well-being from this perspective neither ignores social divisions as happens in orthodox sociological analyses, nor promotes an additive approach in which different forms of oppression are placed on a hierarchy of ascribed importance at the points at which they come into being or are dismantled. Unlike Marxist perspectives, an anti-racist feminist one does not condone a hierarchy of oppression subordinating gender inequality to class (see Offe 1984) or race (see Robinson 1983). Consequently, black women would not be asked to prioritise dealing with classism and racism before engaging in eliminating the injustice arising from sexism. Rather, recognising that as *black women* they would be experiencing class, 'race', and gender-based inequality simultaneously, they would be encouraged to undertake action which tackles the three together. Adopting this approach may well cause black women to oppose activities antithetical to their interests, including those initiated by black men. This has happened, for example, to Women Against Fundamentalism.[4]

This approach also recognises that social divisions interact with each other and come into play simultaneously. Thus, an elder black lesbian woman will be identified as an individual whose experience reflects her being subjected to oppression emanating from each of these divisions, all at the same time. People relate to her as an elder black lesbian woman without giving one social division precedence over the others. As her experience is tempered by the simultaneous impact of ageism, racism, heterosexism, and sexism, she requires all four of these divisions to be addressed together for her welfare needs to be fully met. This principle holds for any other social division impinging on her.

An anti-racist feminist analysis accepts the political nature of the social work enterprise and is informed by the idea that both employment in social work and its practice are racially and sexually structured (Mama 1989; Adams 1989). Acknowledging that the economy is organised according to a sexist and racist division of labour, it places both 'race' and gender on the social work agenda and tries to disentangle the politics responsible for subordinating the interests of women and black people. It also examines their position and explains why they do so badly in it, and elaborates on the dominance of certain forms of policy and practice.

Moreover, an anti-racist feminist analysis places individuals in their social context. In doing so, it makes sense of individuals as both the products of the social forces which operate on them and as people who can influence the social relations in which they participate. Thus, neither women nor black people are deemed passive victims who have things done to them by others. Instead, they are presented as active beings who form their own history as well as have it formed for them. Whether or not they individually resist their position, their lives evolve in the context of struggles against conditions constraining the choices open to them. Despite individual objectives, their efforts towards equality may fail and contribute towards their continued oppression. This happens when women social workers enforce traditional domesticity on women clients (Hudson 1985) who may have originally sought social work intervention in the hope of gaining allies in developing alternative lifestyles. For example, a lesbian mother seeking custody of her child finds that the woman social worker has recommended the heterosexual father (Hanscombe and Forster 1982); a black social worker supports white colleagues' rejection of a black family for fostering black children because they adhere to traditional lifestyles. An anti-racist feminist approach does not presume that the oppressed person is always right. But it does argue that decisions should not simply reinforce dominant stereotypes. Therefore, it stands against the uncritical implementation of conservative approaches which disregard the damage traditional moralism imposes on women because their main concerns are controlling women and maintaining social stability (Glazer 1988). In pressing for the recognition of a diversity of family forms, anti-racist feminism highlights its attempts to avoid the dualism characterising orthodox analyses and practice. Dualism dichotomises the world by positing an artificial division between the private and public domains. This penalises women and ignores the interconnected nature of social relations and interdependency between people (Stanko 1985).

For example, traditional intervention encourages women to remain with violent partners by making them feel responsible for their plight and stigmatising them for striking out on their own (Binney *et al.* 1981; Mama 1989). An anti-racist feminist social worker draws strength and insights from her own experience of oppression to empower women, develop their emotional resources, link private troubles with the social forces affecting their situations, and offer practical support without undermining their choice of single parenthood. She would inform women of resources such as Women's Aid refuges which provide temporary shelter and put them in touch with other women who have undergone similar experiences. Living together and talking about their lives enables women to attribute responsibility for the violence perpetrated against them to the men who beat them, to castigate a system which values women so slightly, and fosters the development of their own confidence. Such interaction enables women to discover for themselves and by the examples of others the viability of alternative lifestyles.

The experience of collective support makes visible the interdependence structuring all social relations, including those shared with violent men, and promotes a belief in the value of the contributions women make in facilitating social intercourse and the legitimacy of their demands for personal fulfilment. In meeting the needs of black women leaving violent partners, anti-racist feminist social workers

189

address the issue of racism alongside that of sexism (Mama 1989). This includes putting black women in contact with other black women similarly placed and acknowledging the burden racism imposes on both refuge life and single parenthood. Racism also restricts other choices available to them, particularly those regarding employment and housing (Mama 1989).

All these considerations require that an anti-racist feminist perspective goes beyond a simple concern with discrimination. Discrimination is about women and black people's limited access to power and resources. To an anti-racist feminist, anti-discrimination measures are oriented towards increasing the access of disadvantaged groups to social resources by merely adapting their responses and making them more sensitive to the needs of women and black workers rather than by challenging existing social relations. Hence, these must be transcended by anti-racist feminist initiatives fostering equality and justice (Durrant 1989).

Summing up, an anti-racist feminist perspective has advantages over other perspectives because it places 'race' and gender on the social work agenda simultaneously. It does not prioritise forms of oppression, according one dominance over the others. And it provides prefigurative forms of practice which can be used to develop further innovative responses in eliminating the oppression of women and black people and ensuring that social work meets their needs.

THE WORKING ENVIRONMENT: THE POSITION OF WOMEN AND BLACK PEOPLE

Our analysis presents a bleak picture for women and black people employed in social work. National government statistics have only recently focused on gender, while a breakdown including 'race' remains outstanding.[5] Thus, national data are primarily about white men. According to the DHSS (1977), approximately two-thirds of social services employees are women and one-third men, thus confirming that social work is predominantly a female occupation. However, these global statistics obscure both a vertical and horizontal sexual segregation in the division of labour which works to the advantage of men (Walton 1975; Howe 1986; Skinner and Robinson 1988). For while women dominate on the lower rungs of the employment ladder such as the basic grades in field social work, men have commandeered the top positions in management including the directorships. While two-thirds of field social workers in social services departments are women, they occupy only 7 per cent of directors' posts (DHSS 1977). The position of black people is particularly appalling. In late-1989, only one black man remained as director of a social services department. Previously, there had been up to five. No black woman has yet been appointed at this level. Although there is a paucity of data about their position and a number of methodological debates surrounding the accuracy of the information collected for black women (see Bruegel 1989), the London Living Standards Survey reveals that they are not only bottom of the heap, but their position relative to black men and white women has progressively deteriorated in recent years (LLSS 1986). This holds despite black women's greater involvement in full-time work and younger age profile (Bruegel 1989; Mama 1989).

Age adversely affects women. While diminishing slightly as one progresses up the career ladder, the proportion of women over 40 exceeds that of men for all grades from the social work assistant upwards. Among basic grade social workers, 35 per cent of women are over 40 compared to 27 per cent of men (DHSS 1977). These statistics reveal nothing regarding black women's position. This age distribution may be the outcome of white women having career breaks to raise children, but the consistency of the pattern at all levels suggests something else is also operating here. Though both black and white women are handicapped by the lack of easily accessible, publicly funded child care facilities, black women are unlikely to take career breaks for child rearing. Their economic circumstances compel them into employment while their children are small (Mama 1989).

Women employees are also held back by employers taking longer to recognise their achievements and acknowledge these through promotion (Popplestone 1980). In other words, women are not readily considered management material, whether they are black or white. Interestingly, the main hurdles occur at middle management level – the point providing training for senior positions (Skinner and Robinson 1988). Additional explanations accounting for white women's poor showing in managerial grades include: women are less likely than men to apply for management posts, interviewing panels prefer men who fit the culture of the enterprise more readily, and women need superior qualifications to compete effectively with men (Popplestone 1980). Skinner and Robinson's (1988) investigations have revealed that women genuinely resist applying for jobs that are remote, alienating, and antithetical to clients' interests. They prefer to continue working with clients in jobs for which they are over-qualified rather than manage people and resources in bureaucratic and impersonal ways (Durrant 1989).

A further differentiation between men and women is revealed when the statistics for field services are compared with those for residential services. Again, white men are over-represented in the managerial grades, but this occurs *to a lesser extent than in the field services*. While 30 per cent of care assistants in children's homes are men, men comprise 40 per cent of the heads of such homes. The corresponding figures are 25 per cent and 52 per cent respectively for hostels for the mentally infirm and handicapped and 14 per cent and 26 per cent respectively for older people's homes (DHSS 1977). This highlights another crucial feature in the sexual segregation of labour: white women do better in areas which are more clearly seen as women's work. This suggests the residential sector is no more than a stepping-stone towards better career prospects in the field sector for white men, while white women are more likely to stay there. It also indicates a hierarchy in the value ascribed to working with different groups. White men are more likely to be located in prestigious child care work than in residential care for older people (Howe 1986). The low status accorded residential work facilitates the employment of black people in this sector. Although they usually occupy its lowest positions, it provides a site for black men, and, exceptionally, black women, to acquire managerial experience (see Durrant 1989).

The structural pitfalls awaiting women managers also deter them from entering management (Skinner and Robinson 1988). Although the mass of women do not expect promotion (Howe 1986), those reaching senior positions are expected to perform to higher standards than men (Skinner and Robinson 1988). Their performance on the job is subjected to constant scrutiny and assessment. This places additional pressure on them to perform according to dominant stereotypes and expectations (Dominelli 1983). Durrant expresses it thus:

> Local authorities don't encourage creativity . . . . You are expected to be a bureaucratic animal, worrying about budgets and the elected members' agenda.
>
> (Durrant 1989: 24–5).

Durrant was the first black woman to reach assistant directorship level in social services, but she left to give expression to her creativity as a manager in an autonomous black organisation.

Additionally, other women expect women managers to change the climate at work by promoting the interests of women. Women do not have similar expectations of male management (WMDG 1982). Women managers are more likely to be working in isolation because of the lack of other women in equivalent ranks. With all this on their shoulders more people notice women's failure (Dominelli 1983). Women reaching these levels are continually negotiating a tension between adhering to organisational norms and fostering improvements in women's position. Hence, women are justifiably wary of embarking on the lonely managerial road (WMDG 1982).

The probation service offers a similarly depressing picture. Black people are disproportionately represented in penal establishments (Home Office 1986a) and seldom find services geared to their specific needs. They rarely (2.5 per cent) feature as employees (Home Office 1988). Most of these are black men at field officer grade (Taylor 1981; Dominelli 1983; Home Office 1988). Many black women work as unpaid volunteers doing translation work. Although white men and women are more equally represented at field officer grade (57 per cent and 43 per cent respectively), this balance has been eroded at the higher reaches of management. Only 9 per cent of chief probation officers were white women (NAPO 1984). Black people have yet to reach this level.

WOMEN AND BLACK PEOPLE AS PRACTITIONERS

An anti-racist feminist perspective draws on the practical experiences of women and black people in changing the circumstances of their lives. This includes learning about new forms of practice from the various campaigns and networks feminists have established as well as from community initiatives developed by black people.

As practitioners, women and black people hold contradictory positions. While they are both oppressed by the system, they can also reinforce the oppression of others through it. This statement is controversial. Radical feminists maintain that women cannot oppress other women because gender oppression relies on men exercising power over women (Dreifus 1973). Similarly, black activists argue that racism is about white people using their power to dominate black people; black people in a position of powerlessness cannot subject others to racial oppression (Robinson 1983). Both these positions reduce power to something which is exercised as a result of biological attributes. Not only is this a form of biological determinism which is unacceptable because it reduces human beings to victim status and therefore incapable of creating their own history, but it also ignores the role women and black people have in both resisting their subordination and reinforcing it through socialisation processes, internalising dominant ideologies, and implementing them in practice. Women and black people do not simply internalise and uphold ideologies of subordination, they also reject and struggle against them (Gilroy 1987), and in doing so create their own history which can challenge the dominant trends and, in some instances, undermine them, for example, feminism, black radicalism.

Additionally, biological determinist positions undervalue those forms of struggle which constitute part of the day-to-day reality of women and black people who are not politically active, but who reject their subordinate status none the less, as does the woman feigning a headache to avoid having sex and a confrontation with her partner for rejecting his advances (Hite 1976); a black woman who cleans a white family's home, knowing she has accepted this job as nothing else was available not because this was all she was fit to do (Morrison 1986); a black man who subordinates white people in his mind while being enraged at being subordinated by them (see, e.g., Wright 1968). Such acts of quiet rebellion will alter neither individual positions nor those of others in similar situations. To achieve this, their perpetrators would have to organise with other women and men sharing a desire to resist the present configuration of relationships and overtly initiate the task of changing them. But these examples do indicate that even women and black people appearing to endorse their predicament do not merely accept their fate. Within their own resources, they are trying to shape their own destiny.

The dynamics of being active creators of their history also apply to social work professionals. They can exert power as well as be constrained by it in their work with clients (Compton and Galaway 1975; Davies 1985). They can exercise power over them when: monitoring behaviour as in supervising offenders; implementing formal statutory provisions such as taking children into care; sectioning mentally ill people; and gatekeeping resources. In their relationships with clients, social workers can act in extremely controlling ways and reinforce both racist and sexist stereotypes. Investigating their practice can illustrate this point.

Case study one: caring for older people: a white family and a white woman social worker[6]

Gladys Jones, aged ninety-one, was referred to social services by her GP as in need of Part III accommodation. She was very frail and could neither cook properly for herself nor clean her house. She had severe arthritis in her legs which greatly limited her mobility. Her daughter Helen lived nearby, but, having her own family to look after and a part-time cleaning job, she could not spend much time with Gladys. Her oldest son, Don, lived in a village five miles away but rarely visited her. Her youngest son had emigrated to Australia.

A woman social worker visited Gladys at home and learnt she did not wish to go into residential accommodation. The social worker was secretly relieved because this was in short supply and her department's policy was to keep people in their homes for as long as possible. Unfortunately, the department lacked the resources to keep Gladys comfortably in the community. For example, despite the small fee payable for home helps, there was a shortage of them for all but the most serious cases. In the social worker's opinion, Gladys was not one of these. She saw the problem as one of marshalling all the resources she could from within Gladys's family. She thus went to see Helen with the intention of getting her to accept responsibility for her mother's welfare. She did not think of contacting Don.

Helen told the social worker she was unable to take major responsibility for her mother's welfare as she had too much on her plate already. She suggested she ask Don. This the social worker did, but was informed he did not get along with his mother and could not offer assistance. The social worker returned to Helen and tried to change her mind, offering her two hours of home help assistance a week to make it easier for her to respond to Gladys's needs. She also promised Gladys a place in a day centre once a week as soon as one became available.

The woman social worker's response in this case reinforces a sexist division of labour orchestrated through familial ties. Her view is that Helen, as the daughter, should assume responsibility for her mother's care. In trying to pursuade Helen to accept this, she is reinforcing sexist stereotypes. Institutional sexism is evident in the department's assumption that women will care for elders in their families and its failure to provide either the appropriate institutional resources or the facilities necessary for society to support people responsibly in the community (Finch 1984). The limited resources at the worker's disposal encourage dependence on sexist stereotypes while undermining her efforts at enforcing them. Without taking gender on as a specific issue neither the social worker nor her department can avoid reinforcing sexism by what they do and don't do. Thus, even economic exigencies have failed to get employer and employee to challenge a division of labour casting women in nurturing roles and excluding men from being drawn into the supportive networks the social worker is seeking to establish.

Case study two: working with black families: a black social worker and a black family

A black woman social worker was asked to investigate a case of suspected child abuse in the Patel family. The Patels had three children, two girls aged six and five and a boy of four. The case had been referred to social services by staff at the nursery five-year-old Djamila attended when she appeared with extensive bruising on her face and arms.

The social worker visited the family and was told the bruising was a result of an accident Djamila had with her tricycle. During her visit the social worker found the mother had been prescribed Depo Provera when her young son was born so that she 'wouldn't get pregnant so easily'. Moeover, she was having the injections regularly without her husband's knowledge because he disapproved of her taking any contraceptive measures. The woman didn't like doing this, but felt she had no other option, and was glad the white male GP had suggested this to her. The social worker knew the health risks attending this course of treatment, the woman did not. However, she decided against informing her of these to avoid endangering the woman's relationship with her husband.

The black social worker in this case is reinforcing both racist and sexist stereotypes. In not informing the woman about the dangers of Depo Provera she is colluding with white people's stereotypes of a rampant sexuality among black women and their use of black women as guinea pigs in testing drugs of questionable merit (see Doyal 1979). Additionally, she is condoning sexist stereotypes by subordinating the woman's health needs and interests to those of her husband and the male GP who treated her life as expendable and in denying the woman the right to negotiate her relationship with her husband.

Both case studies reveal how easy it is for social workers, acting from the best of intentions, to add to the oppression experienced by their clients. In doing this, their practice reinforces the *status quo* and does a disservice to the clients concerned.

CONSTRUCTING ALTERNATIVE FORMS OF PRACTICE: FEMINIST AND BLACK APPROACHES

Feminists and black community activists have organised collectively to create alternative forms of welfare provisions which confront directly the issues of gender and 'race' oppression. For feminists, this includes initiatives in the statutory social services and autonomous provisions in the voluntary sector such as Women's Aid refuges, rape crisis centres, incest survivor groups, and feminist therapy (Dominelli and McLeod 1989). These have taken gender as their starting point and have explicitly set out to meet the welfare needs of women, often without reference to men's needs (see Marchant and Wearing 1986). This last point is changing as feminists realise that to improve the lot of women they must simultaneously change the position of men and children (see Dominelli and McLeod 1989; Dominelli 1989). In tackling women's experience of sexism, feminist social workers have re-defined social problems. Additionally, they have developed forms of practice which endorse egalitarian relations between women, build women's confidence in their ability to control their lives and choose the lifestyles they wish to enjoy (Marchant and Wearing 1986; Brook and Davis 1985; Dominelli and McLeod 1989).

In the absence of state provisions meeting their welfare needs, black men and women have also organised to promote their welfare in autonomous identity groups within both social services and the voluntary sector (Adams 1989). Among other initiatives, these include the Black Families Unit (Small 1984), resource centres for black people (Sondhi 1982), black women's refuges (Guru 1987), residential accommodation for black elders (ASRA 1981). These have confronted black people's experience of racism and fostered pride in their achievements, strengths, and ability to act collectively.

By taking an approach rooted in the experience of women and black people, feminists and black activists have challenged the *status quo* and have created prefigurative forms of practice which can serve as useful indicators of the kinds of provisions endorsed by a welfare system which places human needs above economic motives, controlling people, and rationing resources. The following case studies indicate the forms that such practice can take.

Case study three: feminist practice in a women's refuge

Sarah fled from her violent partner one rainy night with her two children, John aged five and Debbie aged three. All they had were the clothes on their backs. They sought accommodation in a Women's Aid refuge and were warmly received by the paid worker and other women and children who had sought sanctuary there. The refuge was very crowded and noisy with children's laughter.

Sarah was very shy at first and found it difficult to adjust to the communal aspects of refuge life, but cherished the privacy provided by her sleeping quarters.

She found sharing experiences with other battered women salutary. She no longer felt alone. Slowly, with their support, she started developing her confidence. A big boost in this direction occurred when she took charge of a refuge fund-raising event and raised £100. Eventually, she began speaking at meetings where women discussed policies and decided how to allocate the work of the refuge.

One of the most testing situations Sarah faced there involved a black woman. Indejit joined them after losing a tooth when her husband beat her up. Although the refuge had an anti-racist policy, its practice failed Indejit. To begin with, she was the only black woman present. Additionally, no provisions for cooking her food according to her religious requirements were available. When she pointed this out, one white woman subjected her to racist abuse. The white woman was repeatedly warned to desist from such behaviour, but ignored this advice. Eventually a meeting of all women in the refuge was called to debate what sanctions to apply to her. They finally decided to throw her out. She was told she could return if she apologised to Indejit and signed a statement agreeing to conform to anti-racist standards of behaviour. Meanwhile, Sarah couldn't help worrying about what would happen to this woman and her child if she didn't find a place to stay and resumed her previous relationship. But equally, she felt she should not have subjected Indejit to constant humiliation.

This case shows how women can organise collectively to support and nurture each other. The refuge operates on the basis of letting abused women rather than professional workers take the role of experts, fostering egalitarian relationships between them, and using their experience and skills to build each other's confidence (Mama 1989). Although operating under stringent financial circumstances because feminists have failed to alter society's existing allocation of resources, they can and do challenge the nature of the relationships among themselves. Notwithstanding the liberality of approach, discipline is maintained to promote social justice while leaving control of their lives in the hands of each woman.

Case study four: black initiatives in the community

Mohinder is 79 years old and has just acquired sheltered accommodation through a black group which has built housing for black people. Mohinder is very pleased with his new abode. He lives free from racial harassment in a complex containing black people of all ages who visit and support each other. The community in which he worked and lived for over thirty years is on his doorstep and he can easily visit his old cronies. They can return his calls with ease as most of them can walk to his place. He is also making friends with the neighbourhood children and has kept them enthralled for hours with his funny stories.

This case reveals how black voluntary groups tackle racism against black elders, but in doing so get trapped in plugging the gaps in statutory provisions. To that extent, they do not challenge the *status quo* (Gilroy 1987). However, in so far as they offer an alternative model of living for their elders – that is, a safe environment which does not exploit family care but facilitates close contact with black communities, these are superior to the residential homes available to white elders. Ageism is tackled directly as old and young mix socially and older people find a useful niche for themselves.

CONCLUSIONS

Sociological analyses are essential in understanding social work dynamics (Leonard 1966). However, an anti-racist feminist analysis transcends the 'race' and gender blindness of classical sociology, helps us understand how traditional welfare practice reproduces sexist and racist stereotypes, and indicates how oppression can be tackled in all its manifestations simultaneously by developing forms of practice which counter prevailing stereotypes. It also places the necessity of transforming existing social relations and social work practice before us.

© 1991 Lena Dominelli

NOTES

1　I use 'race' in quotation marks to denote reference to a sociological category, not a biological one.
2　The definition of 'black people' covers people of both Afro-Caribbean and Asian descent.
3　Social work agencies operating in the private sector are excluded from this analysis as their role in implementing racist and sexist stereotypes lacks adequate documentation. Though scant, the evidence suggests their activities also endorse these.
4　Women Against Fundamentalism: this organisation was formed by black women who oppose fundamentalist Islamic groups demanding the banning of Salman Rushdie's novel, *The Satanic Verses*, on the grounds that these consist largely of black men pushing fundamentalist religious beliefs which negate the needs of women and deny Islamic critical traditions. Although white people and the media treat these men as if they represent the entire black community, Women Against Fundamentalism maintains they do not speak for black women (Sahgal 1989).
5　We are reduced to using dated national statistics compiled by the DHSS in 1977 because data identifying the current 'race' and gender composition of the social services work-force are not available. However, analyses of several authorities outside London reveal that little has changed in the intervening years. White men still dominate in management. For example, a local authority noted for its equal opportunities procedures reorganised in 1989 with the following depressing results. Residental services and day care are excluded as their reorganisation is pending.

Table 9.1 The 'race' and gender composition of a social services
department in the West Midlands

Position	Post-reorganisation				Pre-reorganisation			
	White men	*White women*	*Black men*	*Black women*	*Number* *White men*	*White women*	*Black men*	*Black women*
Director	1	–	–	–	1	–	–	–
Deputy director	2	–	–	–	2	–	–	–
Assistant director	2	–	–	–	NA			
Operational sector managers	5	4	–	–	NA			
Area managers	NA				3	–	–	–
Deputy area managers	NA				3	3	–	–
District managers	NA				12	3	1	
Service group managers	10	5	1	1	NA			
Total	20	9	1	1	21	6	1	–

Note NA means post did not exist

6 The case materials are derived from my research into this area.

Chapter Ten

KNOWLEDGE, POWER, AND THE SHAPE OF SOCIAL WORK PRACTICE

DAVID HOWE

In this chapter I explore the distribution of power within the occupation of social work. Of particular help in this task is Freidson's (1986) identification of three types of member within any profession: practitioners, administrators, and teacher-researchers. Each member holds a different view on the use and interpretation of the profession's formal knowledge. These different views lead to different ideas about what is to be recognised as good and appropriate practice. However, power is rarely shared equally between the three members of the profession. The member with the most power will have the greatest influence on the content and purpose of practice. Although the distribution of power within a profession is never permanently fixed, in the case of social work I argue that administrators (welfare managers) currently have the lion's share of power. Practitioners and teacher-researchers are left with significant pockets of freedom, but nevertheless the broad shape of practice is formed within the cognitive purview of the manager.

PROFESSIONAL CONTROL IN SOCIAL WORK

What takes place when 'social worker meets client'? For a long time it was presumed that what did take place was essentially a private, professional matter between the worker and her client. What was achieved and experienced was simply a product of that worker's way of doing things. The social worker constructed her own practice.

But sociologists, pondering the nature of the professions, have questioned this presumption. Upon closer examination, it seems that what the social worker thinks and does is influenced by many people who appear, at first sight, to lie well outside the relationship between worker and client. This observation upsets any cosy notion that social work is an activity simply defined by social workers. Early attempts to understand the nature of the professions had encouraged social workers to believe that they could define their own work along professional lines. Abstracting what seemed to be the main characteristics of professions such as law and medicine, it appeared that all any other aspiring occupation needed to do was to acquire the requisite traits – such as a body of knowledge, a code of ethics, and a longish period of training – and they too would turn into the real thing. But this clean, neat, though ultimately naïve picture of the service-oriented, public-minded professional did not last.

Throughout the 1940s and 1950s, American sociologists repeatedly observed the self-interested behaviour of professional workers. By the 1960s, the professions came under even more exacting scrutiny from critical theorists who recognised that the established professions, far from being passive recipients of society's gratitude for their selfless works, actually fought and manoeuvred, politicked and campaigned for control over what they could do, how they could do it, and with whom they could do it. Medicine and law have been supremely successful in this exercise: they are able to define both the needs of the consumer and the manner in which they are to be met, and to control the production of knowledge and the use to which it might be put. According to Larson (1977, 1980), professions are occupational groups which have developed a market for their expertise. The state gives them exclusive control over the knowledge and skills which inform their work. It is to these occupations that government authorities turn to seek the 'correct' understanding of such things as illness or the laws of social behaviour. In short, the professions are occupational groups that have gained large measures of control over their work. Other occupational groups, including social workers, teachers, and nurses, have been less successful in establishing self-control and so fall short on the status and rewards that occupational self-control brings.

Most of the writing by social workers about social work has failed to keep up with developments in the sociology of the professions. Social work is still discussed by its practitioners as if they are a group capable of determining all that they do. Their sneaking regard for the front-line worker received an interesting and clever boost from Lipsky. Maybe, he argues, occupations like school-teaching and social work do not appear to have the power or trappings of the high-status professions, but this does not mean that they carry out the biddings of their employers and the rules of their organisation in a passive and compliant manner. Lipsky argues that the day-to-day on-the-job decisions of these 'street-level bureaucrats', 'the routines they establish, and the devices they invent to cope with uncertainties and work pressures, effectively *become* the public policies they carry out' (1980: xii). The discretion required when the worker is faced with complex and unpredictable cases produces not only the practice of that agency, but in effect its policy too. Lipsky recognises that this discretion (a combination of 'compassion and flexibility') takes place within a given system of rules and regulations. Nevertheless, the modifications and interpretations that the street worker has to make in order for his or her job to become possible and sustainable mean that what actually occurs in practice may not look much like what the organisation's managers prescribe in theory.

However, in spite of Lipsky's generous estimation of the street-level power of social workers, others have developed the idea that social workers enjoy very little real power or professional freedom. Echoing the work of people like Johnson (1972) and Larson (1977), the assertion is that social workers define neither the purpose of their work nor the means by which it is carried out. Except in matters of style, all the substantive elements of their work are determined by others, either directly in the form of managerial command or indirectly through the distribution of resources, departmental policies and procedures, and ultimately the framework of statutes and legislation that create both welfare clients and welfare agencies (Howe 1986).

Debates about social work have been forced to recognise that it does not exist discretely, independent of its organisation and political context. What social workers think and do can be understood only in relation to the intellectual, ideological, and material surroundings in which they find themselves. The conclusion is that much of social work practice is not defined by front-line practitioners, but many key areas of practice are determined and constructed within welfare organisations. I remain impressed with analyses which reveal social work to be largely a state-sponsored, agency-based, organisationally-tethered activity. It is not wise to tackle any examination of social work without taking note of this formidable context.

KNOWLEDGE AND POWER

Professional groups possess knowledge to which others do not readily have access but which is believed to be of value to the community. It is not routine knowledge. It is knowledge that can be used to tackle personal, social, and technical problems. Those who possess such expert knowledge may gain in remuneration, honour, and status. They may also acquire power which increases if individual members are able to organise themselves into professional associations. Although knowledge can help achieve power, it is more profitable to ask who holds it, what they do with it, and what particular kind of knowledge they have. However, not all or any knowledge brings about power. Indeed, the knowledge valued by the powerful determines to some extent what is to be counted as relevant knowledge. This has the added bonus of helping to sustain the power of those who already have it:

> Since knowledge is never a simple, 'objective' reflection of reality but always represents selection and interpretation, and since it shapes (as well reflects) our ideas of what ought to be, groups in control of a certain body of knowledge have far-reaching influence also in another way: they define the situation for the untutored, they suggest priorities, they shape people's outlook on their life and world, and establish standards for judgements in the different areas of expertise – in matters of health and illness, order and justice, administration of the commonwealth, the organised use of force, the design and deployment of technology, the organisation of production.

> (Rueschmeyer 1986: 104)

However, the sociology of the professions has tended to equate the professional with the front-line practitioner – the doctor who treats patients, the teacher in the classroom, or the social worker with her client. This simple picture has been refined with the recognition that managers and executives, trainers and researchers are involved every bit as much in the occupation's endeavours: the part which they play in the ultimate expression of the occupation's activities requires that they be considered as important members of the profession in question (Freidson 1986; Rueschmeyer 1986: 133). Not only do we have to consider the type of knowledge held and the professional group holding it, we also need to examine which members of the profession have influenced and sponsored that knowledge. Moreover, within this enlarged view of the profession, different members have different amounts of power, so that one group's view of what knowledge counts may hold sway to varying degrees in different situations. Freidson identifies three types of member within any profession, each seeing the world from a different angle:

> Practitioners, administrators and teacher-researchers are each in a position to exercise different powers over client services and material production. Each has a different perspective on the relevance and use of the profession's formal knowledge in the different tasks each performs. This creates differences in what knowledge is actually employed.
>
> (Freidson 1986: xiii–iv)

Moreover, the type of formal knowledge which prevails helps to shape the kind of organisation that best suits the application of that type of knowledge. Once the organisation has come into being it tends to seek and demand more of that kind of knowledge to support and promote its kind of thinking and practice. However, the professions and their organisation do not see themselves this way. 'They tend to view their role as determined by the logic inherent in problems, circumstances and technology' (Rueschmeyer 1986: 107). But the inherent logic perceived will vary between administrators, practitioners, and researchers. Thus there is no constant, homogeneous, coherent, and consistent body of knowledge within a stated profession. Groupings within the profession compete to articulate their understanding of situations. No single group can unequivocally define the profession, its aims and methods, without another group wishing to vary that definition. But the distribution of power varies within the profession so that some perspectives are more consequential than others. Dominant factions are more able to set the boundaries and the terms of thought in which everyone else operates. Not only do many of their practices determine which types of knowledge prevail but also those types of knowledge are likely to be the ones with which they are most adept and familiar, thus providing further support to their position of power.

Freidson examines the way in which different groups utilise certain types of professional knowledge and 'transform' them to suit their perspective and interests. Knowledge emanates from and is developed in many professional arenas – front-line practice, management policy meetings, university research units. But such knowledge does not remain inviolate. Different groups with different duties and interests transform, modify, and adapt it to handle the situation as they see it and as they experience it. For example, we might observe that

206

THE SHAPE OF SOCIAL WORK PRACTICE

trainers and researchers concern themselves with the rigour and consistency of professional performances and things which are intellectually 'interesting', while administrators are keen to establish practices which are consistent, regular, and standardised. Administrators, notes Freidson (1986), make selections from the upwelling knowledge pool that best fit their view of the organisation's purpose. They proceed to 'reduce what they select to an artificially limited and consistent set of rules, guidelines or procedures. . . . Formal knowledge is simplified and rationalised, given greater formality than it actually possesses' (1986: 226). The practitioner is in receipt of both these perspectives, but she has to deal with actual situations that have a habit of escaping the conceptual rules of trainers and the bureaucratic procedures of managers. Lipsky's arguments start with very similar observations. Practitioners seek quality of performance and not organisational consistency and they use research knowledge as a loose guiding framework to meet each unique practice situation. There is a 'primacy of experience over theoretical knowledge' (Zussman quoted in Freidson 1986: 216).

> The rank-and-file, therefore, must simultaneously take those formal rules into account, take their understanding of their discipline's formal knowledge into account, and cope with the practical exigencies of their work situation. Just as they are likely to take liberties with their formal knowledge they learned in school and read about in professional journals, so are they likely to take liberties with the guidelines promulgated by their supervisors and managers.
>
> (Freidson 1986: 216–17)

However, while practitioners bend and adapt the theories and the regulations, trainers, researchers, and managers attempt to control the practitioner's performance. Both take a broader view but for different reasons.

> Academics are likely to be concerned with the way practitioners deviate from cognitively defined performance standards and goals, while administrators are more likely to be concerned with deviation from administratively defined standards and goals that are adapted to the organisation's needs rather than concerned with the integrity of knowledge itself.
>
> (Freidson 1986: 213)

There is a flow of knowledge and observation between each of

207

these three groups. As a piece of knowledge crosses the boundary between one group perspective and another, it is transformed into the vocabulary, interests, and outlook of the host perspective. Thus, a piece of knowledge might be subject to 'situational judgements' by practitioners, formal knowledge criteria by academics, and tests of economy and procedural consistency by managers. But the power of each group over the final expression of the occupation's practice varies, with the more powerful tending to set the conceptual and practical climate for the front-line performance.

Wilding (1982) notes that power may be held over a number of key areas. These include the definition of needs and problems, policy, resource allocation, and the content and style of service responses. Practitioners, administrators, and trainer-researchers have differential access to these powers, so, although each group retains some elements of freedom, the size and scope of the discretionary domain in which it can transform a piece of knowledge depend entirely on the power it enjoys. The more power the group possesses, the greater is its ability to establish its preferred knowledge outlook on the other groups. Managers, for example, are obliged to 'operationalise' political statutes but, in turn, the administrative arrangements they make may reach down and penetrate aspects of the rank-and-file worker's practice.

But even this more elaborate analysis of professional power and knowledge is too simple. Beyond the margins of the professional group lie others who may have views about what the professional should be up to. Larger normative waves can roll through the way problems are recognised and resolved. Social work in particular is susceptible to the views of politicians, the media, and public opinion. Wilensky (1962) observes that there is an unwillingness by politicians and the public to 'recognise the need for special competence in an area where everyone is an "expert"'. For example, newspaper editors, politicians, and pillars of the local society are all likely to pronounce on how best to handle juvenile delinquents or the parents of abused children. Thus, the power to define key aspects of professional practice may actually lie outside the profession itself, weakening its position and the hold which it may have over its own knowledge base.

Although this may not be surprising in social work, the argument transfers to and applies equally well in other fields. For example, Rueschmeyer discusses scientific knowledge in this fashion. 'The autonomy of research . . . is never complete because even the most autonomous institutions of science do not sever all relations with the rest of society' (1986: 114). Research in science does not simply follow the logic of its own development. Rather, it is influenced by governmental, industrial, and ideological concerns. The questions asked, the problems addresed, and the answers found are largely shaped by economic and political interests. The tune is invariably called by those who pay the piper.

CHILD PLACEMENTS IN SOCIAL WORK

There is no obvious place to start when attempting to track the origins and career of a piece of professional knowledge. Researchers develop their ideas when they examine the practice of front-line workers. Managers adopt and adapt some of these ideas in the light of what practitioners are doing already and what they would like them to do in the future. In turn, rank-and-file operators receive theoretical advice from academics, procedural guidelines from managers, and then have to face the exigencies and idiosyncrasies of each client and his or her unique situation.

Using child care placement practice as an example, I shall start, arbitrarily, with the findings of researchers and briefly consider how the knowledge they produce is transformed as it enters the occupational province of the manager and the practitioner. I allow each professional perspective to carry some power in asserting the legitimacy of its knowledge base, but I intend to recognise the researcher-manager axis as the most potent, though even this exhibits a distinct tilt towards the manager.

There are some strong examples to be found in which social services managers take the results of a piece of academic research and use it to re-write their department's policy and practice in a particular field. Sometimes literally overnight, social workers find that either a particular resource is no longer available or they are required to pursue a set of goals whether they like them or not. Of course, many practitioners are able to subvert or modify procedural demands but nevertheless they find themselves working in a world which has boundaries and outlooks not of their making.

A good example is to be found in Warwickshire Social Services Department (DHSS 1987). Accepting that on the whole residential care for children was a bad and damaging experience, the senior managers decided to reduce the department's 'dependency on residential services for children and young people'. 'The belief that every child has the right to a family life has been the guiding principle of Warwickshire Social Services Committee since the mid 1970s. . . . The success of these policies was even greater than we had at first anticipated and enabled us to close our last two children's homes in 1986.' Any social worker who assesses a child and is led to conclude that, say, a residential therapeutic home would best meet the needs of her child finds that no such resource is available in Warwickshire and that such an assessment on her part is held to be the product of unsound thinking. Her assessment and her practice in this field are constrained within the policy and resources laid down by the Committee and its senior managers.

Packman (1986) has explored some of those practices which involve the decision whether or not to admit a child into care. She found that departments were certainly aware of research which suggested that many children might have been better left at home or that social workers in the past had too readily removed children from their homes on the dubious grounds that this was in their best interests. The idea that children should not be in care and in fact might fare better at home has that magic quality, irresistible to managers, of being both cheaper and morally more wholesome. Packman's research method relied heavily upon the subjective accounts of social workers, children, and their parents. Her feeling was that policy and practice in this field had over-simplified earlier research findings, becoming in the process too dogmatic, inflexible, and insensitive to the personal characteristics of each new situation. In particular, as social workers pursued the new policies, they appeared to ignore the views of parents. The aim, in many cases, was simply to keep children out of care even in those cases where the parents and the child were asking for admission into care. Packman concluded:

> Statements that assert that 'admission to care should be a last resort' or that 'it is to be prevented at all costs', and policies which equate low admission rates with good child care, for example, seem to us singularly unhelpful – yet they were much in evidence in depart-mental documents and in discussions with staff at many levels.
> (Packman 1986: 197)

Perhaps the most widespread example affecting child care place-ment practice is the use (and some would say abuse) of the principle of 'permanence'. Again, the origins of the principle might be located with the findings of a small number of established and influential researchers. Throughout the 1970s there was growing recognition and concern that too many children were drifting through their time in care. There appeared to be no clear long-term plans for their future childhood. In 1976, Rowe stated:

It is our conviction that no child can grow emotionally while in limbo, never really belonging to anyone except on a temporary and ill-defined or partial basis. He cannot invest except in a minimal way (just enough to survive) if tomorrow the relationship may be severed. . . . To grow, the child needs at least the promise of permanency in relationships and some continuity of environment.

The social work world was shocked by the realisation that there were up to 7,000 children waiting for foster homes or to be adopted and for whom no definite placement plans existed. The research of Rowe and Lambert (1973) helped to swell the tide of findings in both the UK and the USA which observed that large numbers of children were drifting through a series of temporary homes. Clearly this state of affairs was not good. The implications of the research for practice seemed clear: there should be a plan to provide every child in care with a permanent home as soon as possible. This 'permanent home' could be the child's original family or a substitute family. In either case the aim would be to offer the child a 'continuity of relationships with nurturing parents or caretakers and the opportunity to establish lifetime relationships' as soon as possible (Maluccio and Fein 1983). Any fudging would be bad for the child's proper development. The permanency principle seemed uncompromising on these matters. It therefore contained a clear but contentious practice implication that, if it could not be established within a reasonably short period of time that the child's own birth parents were able to secure the return home of their son or daughter, then a *permanent* substitute home, preferably leading to adoption, should be found. Of course, it was hoped that if the parents could not resume care of their child in a relatively short period of time they would agree that it was in their child's best interests to be adopted and that all contact with them as natural parents would cease. However, if their agreement could not be secured, there was provision in the 1975 Adoption Act to dispense with the consent of the parents and thus 'free' the child for adoption. 'Furthermore,' note Thoburn *et al.* (1986: 3), 'in contradiction to currently held views of social work practice with foster children, [Goldstein and his colleagues] argued that for many children contacts with birth parents tended to impede the growth of attachments and render the placement vulnerable, and so should cease.'

During the 1980s most social services departments began to examine their child placement practices in the light of the research findings. A large number developed policies that captured the principles of permanence. The social worker, found guilty of allowing drift and impermanence in the past, could not be trusted on her own to keep to the new and more rigorous standards. Administrative mechanisms were devised to ensure that plans were made and kept; managers, who in all likelihood had never met the child or the parents, would chair assessment meetings and placement reviews; the guiding principle would be the achievement of a permanent home as soon as possible, and there would be no place for those who were faint-hearted or hesittant or not yet certain.

The enthusiastic adoption of permanency planning challenged the field practitioner's ability to devise her own plans for a child in care, and in many hands it created a blunt and rigid principle that dismissed all attempts to introduce variation and compromise into discussions about the child's future. Although ideally it would be good if the natural parents could have their child back, practitioners must not be squeamish about pushing the child on for adoption if a return home did not look a distinct and early possibility. Kent Social Services is typical in its child care policy. Here is an extract from the department's pamphlet *Planning for Permanence: Children and Families Policy Statement* (1986):

> If the permanence of the natural family cannot be assured either by preventing the child coming into care or by early rehabilitation, permanent substitute families must be found. Adoption offers the best assurance of permanence for children entering care under the age of 10. . . . No child who comes into care under the age of ten should remain in care for more than two years except with the written agreement of the Area Director. Decisions on whether rehabilitation is possible will be taken within 6 months of coming into care. Where rehabilitation has been shown to be impossible then a permanent substitute home should be sought which offers a permanent relationship and legal security with persons who can act as parents. This will normally mean adoption. . . . An assessment will be made of the needs and circumstances of a child aged over 10 when coming into care. A decision will be made within six

months of coming into care on whether rehabilitation is likely to be possible or whether it would be advisable to place an older child in a permanent substitute home through adoption.

In seeking to establish time limits and exact behavioural criteria on the decisions made by parents and social workers, managers both rationalised and systematised the findings of the researchers. And if social workers found their freedom of manoeuvre restricted and researchers winced at the over-simplification of their evidence, then parents of any child in care became positively alarmed. It is hardly surprising that the general fear of many parents involved with social services was that once their child was in care they might never see him or her again. So, although the demand for clearer and firmer thinking for children in care was welcomed by social workers, the zeal of many practitioners and managers distorted the original wisdom of the principle as they transformed it into policy and practice.

By 1984 there was an official note of caution in the Report given by the House of Commons Social Services Committee (quoted in Thoburn *et al*. 1986: 1), 'There is at the moment,' observes the Report, 'considerable confusion over the significance of the search for "permanence" in a placement. It should not become a synonym for adoption. . . . Adoption is only one eventual outcome among many.' So, although adoption may well be appropriate for some children, 'we must sound notes of warning. There is some danger that a new bandwagon is rolling connecting adoption with the idea of permanence.' Indeed, even before these warning notes were sounded, researchers were busy refining the concepts and evidence that informed good placement practice. I have already mentioned Packman. Morris (1984) reviews some of the literature that reflected unhappiness about practices which severed all contact with parents. This fresh evidence was suggesting that children, even adopted children, might benefit from continued contact with their natural parents, wherever they might be 'permanently' placed. Fisher *et al*. (1986) confirmed Packman's work, believing that many parents and their children might benefit from children being in care for a short period, that care should not necessarily be avoided at all costs, and that the child in care should not be placed automatically on the conveyor belt of permanency planning.

We see therefore that the shape of child care practice does not remain fixed. It changes as knowledge is continuously generated, and it is transformed as it leaves one occupational group and enters the intellectual and practical domain of another. But this is not a random process: the more powerful groups control much of the shape of practice and, at present, managers appear to hold most of this power.

MANAGERS AND THE CONSTRUCTION OF PRACTICE

When social worker and client meet, words are said, things are done, decisions are made. The meeting is contoured and can be mapped along several dimensions which reveal the influences that shape the topography of the professional encounter. The implied pessimism about the shrinking power base of the practitioner and her inability to govern large parts of her practice has been used as evidence to illustrate the thesis of 'the proletarianization of the professional' (Derber 1982) in which the professional loses control of key elements of his or her practice. Managers seek to create regular and predictable task environments so that routine responses can be prescribed in set situations. They attempt to define both the work and the way the organisation's functionaries will react. Thus, in a pre-identified situation, the social worker is expected to act in a pre-programmed way. Work becomes both fragmented and standardised. By increasing rules, routines, and procedures, the manager diminishes the area of professional discretion available to the social worker. The design and conception of work shifts from the practitioner to the manager. Clients and their needs are no longer defined by field-workers but by administrators. What clients 'mean' to welfare organisations is determined by legislation and policy, resources and administrative procedures:

> Particular client groups are 'standardised' by the processing procedures and structures of the organisation. The idiosyncrasies (intrinsic uncertainties) of individual clients are subdued or lost in the standardising process. The client group, as the organisation's 'raw material', is defined through statute, procedure, method of process and resources available. As interpreters of statute and designers of work, managers control the content of work. Their understanding penetrates the organisation and practice so that workers think and act in terms of the organisation's perceptions of the client groups.
>
> (Howe 1986: 134)

These strategies iron out large elements of uncertainty that individual clients might otherwise present to the organisation. Removing uncertainty by administrative definition allows responses and resources to be deployed in a more regular and routine fashion. Control increasingly rests with the senior managers who define clients and design responses.

Derber develops many of these ideas. He recognises two types of 'proletarianization':

> These two ways in which workers lose control of their work more broadly concern the means and ends of labor. The loss of control over the process of the work itself (the means), incurred whenever management subjects its workers to a technical plan of production and/or a rhythm or pace of work which they have no voice in creating, can be called *technical* proletarianization. . . . The loss of control over the product can be viewed broadly as the loss of control over the ends of one's work. Called here *ideological* proletarianization, it will refer to a loss of control over the goals and social purposes to which one's work is put. . . .
>
> Ideological proletarianization creates a type of worker whose integrity is threatened by the expropriation of his values or sense of purpose rather than his skill. It reduces the domain of freedom and creativity to problems of technique; it thus creates workers, no matter how skilled, who act as technicians or functionaries. Moral, social, and technological issues are subtly removed from the purview of the worker, as he loses control of his product and his relation to the larger community.
>
> (Derber 1982: 169, 172)

Jamous and Peloille (1970) suggest that in professional practices there is a ratio between the amount of 'indeterminacy' and the amount of 'technicality' in the work done. Indeterminacy refers to that component of work which is based on specialised knowledge, its interpretation, and the use of professional judgement. The skills and knowledge required can be learned only after long training and much experience. Technicality describes those aspects of the job which arise when the work is approached logically, systematically, and rationally. Such an approach opens the way for the work to be programmed and subjected to routine practices. In work which has been technically systematised, the practitioner does not need to interpret knowledge, make judgements, or use experience in order to do the job well.

In so far as professional occupations seek bodies of knowledge which are scientific or systematic, there is always the prospect that their knowledge and skills base can be codified and easily prescribed. This is the first step in developing routine practices. In cases where this happens, the occupation becomes liable to external control and design. The profession is said to experience de-skilling. Occupations which maintain professional status manage to keep a large measure of indeterminacy in their practice. New knowledge and techniques, personal styles and special competences cannot easily be reduced to systematic and routinised knowledge. The profession's esoteric body of knowledge continues to need considerable *interpretation* before it can be applied appropriately and effectively. The maintenance of these indeterminacies acts as a barrier to managerial regularisation. The profession remains in control of its own cognitive base, training, and practice. It continues to define the needs of the consumer and the way these are to be met. To the extent that the profession's knowledge and skills are valued and remain under its control, power accrues to that profession.

There is thus a tension within any professional occupation. On the one hand, as it develops understanding and control over its subject matter (for example, human bodies, legislation, money markets), it can predict the relationship between its practices and their outcome. A systematic body of knowledge is created; there are rules, procedures, and solutions available. In this regularised form, such knowledge and procedures can be transferred and taught to the next generation of practitioners. But on the other hand, to the extent that the occupation can systematically formulate its knowledge, practices, and outcomes, the work is prey to routinisation, de-skilling, and organisational regulation, and these are the strategies of managers.

Turner (1987; 145–6) gives the example of pharmacy as an occupation that has developed a very precise and systematic knowledge base that allows little interpretation by its practitioners. Nor has pharmacy developed a clear counselling role with patients. This remains with the physician. Pharmaceutical practice is standardised and the products of practice remain under the control and direction of the medical profession.

Social work is an interesting example of an occupation that still hovers on the edge of being a fully fledged profession. If occupational self-control is an important measure by which an occupation might gauge its professional prospects, then social work, at first sight, looks as if it is losing grip on its ambitions. Social work, particularly in large-scale welfare bureauracies such as social services and probation departments, seems to be more and more under the control and direction of managers and their knowledge base. Less and less is the social work practitioner able to interpret situations in the light of her own professional knowledge and experience. As the amount of 'technicality' increases in her job, so the area of 'indeterminacy' decreases. Many aspects of the social worker's job now involve carrying out bureaucratic functions and administrative tasks in the field setting. But not only is the social worker losing control over many of her technical skills; she is finding that the ideological purposes of her work are increasingly being defined by managers as they interpret and operationalise legislation, policy, and budgets. Many traditional social work skills and knowledge bases become redundant in managerially designed practices with their emphasis on rule following, procedural propriety, and administrative clarity. The indeterminacy that is present in many social work practices such as professional diagnosis and therapeutic intervention is simply defined as not relevant to the work of a modern welfare bureaucracy. It is not so much that social work has now not got a refined and esoteric body of knowledge; it is more that large parts of that body of knowledge are denied expression and relevance.

Training is increasingly being shaped by what a manager thinks a good social worker should look like. The Central Council for Education and Training in Social Work, the body that prescribes the content of social work training, has turned to managers for advice about what a trained social worker should know and do. Inevitably, the managers' definition of a good social worker suits their way of seeing and doing things. By handing over some control of the training process to managers, the amount of 'technicality' in the make-up of the social worker's practice is bound to increase while the amount of 'indeterminacy' and worker discretion inevitably must decrease. Managers seek to regularise the 'task environment' and the practices of the organisation. They have knowledge and skills that take them in this direction. They are looking for competent functionaries, not independent practitioners. But in conceding this amount of control to managers, trainers (or at least the CCETSW) are limiting the part that practitioner knowledge can play in defining and shaping social work practice. In effect, social work becomes redefined in this process so that the hallmark of a good social worker is administrative competence rather than independent thought and judgement. The result is that competition between managers and practitioners to define problems and the manner of their resolution is diminished. The practitioner, through her training, simply learns to think and practise as the manager would wish her to.

Child abuse work is increasingly defined in the language of the administrator. The statutory duty to investigate defines how the client is to be viewed and how the worker is to proceed. The state, with its views about social behaviour and standards, brings client and worker together. In all probability, the worker will be following a set of procedures which may instruct her what to observe and note, who to inform, and what to do. Assessments are made largely within the discourse of child care law and the procedures that now inform all child abuse work. To operate within codes, laws, and procedures is to think and practise within the knowledge domain of the manager. The social worker can be given discretion but it is understood that she will use it only within the framework of thought that underpins the organisation. Just in case she slips out of her cognitive blinkers, managers use other techniques to control the activities of practitioners at a distance. Rules, resources, and routines can define what a social worker might do in a set situation, without a manager looking over her shoulder. Law (1986b: 254) has argued that 'documents, devices and drilled people' allow those at the centre to control those at the boundaries of an organisation's activities. Talking of Portuguese sailors in the fifteenth century, but with surprising relevance to the modern world, Law observes that through documents, devices, and drilling, practitioners 'would act as they should at a distance so long as they were properly chosen and placed in the right location within an appropriately designed structure' (1986b: 254).

CONCLUSION

A piece of practice can never be an entirely fixed affair. Its shape changes in response to the relative powers of practitioners and researchers, managers and clients. Its shape changes, too, in time: past practices are not always the same as today's and social work in the future may vary yet again. As we have seen, these changes reflect the amount of control held by each of the main occupational groups that together make up the profession of social work. However, the current shape of social work seems to lie largely in the hands of managers. We see field practitioners with less autonomy and less discretion as managers control more of the technical and ideological content of practice.

But social workers and their work are difficult to fix absolutely. Clients do not always succumb to the organisation's definition of who they are and what they are. To the extent that they remain unpredictable in critical areas, the ways of the expert practitioner are more effective than the inflexible prescriptions of the administrator. Practitioners hold on to pockets of freedom and develop favoured skills. Practitioner freedom might remain for two reasons:

1. The area over which the rank-and-file worker retains freedom and control is not yet wholly amenable to routine and standardised practice procedures, still requiring *in situ* judgements and discretionary responses. For example, departments may accept that counselling is necessary in cases of terminal illness or marital conflict but there is no routine response or resource available other than the practitioner's own time and skills.

2. The style and manner of practice are largely irrelevant to the legal and resource concerns of managers, and the practitioner is left to get on with it. So long as she is *involved*, it does not matter how she conducts herself. Much family work seems to fall in this category. For example, the worker may use a person-centred approach or the techniques of family therapy to tackle the situation as she sees it. However, if clients did begin to exhibit behaviours which the organisation felt to be of direct relevance to its operations (for example, they had resource costs, revealed anti-social conduct, or threatened someone's physical or developmental well-being) and which were not responding to the efforts of the practitioner, the discretionary control allowed the social worker would be withdrawn. The case would then be placed under the tighter procedures of the agency and the social worker's practice would be prescribed in greater detail. Organisational definitions of the problem and the response required replace those of the practitioner. Instead of attempting to cure people, behaviours and situations are 'battened down' by the use of statutory and procedural instruments. These instruments seek only to control and contain worrisome situations. If the worker fails to move into a procedural mode once the situation warrants it, her responses will be managed either directly through command or indirectly by an obligation to follow the rules.

Cynically, I might conclude that practitioners have the greatest freedom to control those areas which matter least to those who define problems, clients, and service responses. But in those areas in which front-line workers have control, they (and their trainers) are able to define their essential occupational selves, though this self has not received major backing and recognition from key and powerful institutions. It is a cognitive base which fails to serve dominant definitions of welfare purposes and responses, though it may satisfy workers and their needs and some of the personal (as opposed to socially defined) needs of the client. The only way most practitioners who feel they have a clear professional knowledge base can control the use of their own theories and practices is to move into new or experimental areas of a department's activities where there is not yet sufficient experience to allow the organisation to develop routines and procedures. Or, failing that, for the practitioner to work in small specialist, voluntary agencies where the professional ethos is allowed full expression.

None of this is necessarily to lament the weakness of the practitioner's ability to control her own knowledge and skill base. Sociologically we must remain curious about the steady shift of power away from the practitioner to the manager. This acknowledgement forces us to recognise that the nature and purposes of social work are not the fixed prerogative of any one occupational group. The tightening of budgets, the public's reaction to child abuse, the insistence that public organisations are run according to the principles of efficiency, economy, and effectiveness, might simply mean that managers and their skills are better placed to respond to these external demands than other groups. If, for example, the overriding concern is said to be the protection of children from dangerous parents, then the procedures and practices that appear best to meet this concern will become dominant. The conclusions of public inquiries into child abuse tend to back administrative practices rather than those of the independent professional. When social worker meets client, the broad shape of her practice, at least within the present balance of power, is defined by statutes, designed by administrators, and driven by managers.

© 1991 David Howe

BIBLIOGRAPHY

Abrams, P. (1977) 'Community care: some research problems and priorities', *Policy and Politics* 6: 125–51.

Abrams, P. (1980) 'Social change, social networks and neighbourhood care', *Social Work Service* 22: 12–23.

Adams, B.N. (1967) 'Interaction theory and the social network', *Sociometry* 30: 50–9.

Adams, M.L. (1989) 'There's no place like home: on the place of identity in feminist politics', *Feminist Review* 31, spring: 22–33.

Agar, M. (1986) *Speaking of Ethnography*, London: Sage.

Alden, P. (1905) *The Unemployed: A National Question*, London: P.S. King.

Allan, G.A. (1979) *A Sociology of Friendship and Kinship*, London: Allen & Unwin.

Allan, G.A. (1985) *Family Life: Domestic Roles and Social Organisation*, Oxford: Blackwell.

Allan, G.A. (1986) 'Friendship and care for elderly people', *Ageing and Society* 6: 1–12.

Allan, G.A. (1988) 'Kinship, responsibility and care for elderly people', *Ageing and Society* 8: 249–68.

Allan, G.A. (1989) *Friendship: Developing a Sociological Perspective*, Hemel Hempstead: Harvester-Wheatsheaf.

Althusser, L. (1971) 'Ideology and ideological state apparatuses', in L. Althusser *Lenin and Philosophy*, London: New Left Books.

Anderson, R. and Bury, M. (eds) (1988) *Living with Chronic Illness*, London: Unwin Hyman.

Anwar, M. (1985) *Pakistanis in Britain*, London: New Century.

Arber, S. and Gilbert, N. (1989) 'Men: the forgotten carers', *Sociology* 23: 111–18.

Armstrong, P. (1980) 'Servicing the professions: spurious legitimacy in the development of vocational training', paper given at British Sociological Association Annual Conference, Lancaster, March.

Armstrong, P. (1982) 'The myth of meeting needs in adult education and community development', *Critical Social Policy* 2 (2): 24–37.

Asian Sheltered Residential Accommodation (ASRA) (1981) *Asian Sheltered*

Residential Accommodation, London: ASRA.

Atkinson, J.M. and Drew, P. (1979) *Order in Court*, Atlantic Highlands, NJ: Humanitas Press.

Atkinson, J.M. and Heritage, J. (eds) (1984) *Structures of Social Action*, Cambridge: Cambridge University Press; Paris: Editions de la Maison des Sciences de l'Homme.

ATSWE (Association of Teachers in Social Work Education) (1985) 'ATSWE written response to Paper 20.3', *ATSWE Newsletter No 44*, University of Leicester, July.

Audit Commission for Local Authorities in England and Wales (1985) *Managing Social Services for the Elderly More Effectively*, London: HMSO.

Baert, P.J.N. (1989) 'Unintended consequences, (un)awareness, and (re)production', paper given at British Sociological Association Annual Conference, Plymouth, March.

Bailey, J. (1980) *Ideas and Intervention: Social Theory for Practice*, London: Routledge & Kegan Paul.

Bailey, R. (1982) 'Theory and practice in social work: a kaleidoscope', in R. Bailey and P. Lee (eds) *Theory and Practice in Social Work*, Oxford: Blackwell.

Baker, R. (1983) 'Is there a future for integrated practice? Obstacles to its development in practice and in education', *Issues in Social Work Education* 3 (1): 3-16.

Baldock, J. and Prior, D. (1981) 'Social workers talking to clients: a study of verbal behaviour', *British Journal of Social Work* 11: 19-37.

Ball, S.J. (1989) Review *Sociological Review* 37 (2): 419-21.

Balla, D.A. (1976) 'Relationship of institution size to quality of care: a review of the literature', *American Journal of Mental Deficiency* 81: 117-24.

Balla, D.A., Butterfield, E.C., and Zigler, E. (1974) 'Effects of institutionalisation on retarded children: a longitudinal cross-sectional investigation', *American Journal of Mental Deficiency*, 78: 530-49.

Bamford, T. (1984) Chair of British Association of Social Workers, quoted in N. Murray, 'Two into one won't go: or will it?', *Community Care* 10 May: 21.

Barash, D. (1979) *Sociobiology: The Whisperings Within*, London: Souvenir.

Barbour, R.S. (1985) 'Dealing with the transituational demands of professional socialisation', *Sociological Review* 33 (3): 495-531.

Barclay Report (1982) National Institute for Social Work Training *Social Workers: Their Role and Tasks*, London: Bedford Square Press.

Barnes, B. (1977) *Interests and the Growth of Knowledge*, London: Routledge & Kegan Paul.

Barnes, B. (1985) *About Science*, Oxford: Blackwell.

Baroff, G.S. (1980) 'On "size" and the quality of residential care: a second look', *Mental Retardation* 18: 113-17.

Barthes, R. (1967) *Elements of Semiology*, London: Cape.

Bartlett, H. (1970) *The Common Base of Social Work Practice*, Washington, DC: National Association of Social Workers.

BASW (1977) *The Social Work Task: BASW Working Party Report*,

Birmingham: British Association of Social Workers.

Bateson, G., Jackson, D., Haley, J., and Weakland, J. (1956) 'Towards a theory of schizophrenia', *Behavioural Science* 1.

Becker, H. (1968) 'Social observation and case studies', in D. Sills (ed.) *International Encyclopedia of the Social Sciences Vol. 11*, New York: Macmillan and The Free Press, pp. 232–8.

Behlmer, G.K. (1982) *Child Abuse and Moral Reform in England 1870–1908*, Stanford: Stanford University Press.

Bell, C. and Newby, H. (1971) *Community Studies*, London: Allen & Unwin.

Bendix, R. (1984) *Force, Fate and Freedom: On Historical Sociology*, Berkeley: University of California Press.

Beresford, P. and Croft, S. (1984) 'Welfare pluralism: the new face of Fabianism', *Critical Social Policy* 19: 19–39.

Berger, P. and Kellner, H. (1982) *Sociology Reinterpreted*, Harmondsworth, Middx: Penguin.

Berger, P. and Luckmann, T. (1967) *The Social Construction of Reality*, Harmondsworth, Middx: Penguin.

Berry, J. (1975) *Daily Experience in Residential Life*, London: Routledge & Kegan Paul.

Betts, K. (1986) 'The conditions of action, power, and the problem of interests', *Sociological Review* 34 (1): 39–64.

Beuret, K. and Stoker, G. (1986) 'The Labour Party and neighbourhood decentralisation: flirtation or commitment?', *Critical Social Policy* 17: 4–22.

Billis, D., Bromley, G., Hey, A., and Rowbottom, R. (1980) *Organising Social Services Departments: Further Studies by the Brunel Social Services Unit*, London: Heinemann.

Binney, V., Harkell, G., and Nixon, J. (1981) *Leaving Violent Men: A Study of Refuges and Housing for Battered Women*, London: Women's Aid Federation.

Bjaarnes, A.T. and Butler, E.W. (1974) 'Environmental variations in community care facilities for mentally retarded persons', *American Journal of Mental Deficiency*, 78: 429–39.

Bogner, A. (1986) 'The structure of social processes: a commentary on the sociology of Norbert Elias', *Sociology* 20 (3): 387–411.

Bolger, S., Corrigan, P., Docking, J., and Frost, N. (1981) *Towards Socialist Welfare Work*, London and Basingstoke, Hants: Macmillan.

Bosanquet, B. (1909) 'The Report of the Poor Law Commission: The Majority Report', *Sociological Review* 11: 109–26, quoted in N. Timms (1983) *Social Work Values: An Enquiry*, London: Routledge & Kegan Paul, p. 71.

Bosanquet, H. (1900) 'Methods of training', *Charity Organisation Society Occasional Papers (Third Series) No 3* in M.J. Smith (1965) *Professional Education for Social Work in Britain: An Historical Account*, London: Allen & Unwin, p. 87.

Boswell, G. (1985) *Care, Control and Accountability in the Probation Service*,

Norwich: UEA Social Work Monographs.

Bott, E. (1957) *Family and Social Network*, London: Tavistock.

Bottomore, T. (1975) *Sociology as Social Criticism*, London: Allen & Unwin.

Bottoms, A.E. & McWilliams, W. (1979) 'A non-treatment paradigm for probation practice', *British Journal of Social Work* 9: 159–202.

Boyers, R. (1979) 'Review of Christopher Lasch, *Haven in a Heartless World*', *New Republic*, 19 February.

Braverman, H. (1974) 'Labour and monopoly capitalism: the degradation of work in the twentieth century', *Monthly Review Press*, New York, pp. 85–123.

Braye, S., Chadwick, C., and Mills, C. (1987) *An Evaluation of Old Hall Family Centre for the Children Society*, unpublished research report.

Brent, London Borough of (1985) *A Child in Trust: The Report of the Panel of Inquiry into the Circumstances surrounding the Death of Jasmine Beckford*, Wembley, Middx: London Borough of Brent.

Brewer, C. and Lait, J. (1980) *Can Social Work Survive?*, London: Temple Smith.

Briggs, A. and Oliver, J. (eds) (1985) *Caring: Experiences of Looking After Disabled Relatives*, London: Routledge & Kegan Paul.

Brody, S.R. (1976) *The Effectiveness of Sentencing*, Home Office Research Study No 32, London: HMSO.

Bromley, D. and Longino, C.F. (1972) *White Racism and Black Americans*, Cambridge, Mass: Schenkman.

Brook, E. and Davis, A. (1985) *Women, the Family and Social Work*, London: Tavistock.

Brown, H. and Alcoe, J. (1987) 'Lifestyles: an approach to training staff in normalisation principles', *Social Work Education* 6 (3): 21–2.

Brown, P., Hadley, R., and White, K.J. (1982) 'A case for neighbourhood-based social work and social services', in Barclay Report, *Social Workers: Their Role and Tasks*, Appendix A, London: Bedford Square Press.

Bruce, S. and Wallis, R. (1983) 'Rescuing motives', *British Journal of Sociology* 34 (1): 61–71.

Bruegel, I. (1989) 'Sex and race in the labour market' *Feminist Review* 32, summer: 49–68.

Bryant, G.A. (1976) *Sociology in Action: A Critique of Selected Conceptions of the Social Role of the Sociologist*, London: Routledge & Kegan Paul.

Bryant, G.A. (1989) 'Towards post-empirical sociological theorising', *British Journal of Sociology* 40 (2): 319–27.

Bulmer, M. (1985) 'The rejuvenation of community studies? Neighbours, networks and policy', *Sociological Review* 33 (3): 430–48.

Bulmer, M. (1986) *Neighbours: The Work of Philip Abrams*, Cambridge: Cambridge University Press.

Bulmer, M. (1987) *The Social Basis of Community Care*, London: Allen & Unwin.

Burns, T.R. (1986) *Actors, transactions and social structure*', in

U. Himmelstrand (ed.) *The Social Reproduction of Organisation and Culture*, London: Sage.

Burrell, G. and Morgan, G. (1979) *Sociological Paradigms and Organisational Analysis: Elements of the Sociology of Corporate Life*, London: Heinemann.

Bury, M. (1986) 'Social constructionism and the development of medical sociology', *Sociology of Health and Illness* 8, (2): 137–69.

Butler-Sloss, E. (1988) *Report of the Inquiry into Child Abuse in Cleveland 1987*, Cm. 412, London: HMSO.

Butterfield, E.C., Barnett, C.D., and Bensberg, G.J. (1966) 'Some objective characteristics of institutions for the mentally retarded', *American Journal of Mental Deficiency*, 70: 786–94.

Button, G. and Casey, N. (1984) 'Generating topic: the use of topic initial elicitors', in J.M. Atkinson and J. Heritage (eds) *Structures of Social Action*, Cambridge: Cambridge University Press; Paris: Editions de la Maison des Sciences de l'Homme.

Byrne, P.S. and Long, B.E. (1976) *Doctors Talking to Patients: A Study of the Verbal Behaviour of General Practitioners Consulting in their Surgeries*, London: HMSO.

Bywaters, P. (1982) 'An interactionist model: an answer or just a better question?', *British Journal of Social Work* 12 (3): 303–18.

Callon, M. (1986) 'Some elements of a sociology of translation: domestication of the scallops and the fishermen of St. Brieuc Bay', in J. Law (ed.) *Power, Action and Belief: A New Sociology of Knowledge?*, London: Routledge & Kegan Paul.

Callon, M. and Latour, B. (1981) 'Unscrewing the big Leviathan: how actors macro-structure reality and how sociologists help them to do so', in K. Knorr-Cetina and A.V. Cicourel (eds) *Advances in Social Theory and Methodology: Towards an Integration of Micro- and Macro-Sociologies*, London: Routledge & Kegan Paul.

Calnan, M. (1987) *Health and Illness: The Lay Perspective*, London and New York: Tavistock.

Campbell, A. (1971) 'Aspects of personal independence of mentally subnormal and severely subnormal adults in hospitals and local authority hostels', *International Journal of Social Psychiatry* 17 (4): 305–10.

Campbell, B. (1988) *Unofficial Secrets: Child Sexual Abuse: the Cleveland Case*, London: Virago.

Carby, H. (1982) 'White woman listen! Black feminism and the boundaries of sisterhood', in Centre for Contemporary and Cultural Studies *The Empire Strikes Back*, London: Hutchinson.

Carew, R. (1979) 'The place of knowledge in social work', *British Journal of Social Work* 9 (3): 349–64.

Carlen, P. (1977) 'Magistrates courts: a game theoretic analysis', in M. Fitzgerald, P. Halmos, J. Muncie, and D. Zeldin (eds) *Welfare in Action*, London: Routledge and Open University Press.

Carrier, J. and Kendall, I. (1973) 'Social policy and social change: explanations of the development of social policy', *Journal of Social Policy* 2 (3): 209–24.

Carter, D. (1985) 'Another blind leap into the dark', *Community Care* 20 June: 27-9.

Casson, P. (1982) *Social Work Courses - Their Structure and Content: CCETSW Study 5*, London: Central Council for Education and Training in Social Work.

Cecil, R., Offer, J., and St. Leger, F. (1987) *Informal Welfare: A Sociological Study of Care in Northern Ireland*, Aldershot, Hants, and Vermont: Gower.

Cicourel, A.V. (1980) 'Language and social interaction: philosophical and empirical issues', *Sociological Inquiry* 50: 1-30.

Clapham, D. (1986) 'Management of the local state: the example of corporate planning', *Critical Social Policy* 14: 27-42.

Clark, M. (1982) 'Where is the community which cares?', *British Journal of Social Work* 12: 453-69.

Clarke, J. (1979) 'Critical sociology and radical social work: problems of theory and practice', in N. Parry, M. Rustin, and C. Satyamurti (eds) *Social Work, Welfare, and the State*, London: Edward Arnold.

Clifton, J. (1981) 'Social workers talking to clients: a comment', *British Journal of Social Work* 11: 39-42.

Cockburn, C. (1977) *The Local State: Management of Cities and People*, London: Pluto.

Cohen, P. (1972) *Modern Social Theory*, London: Heinemann.

Cohen, S. (1975) 'It's all right for you to talk: political and sociological manifestos for social action', in R. Bailey and M. Brake (eds) *Radical Social Work*, London: Edward Arnold.

Cohen, S. (1980) *Folk Devils and Moral Panics*, 2nd edition, Oxford: Martin Robertson.

Cohen, S. (1985) *Visions of Social Control*, Cambridge: Polity Press.

Cohen, S. and Scull, A. (eds) (1983) *Social Control and the State*, Oxford: Martin Robertson.

Cohen, S. and Scull, A. (1983) 'Social control in history and sociology', in S. Cohen and A. Scull (eds) *Social Control and the State*, Oxford: Martin Robertson.

Cole, J.R. (1970) 'Patterns of intellectual influence in scientific research', *Sociology of Education* 43: 377-403.

Collett, S.J. (1989) 'Women before the courts: probation practice and criminal justice', unpublished MA (Econ.) dissertation, University of Manchester.

Compton, B. and Galaway, B. (1975) *Social Work Processes*, Homewood, Ill: The Dorsey Press.

Cooley, C. (1902) *Human Nature and the Social Order*, New York: Charles Scribner.

Cooper, D. and Ball, D. (1987) *Social Work and Child Abuse*, Basingstoke, Hants: Macmillan.

Corby, B. (1986) 'After The Beckford Inquiry', *Community Care* 594: 18-19.

Corby, B. (1987) *Working with Child Abuse*, Milton Keynes: Open University Press.

Corrigan, P. and Leonard, P. (1978) *Social Work Practice Under Capitalism*, London: Macmillan.

Coull, B. (1986) 'Review: distance learning in social work education', *Issues in Social Work Education* 6 (1): 67–9.

Coyle, A. and Skinner, J. (1988) *Women and Work: Positive Action for Change*, London: Macmillan.

Craib, I. (1984) *Modern Social Theory from Parsons to Habermas*, Brighton: Wheatsheaf.

Crow, G. (1989) 'The use of the concept "strategy" in recent sociological literature', *Sociology* 23 (1): 1–24.

Crow, G. and Allan, G. (1990) 'Constructing the domestic sphere: the emergence of the modern home in post-war Britain', in H. Corr and L. Jamieson (eds) *The Politics of Everyday Life*, London: Macmillan.

Culler, J. (1975) *Structuralist Poetics*, London: Routledge & Kegan Paul.

Curnock, K. and Hardiker, P. (1979) *Towards Practice Theory: Skills and Methods in Social Assessments*, London: Routledge & Kegan Paul.

Cypher, J. (1983) 'Introduction', in Social Work Today *The Concise Barclay: A Digest and Commentary*, Birmingham: Social Work Today Publications.

Dahrendorf, R. (1968) *Essays in the Theory of Society*, London: Routledge . & Kegan Paul.

Dale, P., Davies, M., Morrison, T., and Waters, J. (1986) *Dangerous Families: Assessment and Treatment of Child Abuse*, London: Tavistock.

Dalgleish, M. (1983) 'Assessments of residential environments for mentally retarded adults in Britain', *Mental Retardation* 21 (5): 204–8.

Daunton, M.J. (1983) 'Public place and private space: the Victorian city and the working-class household', in D. Frazer and A. Sutcliffe (eds) *The Pursuit of Urban History*, London: Edward Arnold.

David, J. (1983) 'Walsall and decentralisation', *Critical Social Policy* 7: 75–9.

Davies, B. (1982) 'Towards a personalist framework for "radical" social work education', in R. Bailey and P. Lee (eds) *Theory and Practice in Social Work*, Oxford: Blackwell.

Davies, M. (1974) 'Social inquiry for the courts', *British Journal of Criminology* 14: 18–33.

Davies, M. (1981) 'Social work, the state and the university', *British Journal of Social Work* 11 (3): 275–88.

Davies, M. (1983) 'Questions to be asked', in T. Philpott (ed.) *A New Direction for Social Work? The Barclay Report and its Implications*, London: Community Care/IPC Business Press.

Davies, M. (1985) *The Essential Social Worker*, 2nd edition, Aldershot, Hants: Gower

Day, P. (1981) *Social Work and Social Control*, London: Tavistock.

Day, P. (1985) 'An interview: constructing reality', *British Journal of Social Work* 15: 487–99.

Day, P. (1987) *Sociology in Social Work Practice*, London and Basingstoke, Hants: Macmillan.

Deacon, B. (1981) 'Social administration, social policy, and socialism', *Critical Social Policy* 1 (1): 43–66.

Deacon, R. and Bartley, R. (1975) 'Becoming a social worker', in
   H. Jones (ed.) *Towards a New Social Work*, London: Routledge &
   Kegan Paul.
Department of Health and Social Security (1977) *Annual Report 1976.*,
   Cmnd 6931, London: HMSO.
Department of Health and Social Security (1987) *The Warwickshire
   Direction: Proceedings of a Seminar 10th November 1987.*
Derber, C. (1982) *Professionals as Workers: Mental Labor in Advanced
   Capitalism*, Boston, Mass: G.K. Hall.
Devine, D. (1985) 'Defective, hypocritical and patronising research',
   Caribbean Times 4 March: 4.
Dingwall, R. (1976) *Aspects of Illness*, London: Martin Robertson.
Dingwall, R. (1977) *The Social Organisation of Health Visitor Training*,
   London: Croom Helm.
Dingwall, R., Eekelaar, J., and Murray, T. (1983) *The Protection of
   Children: State Intervention and Family Life*, Oxford: Blackwell.
Ditton, J. (1980) *The View from Goffman*, London: Macmillan.
Dominelli, L. (1983) *Women in Focus: Community Service Orders and Female
   Offenders*, Coventry: University of Warwick.
Dominelli, L. (1986) 'Father-daughter incest: patriarchy's shameful
   secret', *Critical Social Policy* 16: 8–22.
Dominelli, L. (1988) *Anti-Racist Social Work*, Basingstoke, Hants, and
   London: Macmillan.
Dominelli, L. (1989) 'Betrayal of trust: a feminist analysis of power
   relationships in incest abuse and its implications for social work
   practice', *British Journal of Social Work* 19 (4): 54–76.
Dominelli, L. and McLeod, E. (1989) *Feminist Social Work*, London and
   Basingstoke, Hants: Macmillan.
Donzelot, J. (1979) *The Policing of Families*, London: Hutchinson.
Doyal, L. (1979) *The Political Economy of Health*, London: Pluto.
Dreifus, C. (1973) *Woman's Fate: Raps From a Feminist Consciousness-Raising
   Group*, New York: Bantam.
Dressel, P. (1984) *The Service Trap: From Altruism to Dirty Work*, New
   York: C.C. Thomas.
Durrant, J. (1989) 'Continuous agitation', *Community Care* 13 July: 23–5.
Duster, T. (1981) 'Intermediate steps between micro- and macro-
   integration: the case of screening for inherited disorders', in
   K. Knorr-Cetina and A.V. Cicourel (eds) *Advances in Social Theory and
   Methodology: Towards an Integration of Micro- and Macro-Sociologies*,
   London: Routledge & Kegan Paul.
Eckstein, H. (1970) 'Case study and theory in political science', in
   F. Greenstein and N. Polsby (eds) *The Handbook of Political Science:
   Strategies of Inquiry Vol. 7*, London: Addison-Wesley.
Edgerton, R.B. (1975) 'Issues relating to the quality of life among
   mentally retarded persons', in M.J. Begab and S.A. Richardson (eds)
   The Mentally Retarded and Society: A Social Science Perspective, Baltimore,
   Md: University Park Press.

'Editorial' ATSWE (Association of Teachers in Social Work Education) (1984) *Issues in Social Work Education* 4 (1): 1–2.

Edwards, J. (1981) 'Subjectivist approaches to the study of social policy making', *Journal of Social Policy* 10 (3): 289–310.

Ehrenreich, B. and Ehrenreich, J. (1979) 'The professional-managerial class', in P. Walker (ed.) *Between Labour and Capital*, Sussex: Harvester Press.

Elias, N. (1978) *What is Sociology?* London: Hutchinson.

Elster, J. (1985) *Making Sense of Marx*, Cambridge: Cambridge University Press.

Epstein, N.B. and Bishop, D.S. (1981) 'Problem-centred systems therapy of the family', in A.S. Gurman and D.P. Kniskern (eds) *Handbook of Family Therapy*, New York: Brunner/Mazel.

Farson, R. (1978) *Birthrights*, Harmondsworth, Middx: Penguin.

Fielding, N. (1984) *Probation Practice: Client Support under Social Control*, Aldershot, Hants: Gower.

Fielding, N. (1988) 'Competence and culture in the police', *Sociology* 22 (1): 45–64.

Finch, J. (1982) 'The sociology of welfare', in R.G. Burgess (ed.) *Exploring Society*, London: BSA.

Finch, J. (1984) 'Community care: developing non-sexist alternatives', *Critical Social Policy* 9: 6–18.

Finch, J. (1989) *Family Obligations and Social Change*, Oxford: Polity Press.

Finch, J. and Groves, D. (1980) 'Community care and the family: a case for equal opportunities?', *Journal of Social Policy* 9: 486–511.

Finch, J. and Groves, D. (eds) (1983) *A Labour of Love*, London: Routledge & Kegan Paul.

Finkelhor, D. (1986) *Sourcebook on Child Sexual Abuse*, Beverly Hills, Ca: Sage.

Fisher, M., Marsh, P., and Phillips, D. (1986) *In and Out of Care: the Experiences of Children, Parents and Social Workers*, London: Batsford.

Fleck, L. (1979) *Genesis and Development of a Scientific Fact*, Chicago: University of Chicago Press.

Flew, A. (1981) *The Politics of Procrustes*, London: Temple Smith.

Flexner, A. (1915) 'Is social work a profession?', *Proceedings of the National Conference of Charity and Corrections*, cited in B. Heraud (1970) *Sociology and Social Work*, Oxford: Pergamon Press, p. 219.

Fogarty, M. and Rodgers, B. (1982) 'Family policy – international perspectives', in R. Rapoport, M. Fogarty, and R. Rapoport (eds) (1982) *Families in Britain*, London: Routledge & Kegan Paul.

Folkard, M.S., Fowles, A.J., McWilliams, B.C., Smith, D.D., Smith, D.E., and Walmsley, G.R. (1974) *IMPACT Intensive Matched Probation and After-Care Treatment: Volume I The Design of the Probation Experiment and an Interim Evaluation*, Home Office Research Study No 24, London: HMSO.

Folkard, M.S., Smith, D.D., and Smith, D.E. (1976) *IMPACT Intensive Matched Probation and After-Care Treatment: Volume II The Results of the Experiment*, Home Office Research Study No 36, London: HMSO.

Foucault, M. (1972) *The Birth of the Clinic*, London: Tavistock.
Foucault, M. (1975) *Discipline and Punish*, Harmondsworth, Middx: Penguin.
Freeman, M. (1983) *The Rights and Wrongs of Children*, London: Frances Pinter.
Freidson, E. (1983) 'The theory of professions', in R. Dingwall and P. Lewis (eds) *The Sociology of Profession*, London and Basingstoke, Hants: Macmillan.
Freidson, E. (1986) *Professional Powers*, Chicago: University of Chicago Press.
Friedrichs, R.W. (1970) *A Sociology of Sociology*, Toronto: Collier-Macmillan.
Froland, C., Pancoast, D.L., Chapman, N.J., and Kimboko, P.J. (1981) 'Linking formal and informal support systems', in B. Gottlieb (ed.) *Social Networks and Social Support*, Beverly Hills, Ca: Sage.
Gammack, G. (1982) 'Social work as uncommon sense', *British Journal of Social Work* 12 (1): 3–21.
Garbarino, J. and Gilliam, G. (1980) *Understanding Abusive Families*, Cambridge, Mass.: Lexington Books.
Garfinkel, H. (1967) 'Good organizational reasons for "bad" clinic records', in H. Garfinkel *Studies in Ethnomethodology*, Englewood Cliffs, NJ: Prentice-Hall.
Garfinkel, H. and Sacks, H. (1970) 'On the formal structures of practical actions', in J. Macknney and E. Tirakion (eds) *Theoretical Sociology*, New York: Appleton Century Crofts.
Garland, D. and Young, P. (eds) (1989) *The Power to Punish*, Aldershot, Hants: Gower.
Geertz, C. (1979) 'From the native's point of view: on the nature of anthropological understanding', in P. Rainbow and W.M. Sullivan (eds) *Interpretive Social Science: A Reader*, Berkeley, Ca: University of California Press, cited in M. Reed (1985) *Redirections in Organisational Theory*, London: Tavistock, p. 145.
Gelles, R. and Cornell, C. (1985) *Intimate Violence in Families*, Beverly Hills, Ca: Sage.
Germaine, L.B. (1983) 'A comment on "Central issues in developing a scheme for specialization in social work education" by Gross, Murphy, and Steiner', *Issues in Social Work Education* 3 (1): 49–53.
Giddens, A. (1976) *New Rules of Sociological Method*, London: Hutchinson.
Giddens, A. (1977) *Studies in Social and Political Theory*, London: Hutchinson.
Giddens, A. (1982) *Profiles and Critiques in Social Theory*, London and Basingstoke, Hants: Macmillan.
Giddens, A. (1984) *The Constitution of Society*, Cambridge: Polity Press.
Gil, D. (1970) *Violence against Children: Physical Abuse in the United States*, Cambridge, Mass: Harvard University Press.
Gil, D. (1975) 'Unravelling child abuse', *American Journal of Orthopsychiatry* 45 (3): 346–56.

Gilbert, G. and Mulkay, M. (1984) *Opening Pandora's Box*, Cambridge: Cambridge University Press.

Gilbert, G.N. and Specht, H. (1977) 'The incomplete profession', in H. Specht and A. Vickery (eds) *Integrating Social Work Methods*, London: Allen & Unwin.

Gilroy, P. (1987) *There Ain't No Black in the Union Jack*, London: Hutchinson.

Ginsburg, N. (1979) *Class, Capital and Social Policy*, London: Macmillan.

Glaser, B. and Strauss, A. (1964) 'Awareness contexts and social interaction', *American Sociological Review* 29: 669–79.

Glaser, B. and Strauss, A. (1967) *The Discovery of Grounded Theory*, London: Weidenfeld & Nicolson.

Glastonbury, B. (1979) *Paying the Piper and Calling the Tune*, London: BASW.

Glazer, N. (1988) *The Limits of Social Policy*, Cambridge, Mass: Harvard University Press.

Glendinning, C. (1983) *Unshared Care: Parents and Their Disabled Children*, London: Routledge & Kegan Paul.

Glucksmann, M. (1974) 'The structuralism of Lévi-Strauss and Althusser', in J. Rex (ed.) *Approaches to Sociology*, London: Routledge & Kegan Paul.

Goffman, E. (1961) *Asylums*, New York: Anchor Books.

Goldberg, E.M. and Stanley, S.J. (1985) 'Task-centred casework in a probation setting: Part 2', in E.M. Goldberg, I. Sinclair, and J. Gibbons (eds) *Problems Tasks and Outcomes: The Evaluation of Task-Centred Casework in Three Settings*, London: Allen & Unwin.

Gordon, L. (1976) *Women's Body, Women's Right: A Social History of Birth Control in America*, New York: Grossman.

Gordon, L. (1989) *Heroes of their own Lives: The Politics and History of Family Violence*, London: Virago.

Gough, I. (1979) *The Political Economy of the Welfare State*, London: Macmillan.

Greater London Council Women's Employment Group (GLC/WEG) (1986) *London Women in the 1980s*, London: GLC.

Green, H. (1988) *Informal Carers: General Household Survey 1985*, London: HMSO.

Greenwell, S. and Howard, B. (1986) 'An exercise in collaboration', *Issues in Social Work Education* 6 (2): 129–36.

Greenwich, London Borough of (1987) *A Child in Mind: The Report of the Commission of Inquiry into the Circumstances surrounding the Death of Kimberley Carlile*, London: Borough of Greenwich.

Griffiths Report (1988) *Community Care: Agenda for Action*, London: HMSO.

Gross, G., Murphy, D., and Steiner, D. (1982) 'Central issues in developing a scheme for specialisation in social work education', *Issues in Social Work Education* 2 (2): 77–94.

Guru, S. (1987) 'An Asian women's refuge', in S. Ahmed, J. Cheetham, and J. Small, *Social Work with Black Children and their Families*, London: Batsford.

Habermas, J. (1972) *Knowledge and Human Interests*, trans. J.J. Shapiro, London: Heinemann.

Hadley, R. and Hatch, R. (1981) *Social Welfare and the Failure of the State: Centralised Social Services and Participatory Alternatives*, London: Allen & Unwin.

Hagstrom, W.O. (1965) *The Scientific Community*, New York: Basic Books.

Haines, J. (1975) *Skills and Methods in Social Work*, London: Constable.

Haines, J. (1985) 'Alternative frameworks for organising the social work syllabus', in R.J. Harris, M. Barker, P. Reading, M. Richards, and P. Youll (eds) *Educating Social Workers*, University of Leicester: Association of Teachers in Social Work Education.

Halliday, T.C. (1985) 'Knowledge mandates: collective influence by scientific, normative, and syncretic professions', *British Journal of Sociology* xxxvi (3): 421–47.

Ham, C. (1980) 'Approaches to the study of policy making', *Policy and Politics* 8 (1): 55–71.

Hamilton, P. (1974) *Knowledge and Social Structure*, London: Routledge & Kegan Paul.

Hanmer, J. and Statham, D. (1988) *Women and Social Work: Towards a Woman-Centred Practice*, Basingstoke, Hants, and London: Macmillan.

Hanscombe, G.E. and Forster, J. (1982) *Rocking the Cradle: Lesbian Mothers and Custody*, London: Sheba Feminist Publishers.

Harbert, W. (1985a) 'Crisis in social work', *Community Care* 21 March: 14–16.

Harbert, W. (1985b) 'Status professionalism', *Community Care* 10 October: 14–15.

Hardiker, P. (1977) 'Social work ideologies in the probation service', *British Journal of Social Work* 7 (2): 131–54.

Hardiker, P. (1981) 'Heart or head: the function and role of knowledge in social work', *Issues in Social Work Education* 1 (2): 85–111.

Hardiker, P. and Webb, D. (1979) 'Explaining deviant behaviour: the social context of "action" and "infraction" accounts in the probation service', *Sociology* 13 (1): 1–17.

Harre, R. (1981) 'Philosophical aspects of the macro-micro problem', in K. Knorr-Cetina and A.V. Cicourel (eds) *Advances in Social Theory and Methodology: Towards an Integration of Micro- and Macro-Sociologies*, London: Routledge & Kegan Paul.

Harris, C.C. (1969) *The Family*, London: Allen & Unwin.

Harris, J.M., Veit, S.W., Allen, G.J., and Chinsky, J.M. (1974) 'Aide-resident ratio and ward population density as mediator of social interaction', *American Journal of Mental Deficiency*, 79: 320–6.

Harris, R.J. (1984) 'CCETSW review of qualifying training', *ATSWE Newsletter No 4 (February)*, University of Leicester: Association of Teachers in Social Work Education, pp. 4–10.

Harris, R.J., Barker, M., Reading, P., Richards, M., and Youll, P. (eds)

(1985) *Educating Social Workers*, University of Leicester: Association of Teachers in Social Work Education.

Harris, R. and Webb, D. (1987) *Welfare, Power and Juvenile Justice*, London: Tavistock.

Hearn, J. (1982) 'Radical social work: contradictions, limitations and political possibilities', *Critical Social Policy* 2 (1): 19–34.

Hechter, M. (1988) 'Rational choice theory and the study of race and ethnic relations', in J. Rex and D. Mason (eds) *Theories of Race and Ethnic Relations*, Cambridge: Cambridge University Press.

Heller, A. (1986) 'The sociology of everyday life', in U. Himmelstrand (ed.) *The Social Reproduction of Organisation and Culture*, London: Sage.

Heraud, B. (1970) *Sociology and Social Work: Perspectives and Problems*, Oxford: Pergamon.

Heraud, B. (1979) *Sociology in the Professions*, London: Open Books.

Heraud, B. (1981) *Training for Uncertainty: A Sociological Approach to Social Work Education*, London: Routledge & Kegan Paul.

Hill, B.K. and Lakin, K.C. (1986) 'Classification of residential facilities for individuals with mental retardation', *Mental Retardation* 24 (2): 107–15.

Hill, M. (1982) 'Street level bureaucracy in social work and social services departments', in J. Lishman (ed.) *Research Highlights No 4: Social Work Departments as Organisations*, Aberdeen: University of Aberdeen.

Hindess, B. (1981) Review, *Sociology* 15 (4): 636–7.

Hindess, B. (1982) 'Power, interests, and the outcomes of struggles', *Sociology* 16 (4): 498–511.

Hindess, B. (1983a) *Parliamentary Democracy and Socialist Politics*, London: Routledge & Kegan Paul.

Hindess, B. (1983b) Review, *Sociology* 17 (1): 125–6.

Hindess, B. (1986a) 'Actors and social relations', in M.L. Wardell and S.P. Turner (eds) *Sociological Theory in Transition*, London: Allen & Unwin.

Hindess, B. (1986b) 'Interests in political analysis', in J. Law (ed.) *Power, Action, and Belief: A New Sociology of Knowledge?*, London: Routledge & Kegan Paul.

Hindess, B. (1986c) Review *Sociological Review* 34 (2): 440–2.

Hindess, B. (1987) *Freedom, Equality and the Market: Arguments on Social Policy*, London: Tavistock.

Hindess, B. (1988) *Choice, Rationality, and Social Theory*, London: Unwin Hyman.

Hite, S. (1976) *The Hite Report: A Nationwide Study on Female Sexuality*, New York. Macmillan.

Hoggett, P. and Hambleton, R. (eds) (1988) *Decentralisation and Democracy: Localising Public Services*, Occasional Paper 28, Bristol: School for Advanced Urban Studies, University of Bristol.

Holme, A. (1985) *Housing and Young Families in East London*, London: Routledge & Kegan Paul.

Holmwood, J.M. and Stewart, A. (1983) 'The role of contradictions in modern theories of social stratification', *Sociology* 17 (2): 234–54.

Holt, J. (1975) *Escape from Childhood: The Needs and Rights of Children*, Harmondsworth, Middx: Penguin.

Home Office (1986a) *Ethnic Minorities: Crime and Policing*, London: HMSO.

Home Office (1986b) 'Reconvictions of those given probation orders', *Home Office Statistical Bulletin* 34 (86).

Home Office (1988) 'Ethnic origins of probation service staff', *Home Office Statistical Bulletin* 24 (88), 15 August: 2.

Howe, D. (1983) 'The social work imagination in practice and education', *Issues in Social Work Education* 3 (2): 77–89.

Howe, D. (1986) 'The segregation of women and their work in the personal social services', *Critical Social Policy* 15: 21–35.

Howe, D. (1986) *Social Workers and their Practice in Welfare Bureaucracies*, Aldershot, Hants: Gower.

Howe, D. (1987) *An Introduction to Social Work Theory*, Aldershot, Hants: Gower.

Howe, D. (1988) Review, *Issues in Social Work Education* 8 (1): 65–6.

Howe, D. (1989a) *The Consumers' View of Family Therapy*, Aldershot, Hants: Gower.

Howe, D. (1989b) 'Family therapy: the other side of the coin', *Social Services Insight* 4 (11), March: 16–17.

Hudson, A. (1985) 'Feminism and social work: resistance or dialogue?', *British Journal of Social Work* 15 (6): 635–55.

Ingleby, D. (1983) 'Mental health and social order', in S. Cohen and A. Scull (eds) *Social Control and the State*, Oxford: Martin Robertson.

Jacobs, S. (1987) 'Scientific community: formulations and critique of a sociological motif', *British Journal of Sociology* xxxviii (2): 266–76.

Jamous, H. and Peloille, B. (1970) 'Changes in the French university – hospital system', in J. Jackson (ed.) *Professions and Professionalisation*, Cambridge: Cambridge University Press.

Johnson, T. (1972) *Professions and Power*, London: Macmillan.

Jones, C. (1979) 'Social work education 1900–1917', in N. Parry, M. Rustin, and C. Satyamurti (eds) *Social Work, Welfare and the State*, London: Edward Arnold.

Jones, C. (1983) *State Social Work and the Working Class*, London and Basingstoke, Hants: Macmillan.

Jones, C. (1989) 'The end of the road? Issues in social work education', in P. Carter, T. Jeffs, and M. Smith (eds) *Social Work and Social Welfare*, Milton Keynes: Open University Press.

Jones, D., Pickett, J., Oates, M., and Barbor, P. (1987) *Understanding Child Abuse*, 2nd edition, Basingstoke, Hants: Macmillan.

Jones, H. (ed.) (1975) *Towards a New Social Work*, London: Routledge & Kegan Paul.

Jones, K. (1983) 'Services for the mentally ill: the death of a concept', in P. Bean and S. MacPherson (eds) *Approaches to Welfare*, London: Routledge & Kegan Paul.

Jones, K. and Fowles, A. (1984) *Ideas on Institutions*, London: Routledge & Kegan Paul.

Jones, R. (1982) 'A comment on "Through experience towards theory: a psychodynamic contribution to social work education" by Mary Barker', *Issues in Social Work Education* 2 (2): 149–52.

Joyce, P., Corrigan, P., and Hayes, P. (1988) *Striking Out: Trade Unionism in Social Work*, London: Macmillan.

Kadushin, A. (1959) 'The knowledge base of social work', in A. Kahn (ed.) *Issues in American Social Work*, New York: Columbia University Press.

Kakabadse, A. (1982) *Culture of Social Services*, Aldershot, Hants: Gower.

Karpf, M. (1931) *The Scientific Base of Social Work*, New York: Columbia University Press.

Kasius, C. (ed.) (1950) *A Comparison of Diagnostic and Functionalist Casework Concepts*, Family Service Association of America, cited in N. Timms (1983) *Social Work Values: An Enquiry*, London: Routledge & Kegan Paul, p. 79.

Kempe, C., Silverman, F., Steele, B., Droegemueller, W., and Silver, H. (1962) 'The battered child syndrome', *Journal of the American Medical Association* 181: 17–24.

Kent Social Services Department (1986) *Planning for Permanence: Children and Families Policy Statement*.

King, R.D., Raynes, N.V., and Tizard, J. (1971) *Patterns of Institutional Residential Care: Sociological Studies in Institutions for Handicapped Children*, London: Routledge & Kegan Paul.

Kirwin, K. (1985) 'Probation and supervision', in H. Walker and B. Beaumont (eds) *Working with Offenders*, Basingstoke, Hants, and London: Macmillan.

Klaber, M.M. (1969) 'The retarded and institutions for the retarded – a preliminary research report', in S.B. Sarason and J. Doris (eds) *Psychological Problems in Mental Deficiency*, New York: Harper & Row.

Klaber, M.M. and Butterfield, E.C. (1968) 'Stereotyped rocking – a measure of institution and ward effectiveness', *American Journal of Mental Deficiency* 73: 13–20.

Knorr-Cetina, K. (1981) 'The micro-sociological challenge of macro-sociology: towards a reconstruction of social theory and methodology', in K. Knorr-Cetina and A.V. Cicourel (eds) *Advances in Social Theory and Methodology: Towards an Integration of Micro- and Macro-Sociologies*, London: Routledge & Kegan Paul.

Knorr-Cetina, K. (1982) 'Scientific communities or transepistemic arenas of research?', *Social Studies of Science* 12: 111–28.

Kuhn, M.H. (1962) 'The interview and the professional relationship', in A.M. Rose (ed.) *Human Behaviour and Social Process: An Interactionist Approach*, London: Routledge & Kegan Paul.

Kuhn, T.S. (1970) *The Structure of Scientific Revolutions*, 2nd edition, Chicago: University of Chicago Press.

Kushlick, A. (1972) 'Evaluating residential services for the mentally handicapped', in G. McLachlan (ed.) *Approaches to Action: a Symposium on Services for the Mentally Ill and Handicapped*, Oxford: Oxford University Press.

Land, H. (1978) 'Who cares for the family?', *Journal of Social Policy* 7: 257–84.

Larson, M. (1977) *The Rise of the Professions*, Berkeley Ca: University of California Press.

Larson, M. (1980) 'Proletarianisation and educated labor', *Theory and Society* 9: 131–75.

Latour, B. (1986) 'The powers of association', in J. Law (ed.) *Power, Action and Belief: A New Sociology of Knowledge?*, London: Routledge & Kegan Paul.

Lave, J. (1986) 'The values of quantification', in J. Law (ed.) *Power, Action and Belief: A New Sociology of Knowledge?*, London: Routledge & Kegan Paul.

Law, J. (1986a) 'On power and its tactics: a view from the sociology of science', *Sociological Review* 34 (1): 1–38.

Law, J. (1986b) 'On the methods of long-distance control: vessels, navigation and the Portuguese route to India', in J. Law (ed.) *Power, Action and Belief: A New Sociology of Knowledge?*, London: Routledge & Kegan Paul.

Law, J. (1986c) 'Power/knowledge and the dissolution of the sociology of knowledge', in J. Law (ed.) *Power, Action and Belief: A New Sociology of Knowledge?*, London: Routledge & Kegan Paul.

Layder, D. (1986) 'Social reality as figuration: a critique of Norbert Elias's conception of sociological analysis', *Sociology* 20 (3): 367–86.

Lee, P. (1982) 'Some contemporary and perennial problems of relating theory to practice in social work', in R. Bailey and P. Lee (eds) *Theory and Practice in Social Work*, Oxford: Blackwell.

Lee, P. and Raban, C. (1988) *Welfare Theory and Social Policy: Reform or Revolution?*, London: Sage.

Leonard, P. (1966) *Sociology in Social Work*, London: Routledge & Kegan Paul.

Leonard, P. (1983) 'Editor's Introduction', in C. Jones *State Social Work and the Working Class*, London and Basingstoke, Hants: Macmillan.

Leonard, P. (1984) *Personality and Ideology: Towards a Materialist Understanding of the Individual*, London and Basingstoke, Hants: Macmillan.

Lévi-Strauss, C. (1963) *Structural Anthropology*, New York: Basic Books.

Lévi-Strauss, C. (1974) *The Savage Mind*, London: Weidenfeld & Nicolson.

Lidz, V. (1981) ' Transformational theory and the internal environment of action systems', in K. Knorr-Cetina and A.V. Cicourel (eds) *Advances in Social Theory and Methodology: Towards An Integration of Micro- and Macro-Sociologies*, London: Routledge & Kegan Paul.

Link, B.G., Cullen, F.T., Frank, J., and Wozniak, J.F. (1987) 'The social rejection of former mental patients: understanding why labels matter', *American Journal of Sociology* 92 (6): 461–500.

Lipsky, M. (1980) *Street-level Bureaucracy*, New York: Russell Sage.

Litwak, E. (1965) 'Extended kin relations in an industrial democratic society', in E. Shanas and G.F. Streib (eds) *Social Structure and the Family*, Englewood Cliffs, NJ: Prentice-Hall.

Llandesman-Dwyer, S. (1981) 'Living in the community', *American Journal of Mental Deficiency* 86: 223–34.

Llandesman, S. and Butterfield, E. (1987) 'Normalisation and deinstitutionalisation of mentally retarded individuals: controversy and facts', *American Psychologist* 42 (2): 809–16.

LLSS (1986) London Living Standards Survey, London: Greater London Council.

Loch, C.S. (1906) *Introduction to the Annual Charities Register and Digest*, 15th edition, London: Longman.

Lorde, A. (1984) *Sister Outsider*, New York: The Crossing Press.

Lukes, S. (1977) *Essays in Social Theory*, London: Macmillan.

Lynch, M. (1985) 'Discipline and the material form of images: an analysis of scientific visibility', *Social Studies of Science* 15: 37–66.

Lynch, M. and Roberts, J. (1982) *The Consequences of Child Abuse*, London: Academic Press.

McCauley, R. (1977) *Child Behaviour Problems*, London: Macmillan.

McCormick, M., Balla, D., and Zigler, E. (1975) 'Resident care practices in institutions for retarded persons', *American Journal of Mental Deficiency* 80: 1–17.

Macleod, M. and Saraga, E. (1987) 'Challenging the orthodoxy: towards a feminist theory and practice', *Feminist Review* 28: 15–55.

Maitland, P. (1983) *The Supervision of Parole: Report of the Southwark Parole Project*, London: Inner London Probation Service.

Maluccio, A. and Fein, E. (1983) 'Permanency planning: a redefinition', *Child Welfare* 62 (3): 195–201.

Mama, A. (1989) 'Violence against black women: gender, race and state responses', *Feminist Review* 32: 30–8.

Mansell, J., Felce, D., Jenkins, J., de Kock, U., and Toogood, S. (1987) *Developing Staffed Housing for People with Mental Handicaps*, Tunbridge Wells, Kent: Costello.

Marchant, H. and Wearing, B. (eds) (1986) *Gender Reclaimed*, Sydney: Hale & Iremonger.

Marglin, S. (1980) 'The origins and functions of hierarchy in capitalist production', in T. Nichols (ed.) *Capital and Labour*, London: Fontana.

Mason, D. (1988) 'Introduction', in J. Rex and D. Mason (eds) *Theories of Race and Ethnic Relations*, Cambridge: Cambridge University Press.

Mayer, J.E. and Timms, N. (1970) *The Client Speaks*, London: Routledge & Kegan Paul.

Mazis S. and Canter, D. (1979) 'Organisational patterns and management practices in institutions for mentally retarded children', in D. Canter and S. Canter (eds) *Designing for Therapeutic Environments: A Review of Research*, Chichester: Wiley.

Mead, G.H. (1967) *Mind, Self and Society*, Chicago: University of Chicago Press.

Measures, P. (1986) 'Professionalism', *Community Care* 17 April: 16–17.

Mellor, R. (1989) 'Urban sociology: a trend report', *Sociology* 23 (2): 241–60.

Meltzer, B., Petras, J.W., and Reynolds, L.T. (1975) *Symbolic Interactionism: Genesis, Varieties, and Criticisms*, London: Routledge & Kegan Paul.

Mepham, J. and Ruben, D. (eds) (1979) *Issues in Marxist Philosophy. Volume II: Materialism*, Brighton, Sussex: Harvester.

Merton, R.K. (1968) *Social Theory and Social Structure*, enlarged edition, Toronto: Collier-Macmillan.

Metropolitan Police and Bexley Social Services (1987) *Child Sexual Abuse Joint Investigation Programme: The Bexley Experiment, Final Report*, London: HMSO.

Miller, E.J. and Gwynne, G.V. (1972) *A Life Apart*, London: Tavistock.

Minty, B. *Child Care and Adult Crime*, Manchester: Manchester University Press.

Mishra, R. (1981) *Society and Social Policy*, 2nd edition, London and Basingstoke, Hants: Macmillan.

Mishra, R. (1986) 'The left and the welfare state: a critical analysis', *Critical Social Policy* 15: 4–19.

Mitchell, J. (1975) *Psychoanalysis and Feminism*, Harmondsworth, Middx: Penguin.

Mitchell, J.C. (1983) 'Case and situation analysis', *Sociological Review* 31 (2): 187–211.

Moffett, J. (1972) *Concepts in Casework Treatment*, London: Routledge & Kegan Paul.

Moore, J. (1985) *The ABC of Child Abuse Work*, Aldershot, Hants: Gower.

Morgan, D.H.J. (1985) *The Family, Politics and Social Theory*, London: Routledge & Kegan Paul.

Morgan, D.H.J. (1989) 'Strategies and sociologists: a comment on Crow', *Sociology* 23 (1): 25–9.

Morris, C. (1984) *The Permanency Principle in Child Care Social Work*, Norwich: University of East Anglia, Social Work Monograph.

Morris, P. (1975) 'Case con: the maturing five year old', *Community Care* 26 November: 18–19.

Morrison, T. (1986) *The Bluest Eye*, London: Triad/Grafton Books.

Mrazek, P. and Ben-Tovim, A. (1981) 'Incest and the dysfunctional family system', in P. Mrazek and C. Kempe (eds) *Sexually Abused Children and their Families*, New York: Pergamon Press.

Munday, B. (1972) 'What is happening to social work students?', *Social Work Today* 15 June: 4–5.

Murray, N. (1983) 'Decentralisation is here to stay', *Community Care* 17 April: 12–14.

National Association of Probation Officers (NAPO) (1984), *NAPO Bulletin* London: NAPO.

Nelson, B. (1984) *Making an Issue of Child Abuse: Political Agenda Setting for Social Problems*, Chicago: Chicago University Press.

Nissel, M. and Bonnerjea, L. (1982) *Family Care of the Handicapped*

Elderly: Who Pays?, London: Policy Studies Institute.

North, M. (1972) *The Secular Priests: Psychotherapists in Contemporary Society*, London: Allen & Unwin.

Offe, C. (1984) *Contradictions of the Welfare State*, ed. J. Keane, London: Hutchinson.

Offer, J. (1983) 'Spencer's sociology of welfare', *Sociological Review* 31 (4): 719-52.

Offer, J. (1984) 'Informal welfare, social work and the sociology of welfare', *British Journal of Social Work* 14 (6): 545-55.

Offer, J. (1985a) 'On the need for a sociology of poverty: comments on the state of research on poverty in the United Kingdom', *Social Science Information* 24 (2): 299-307.

Offer, J. (1985b) 'Social policy and informal welfare', in M. Brenton and C. Jones (eds) *The Year Book of Social Policy in Britain 1984-5*, London: Routledge & Kegan Paul.

Ong, B. (1985) 'The paradox of "wonderful children": the case of child abuse', *Early Child Development and Care* 21: 91-106.

Outhwaite, W. (1983) Review, *Network No 25*, London: British Sociological Association, p. 17.

Packman, J. (1986) *Who Needs Care? Social Work Decisions About Children*, Oxford: Blackwell.

Pakulski, J. (1986) 'Leaders of the Solidarity movement: a sociological portrait', *Sociology* 20 (1): 64-81.

Paley, J. (1984) 'The devolution of knowledge in social work education', *Social Work Education* 3 (2): 19-21.

Parker, H.J. (1974) *View from the Boys: A Sociology of Down-Town Adolescents*, Newton Abbot, Devon, and London: David & Charles.

Parker, R. (1981) 'Tending and social policy', in E.M. Goldberg and S. Hatch (eds) *A New Look at the Personal Social Services*, London: Policy Studies Institute.

Parker, R. (1982) 'Family and social policy: an overview', in R. Rapoport, M. Fogarty, and R. Rapoport (eds) *Families in Britain*, London: Routledge & Kegan Paul.

Parry, N. and Parry, J. (1979) 'Social work, professionalism, and the state', in N. Parry, M. Rustin, and C. Satyamurti (eds) *Social Work, Welfare and the State*, London: Edward Arnold.

Parsloe, P. (1985) Review, *Issues in Social Work Education* 5 (2): 158-9.

Parsons, T. (1943) 'The kinship system of the contemporary United States', *American Anthropologist* 45: 22-38.

Parsons, T. (1954) *Essays in Sociological Theory*, New York: The Free Press.

Parton, N. (1979) 'The natural history of child abuse: a study in social problem definition', *British Journal of Social Work* 9 (4): 431-53.

Parton, N. (1985) *The Politics of Child Abuse*, London: Macmillan.

Pearson, G. (1975) *The Deviant Imagination: Psychiatry, Social Work, and Social Change*, London and Basingstoke, Hants: Macmillan.

Pearson, G. (1983) 'The Barclay Report and community social work',

Critical Social Policy 2 (3): 78–86.

Pelton, L. (1978) 'Child abuse and neglect: the myth of classlessness', *American Journal of Orthopsychiatry* 48 (4): 608–17.

Philp, M. (1979) 'Notes on the form of knowledge in social work', *Sociological Review* 27 (1): 83–111.

Pierson, C. (1984) 'New theories of state and civil society: recent developments in post-marxist analysis of the state', *Sociology* 18 (4): 563–71.

Pill, R. and Stott, N.C.H. (1982) 'Concepts of illness causation and responsibility: some preliminary data from a sample of working class mothers', *Social Science and Medicine* 16: 43–52.

Pincus, A. and Minahan, A. (1973) *Social Work Practice: Mode and Method*, Itasca, Ill. Peacock.

Pinker,R. (1974) 'Social policy and social justice', *Journal of Social Policy* 3: 1–19.

Pinker, R. (1982) 'An alternative view', in Barclay Report *Social Workers: Their Role and Tasks*, Appendix B, London: Bedford Square Press.

Pinker, R. (1983a) 'Social welfare and the education of social workers', in P. Bean and S. Macpherson (eds) *Approaches to Welfare*, London: Routledge & Kegan Paul.

Pinker, R. (1983b) 'Social work is casework', in T. Philpott (ed.) *A New Direction for Social Work? The Barclay Report and its Implications*, London: Community Care/IPC Business Press.

Pinker, R. (1984a) 'The threat to professional standards in social work education: a response to some recent proposals', *Issues in Social Work Education* 4 (1): 5–15.

Pinker, R. (1984b) 'The balloon has reached bursting point', *Community Care* 9 August: 18–19.

Pinker, R. (1986) 'Time to stop CCETSW in its tracks', *Community Care* 18 September: 21–2.

Pithouse, A. (1987) *Social Work: The Social Organisation of an Invisible Trade*, Aldershot, Hants: Avebury.

Popplestone, R. (1980) 'Top jobs for women: are the cards stacked against them?' *Social Work Today* 12 (4): 12–15.

Poulantzas, N. (1975) *Classes in Contemporary Capitalism*, London: New Left Books.

Pratt, J. and Grimshaw, R. (1985) 'A study of a social work agency: the occupational routines and working practices of the education social work service', *Sociological Review* 33 (1): 106–35.

Radzinowicz, L. (1958) (ed.) *The Results of Probation: A Report of the Cambridge Department of Criminal Science*, London: Macmillan.

Rapoport, R., Fogarty, M., and Rapoport, R. (eds) (1982) *Families in Britain*, London: Routledge & Kegan Paul.

Reavley, W. and Gilbert, M. (1978) 'The behavioural treatment approach to potential child abuse - two illustrative cases', *Social Work Today* 7: 166–8.

Reed, M. (1985) *Redirections in Organisational theory*, London: Tavistock.

Rees, S. (1978) *Social Work Face to Face*, London: Edward Arnold.
Rein, M. (1976) *Social Science and Public Policy*, Harmondsworth, Middx: Penguin.
Report to Joint Working Party (1986) Association of Teachers in Social Work Education, Joint University Council Social Work Education Committee, Standing Conference of Heads of CQSW Courses *Preparing for Practice: Towards a Future Educational Strategy in Social Work*, June.
Rescher, N. (1969) *Introduction to Value Theory*, Englewood Cliffs, NJ: Prentice-Hall.
Rex, J. (1973) *Discovering Sociology: Studies in Sociological Theory and Method*, London: Routledge & Kegan Paul.
Rex, J. (1988) 'The role of class analysis in the study of race relations', in J. Rex and D. Mason (eds) *Theories of Race and Ethnic Relations*, Cambridge: Cambridge University Press.
Rex, J. and Moore, R. (1967) *Race, Community and Conflict*, Oxford: Oxford University Press.
Richards, M. and Righton, P. (1979) *Social Work Education in Conflict*, National Institute For Social Work Papers No 10, London: National Institute for Social Work.
Ricoeur, P. (1971) 'The meaning of the text: meaningful action considered as a text', *Social Research* 38 (3): 531–42.
Rimmer, L. and Wicks, M. (1983) 'The challenge of change: demographic trends, the family and social policy', in H. Glennerster (ed.) *The Future of the Welfare State: Remaking Social Policy*, London: Heinemann.
Roberts, C. and Roberts, J. (1982) 'Social enquiry reports and sentencing', *Howard Journal of Criminal Justice* 21: 76–93.
Robinson, C. (1983) *Black Marxism; The Making of the Black Radical Tradition*, London: 2nd Press.
Robinson, T. (1978) *In Worlds Apart*, London: Bedford Square Press.
Rojek, C. (1986) 'Problems of involvement and detachment in the writings of Norbert Elias', *British Journal of Sociology* xxxvii (4): 584–96.
Rojek, C., Peacock, G., and Collins, S. (1988) *Social Work and Received Ideas*, London: Routledge.
Room, G. (1979) *The Sociology of Welfare*, Oxford: Blackwell and Martin Robertson.
Rooney, B. (1987) *Resistance and Change*, Liverpool: Liverpool University.
Roos, J.P. (1973) *Welfare Theory and Social Policy*, Helsinki-Helsingfors: Societas Scientiarum Fennica.
Rose, D. (1989) 'Big money turns the key: how government policy on private prisons was diverted by skilful lobbying', *Guardian* 11 January: 25.
Rosen, A. (1972) 'Residential provision for mentally handicapped adults', in G. McLachlan (ed.) *Approaches to Action: A Symposium on Services for the Mentally Ill and Handicapped*, Oxford: Oxford University Press.

Rossiter, C. and Wicks, M. (1982) *Crisis or Challenge?*, London: Study Commission on the Family.

Rowe, J. (1976) *Keynote Address*, First Australian Adoption Conference.

Rowe, J. and Lambert, L. (1973) *Children Who Wait*, London: ABAA.

Rueschmeyer, D. (1986) *Power and the Division of Labour*, Cambridge: Polity Press.

Rush, F. (1980) *The Best Kept Secret: Sexual Abuse of Children*, Englewood Cliffs, NJ: Prentice-Hall.

Ryle, G. and Findlay, J. (1972) 'Use, usage, and meaning', in Open University Language and Learning Course Team *Language in Education*, London: Routledge and Open University Press.

Sacks, H. (1984) 'Notes on methodology', in J.M. Atkinson and J. Heritage (eds) *Structures of Social Action*, Cambridge: Cambridge University Press; Paris: Editions de la Maison des Sciences de l'Homme.

Sacks, H., Schegloff, E., and Jefferson, G. (1978) 'A simplest systematics for the organization of turn taking for conversation', in J. Schenkein (ed.) *Studies in the Organization of Conversational Interaction*, New York: Academic Press.

Sadock, J. (1974) *Towards a Linguistic Theory of Speech Acts*, New York: Academic Press.

Sahgal, G. (1989) 'Women march against fundamentalism', *Spare Rib* 203, July: 46.

Sainsbury, E., (1985) 'Diversity in social work practice: an overview of the problem', *Issues in Social Work Education* 5 (1): 3–12.

Sapir, E. (1966) *Culture, Language and Personality*, Berkeley and Los Angeles: University of California Press.

Sargent, J. (1985) 'The use of self in teaching social work', in R.J. Harris, M. Barker, P. Reading, M. Richards, and P. Youll (eds) *Educating Social Workers*, University of Leicester: Association of Teachers in Social Work Education.

Saussure, F. de (1974) *Course in General Linguistics* (1916), trans. W. Baskin, London: Collins.

Scarre, G. (1980) 'Children and paternalism', *Philosophy* 55: 117–24.

Scheler, M. (1970) *Problems of a Sociology of Knowledge*, London: Routledge & Kegan Paul.

Scholes, R. (1974) *Structuralism In Literature*, New Haven, Conn.: Yale University Press.

Schwartz, D. (1973) 'The invocation of legal norms: an empirical investigation of Durkheim and Weber', *American Sociological Review* 28: 340–54.

Scott, A. (1988) 'Imputing beliefs: a controversy in the sociology of knowledge', *Sociological Review* 36 (1): 331–56.

Scull, A. (1989) 'Community corrections – panacea, progress, or pretence?', in D. Garland and P. Young (eds) *The Power to Punish*, Aldershot, Hants: Gower.

Searle, J. (1969) *Speech Acts: An Essay in the Philosophy of Language*,

Cambridge: Cambridge University Press.

Seed, P. (1977) *The Expansion of Social Work in Britain*, London: Routledge & Kegan Paul.

Sharp, R. (1980) *Knowledge, Ideology and Politics of Schooling: Towards a Marxist Analysis of Education*, London: Routledge & Kegan Paul.

Sharron, H. (1983) 'The NSPCC: moral panic and distortion in social policy', *Guardian* 30 November: 12.

Shaw, I. (1975) 'Making use of research', in H. Jones (ed.) *Towards a New Social Work*, London: Routledge & Kegan Paul.

Shaw, J. (1974) *The Self in Social Work*, London: Routledge & Kegan Paul.

Sheppard, B. (1980) 'Research into aspects of probation', Home Office Research Unit, *Research Bulletin* 10: 23–5.

Sibeon, R.A. (1981) 'The nature of social work: a social constructionist approach', *Issues in Social Work Education* 1 (1): 45–64.

Sibeon, R.A. (1982) Review, *Sociological Review* 30 (3): 509–12.

Sibeon, R.A. (1989) 'Cognitive indeterminacy and technical rationality in professional social work', paper given at British Sociological Association Annual Conference, Plymouth, March.

Silverstein, A.B.A. (1968) 'A dimensional analysis of institutional differences', *The Training School Bulletin* 64: 102–4.

Simmel, G. (1971) *On Individuality and Social Forms: Selected Writings*, Chicago: University of Chicago Press.

Simon, B.S. (1967) *The Nature and Objectives of Professional Education*, University of Leicester: Association of Social Work Teachers Annual Meeting, February.

Simpkin, M. (1979) *Trapped within Welfare*, London: Macmillan.

Simpkin, M. (1982) Review, *Critical Social Policy* 1 (3): 92–4.

Sinclair, I. and Thomas, D.N. (1983) *Perspectives on Patch*, NISW Paper No 14, London: National Institute of Social Work.

Skinner, J. and Robinson, C. (1988) 'Who cares? Women and the social services', in Coyle, A. and Skinner, J. *Women and Work: Positive Action for Equal Opportunities*, London: Macmillan.

Small, J. (1984) 'The crisis in adoption', *International Journal of Psychiatry* 30, spring: 129–41.

Small, N. (1987) 'Putting violence towards social workers into context', *Critical Social Policy* 19: 40–51.

Smart, B. (1985) *Foucault, Marxism and Critique*, London: Routledge & Kegan Paul.

Smart, B. (1989) 'On discipline and social regulation – a review of Foucault's genealogical analysis', in D. Garland and P. Young (eds) *The Power To Punish*, Aldershot, Hants: Gower.

Smith, C.J. and Giggs, J.A. (1988) *Location and Stigma*, London: Unwin Hyman.

Smith, D. (1965) 'Front line organisation of the state mental hospital', *Administrative Science Quarterly* 10: 381–99.

Smith, G. (1977) 'The place of professional ideology in the analysis of social policy: some theoretical conclusions from a pilot study of the children's panels', *Sociological Review* 25 (4): 843-65.

Smith, G. (1979) *Social Work and the Sociology of Organisations*, revised edition, London: Routledge & Kegan Paul.

Sondhi, R. (1982) 'An Asian resources centre', in J. Cheetham (ed.) *Social Work and Ethnicity*, London: Allen & Unwin.

Spencer, H. (1867) *First Principles*, 2nd edition, London: Williams & Norgate (first published in 1862).

Spencer, H. (1893) *The Principles of Ethics, Vol. 2*, London: Williams & Norgate.

SSORU (1974) Social Science Organisation Research Unit, Brunel Institute of Organisation and Social Studies *Social Services Departments: Developing Patterns of Work and Organisation*, London: Heinemann.

Stacey, M. (1988) *The Sociology of Health and Healing*, London: Unwin Hyman.

Stanko, E. (1985) *Intimate Intrusions: Women's Experiences of Male Violence*, London: Routledge & Kegan Paul.

Stanley, S.J. and Murphy, M. (1984) *Inner London Probation Service Survey of Social Enquiry Reports*, London: Inner London Probation Service.

Stedman Jones, G. (1971) *Outcast London*, London: Clarendon Press.

Stevenson, O. (1970) 'The knowledge base for social work', *British Journal of Social Work* 1 (2): 225-37.

Stevenson, O. (1981) *Specialisation in Social Services Teams*, London: Allen & Unwin.

Straus, M., Gelles, R., and Steinmetz, S. (1980) *Behind Closed Doors: Violence in the American Family*, Darden City, NY: Anchor/Doubleday.

Strauss, A., Schatzman, L., Ehrlich, D., Bucher, R., and Sabshin, M. (1973) 'The hospital and its negotiated order', in G. Salaman and K. Thompson (eds) *People and Organisations*, London: Longman.

Sudnow, D. (1965) 'Normal crimes: sociological features of the penal code in a public defender's office', *Social Problems* 12: 255-76.

Sullivan, M. (1987) *Sociology and Social Welfare*, London: Allen & Unwin.

Sutton, C. (1979) *Psychology for Social Workers and Counsellors*, London: Routledge & Kegan Paul.

Taylor, W. (1981) *Probation and After-Care in a Multi-Racial Society*, London: Commission for Racial Equality.

Thoburn, J., Murdoch, A., and O'Brien, A. (1986) *Permanence in Child Care*, Oxford: Blackwell.

Thomason, B.C. (1982) *Making Sense of Reification: Alfred Schutz and Constructionist Theory*, London and Basingstoke, Hants: Macmillan.

Thorpe, J. (1979) *Social Inquiry Reports: A Survey*, Home Office Research Study No 48, London: HMSO.

Timms, N. (1983) *Social Work Values: An Enquiry*, London: Routledge & Kegan Paul.

Timms, N. and Timms, R. (1977) *Perspectives in Social Work*, London: Routledge & Kegan Paul.

Timms, N. and Watson, D. (eds) (1978) *Philosophy in Social Work*,

London: Routledge & Kegan Paul.

Tizard, J. (1964) *Community Services for Mentally Handicapped People*, London: Oxford University Press.

Tonnies, F. (1955) *Community and Association*, translated by C.P. Lommis, London: Routledge & Kegan Paul (first published in German in 1887).

Townsend, M. (1911) *The Case Against the Charity Organisation Society*, Fabian Tract No 158, London.

Townsend, P. (1979) *Poverty in the United Kingdom*, Harmondsworth, Middx: Penguin.

Turner, B.S. (1987) *Medical Power and Social Knowledge*, London: Sage.

Turner, R. (1972) 'Some formal properties of therapy talk', in D. Sudnow (ed.) *Studies in Social Interaction*, New York: The Free Press; London: Collier-Macmillan.

Tuson, G. (1989) letter 'A false dichotomy in community social work', *Social Work Today* 22 June: 13.

Twelve Students, Applied Social Work Course, School of Social Work, Manchester University (1989) letter 'Breath of fresh air over social work training', *Social Work Today* 6 April: 10.

Twigg, J. (1989) 'Models of carers: how do social care agencies conceptualise their relationship with informal carers?', *Journal of Social Policy* 18: 53–66.

Ungerson, C. (1987) *Policy is Personal: Sex, Gender and Informal Care*, London: Tavistock.

University Grants Committee (1989) *Report of the Review Committee on Sociology*, London: University Grants Committee.

Urry, J. (1981) 'Sociology as a parasite: some vices and virtues', in P. Abrams, R. Deem, J. Finch, and P. Rock (eds) *Practice and Progress: British Sociology 1950–1980*, London: Allen & Unwin.

Vance, F.L. (1968) 'The psychological interview as a discovery machine', in C.A. Parker (ed.) *Counselling Theories and Counsellor Education*, Boston, Mass: Houghton Mifflin.

Vyvyan, C. (1987) 'The Registered Homes Act, 1984: reform and response', in M. Brenton and C. Ungerson (eds) *The Year Book of Social Policy*, London: Longman.

Wagner, Lady (1988) *Residential Care: A Positive Choice*, London: NISW.

Walker, A. (1981) 'Social policy, social administration and the social construction of welfare', *Sociology* 15 (2): 225–50.

Walker, A. (ed.) (1982) *Community Care: The Family, The State and Social Policy*, Oxford: Blackwell.

Walker, H. and Beaumont, B. (1981) *Probation Work: Critical Theory and Socialist Practice*, Oxford: Blackwell.

Walker, H. and Beaumont B. (1985) (eds) *Working with Offenders*, Basingstoke, Hants, and London: Macmillan.

Wallis, R. and Bruce, S. (1983) 'Accounting for action: defending the commonsense heresy', *Sociology* 17 (1): 97–111.

Walton, R. (1975) *Women in Social Work*, London: Routledge & Kegan Paul.

Ward, L. (1984) 'Planning for people: developing a local service for people with mental handicap, 1: Recruiting and training staff', *King's Fund Project Paper 47*, London.

Wardell, M.L. and Turner, S.P. (eds) (1986) *Sociological Theory in Transition*, London: Allen & Unwin.

Warham, J. (1973) 'Social administration and sociology', *Journal of Social Policy* 2 (3): 193–207.

Webb, A. (1980) 'The personal social services', in N. Bosanquet and P. Townsend (eds) *Labour and Equality*, London: Heinemann.

Webb, D. (1981) 'Themes and continuities in radical and traditional social work', *British Journal of Social Work* 11 (2): 143–58.

Webb, D. (1985) 'Social work and critical consciousness: rebuilding orthodoxy', *Issues in Social Work Education* 5 (2): 85–102.

Webb, D. (1987) Review, *Issues in Social Work Education* 7 (2): 157–60.

Webb, D. (1988) Notes for the Lincoln conference.

Webb, D. and Evans, R. (1976) 'Sociology and social work practice: explanation or method?', paper given at National Deviancy Conference, London.

Weinstein, J. (1986) 'Angry arguments across the picket line: left labour councils and white collar trade unionism', *Critical Social Policy* 17: 41–60.

Welsh Office (1983) *All Wales Strategy for the Development of Services for Mentally Handicapped People*.

Welsh Office (1986) *A Home of Their Choice*.

Wenger, G.C. (1984) *The Supportive Network*, London: Allen & Unwin.

Whittington, C. and Bellaby, P. (1979) 'The reason for hierarchy in social services departments: a critique of Elliott Jaques and his associates', *Sociological Review* 27 (3): 513–39.

Whittington, C. and Holland, R. (1985) 'A framework for theory in social work', *Issues in Social Work Education* 5 (1): 25–50.

Whorf, B. (1956) *Language, Thought and Reality*, New York: MIT Press and Wiley.

Wilding, P. (1982) *Professional Power and Social Welfare*, London: Routledge & Kegan Paul.

Wilensky, H. (1962) 'The dynamics of professionalism: the case of the hospital administrator', *Hospital Administration* 7: 2.

Wilkin, D. (1979) *Caring for the Mentally Handicapped Child*, London: Croom Helm.

Wilkinson, P. (1971) *Social Movement*, London: Pall Mall Publications.

Williams, M. (1977) *Groundless Belief*, Oxford: Blackwell.

Williams, R.G.A. (1983) 'Concepts of health', *Sociology* 17 (2): 185–205.

Williams, S. (1986) 'Appraising Goffman', *British Journal of Sociology* xxxvii (3): 348–69.

Willis, A. (1986) 'Help and control in probation: an empirical assessment of probation practice', in J. Pointing (ed.) *Alternatives to Custody*, Oxford: Blackwell.

Willmott, P. (1987) Friendship Networks and Social Support, London:

Policy Studies Institute.

Wilson, A. (1986) *But My Cows Ain't Coming to England*, London: Institute of Race Relations.

Wilson, D. (1974) 'Uneasy bedfellows', *Social Work Today* 5 (1): 9–10.

Wilson, T. (1971) 'Normative and interpretive paradigms in sociology', in J. Douglas (ed.) *Understanding Everyday life*, London: Routledge & Kegan Paul.

Wolfensberger, W. (1972) *The Principle of Normalisation in Human Services*, Toronto: NIMR Leonard Crainford.

Wolfensberger, W. (1988a) 'Common assets of mentally retarded people that are commonly not acknowledged', *Mental Retardation* 26 (2): 63–70.

Wolfensberger, W. (1988b) 'Reply to "All people have personal assets"', *Mental Retardation* 26 (2): 75–6.

Women and Management Discussion Group (WMDG) (1982) 'Women and management', at the *Feminism and Social Work Conference*, Goldsmiths' College, London, November.

Woodroofe, K. (1962) *From Charity to Social Work*, London: Routledge & Kegan Paul.

Wootton, A. (1975) *Dilemmas of Discourse: Controversies about the Sociological Interpretation of Language*, London: Allen & Unwin.

Wootton, B. (1959) *Social Science and Social Pathology*, London: Allen & Unwin.

Wright, R. (1968) *Native Son*, London: Penguin.

Wright, R. (1977) *Expectations of the Teaching of Social Work on Courses Leading to the CQSW: Consultative Document 3*, London: Central Council for Education and Training in Social Work.

Wuthnow, R., Hunter, J.D., Bergesen, A., and Kurzweil, E. (1984) *Cultural Analysis: The Work of Peter L. Berger, Mary Douglas, Michel Foucault and Jurgen Habermas*, London: Routledge & Kegan Paul.

Yelloly, M. (1980) *Social Work Theory and Psychoanalysis*, London: Van Nostrand Reinhold.

Young, A. and Ashton, E. (1956) *British Social Work in the Nineteenth Century*, London: Routledge & Kegan Paul.

Young, K. (1977) 'Values in the policy process', *Policy and Politics* 5 (3): 1–22.

Young, P. (1979) 'Foreword', in K. Curnock and P. Hardiker *Towards Practice Theory: Skills and Methods in Social Assessments*, London: Routledge & Kegan Paul.

NAME INDEX

SUBJECT INDEX